LOVERS

FOR

LIFE

GUERRILLA TACTICS TO GET YOUR
RELATIONSHIP BACK ON TRACK

Sharyn Wolf, CSW

Thorsons
An Imprint of HarperCollinsPublishers

For
Derek, Sherrie Rose, Alison,
Michelle, and Hannah Li

Thorsons
An Imprint of HarperCollins*Publishers*
77–85 Fulham Palace Road,
Hammersmith, London W6 8JB

First published in the US by Penguin 1997
Published by Thorsons 1998

1 3 5 7 9 10 8 6 4 2

A catalogue record for this book is available
from the British Library

ISBN 0 7225 3581 3

Printed and bound in Great Britain by
Caledonian International Book Manufacturing Ltd, Glasgow

ACKNOWLEDGEMENTS

I couldn't have completed this three-year project without help. And I got it all along the way. The generosity of others came in many forms. I want to offer grateful thanks to the following people:

Nancy Rose, my lawyer, by sticking by me and fighting for the integrity of this book. I also want to thank Bob Levine and Conrad Rippy for their hard work in taking on this project and seeing it through.

Deb Brody, my editor, for her smart input and for the chance to work by her side. Deb is so wonderful to work with that I'd keep writing just to spend more time with her.

Ross Klavan and Charles Salzberg – placed here alphabetically. Thank you for reading drafts, drinking draughts, commiserating, always being a phone call away, teasing me mercilessly, and taking my mind off my troubles by doing the best lunch in town.

My parents, Milton and Norma Rubin, for support, understanding, and a nice place to visit during the writing of the book.

Michelle Wolf, Tom Wolburst, and Debra Wolf, for reading the early drafts and offering encouragement. Michelle, thank you for your editing notes. Tom, thank you for providing some great phrases which I borrowed.

Maureen Baron, thank you for your careful reading of an endless first draft and for finally setting me in the right direction.

My wonderful women's group, who offered support, grounding, and deep listening: Lois Greifer, Harriet Hoffman, Toby Silverman, Caryn Stark, and Bonnie Zindel.

The 92nd Street Y, the Boston Center for Adult Education, Discovery U, Leisure Learning, and Bruce Mezei and Tim Dwyer in Calgary, Alberta, for offering me wonderful places to run my workshops.

Peggy Papp, for excellent material about couples, for her wisdom, and for her commonsensical point of view.

Mark Finn, thank you for great 'front-line' instruction in couples therapy and couples therapy techniques.

Thanks to the staff of Radio Mexico for great margaritas and food.

Publicists Yvonne Orteg and Lisa Johnson, for their hard work in promoting this book.

Oprah Winfrey and her entire staff. Their support of my work through the years has made a wonderful difference in my career.

Dr. Martin Post for keeping me healthy in spite of my best efforts to get sick enough to put this book aside.

Bill Pullman, Jamie Thompson, and Big Town Productions for their interest in my work and for bringing some excitement into my life.

The following people told me stories, offered suggestions and support, and some helped me come up with a title for my book. I want to thank them all: Sallie Raynor, Michael Mark, Juliet Haffner, Donna Zerwitz, Carol Fredette, Ildy Herczeg, Michael Brook, Laura George, Gary Keske, Sarah Mills, Perry Beekman, Laura Schalk, Daryl Sherman, Karen Armstrong, Linda Antoniucci, Sparky Jones, Doris Germansky, Deborah Henson-Conant, Jody Watkins, Lyn Meehan, Victoria Watson, Michael Shaw, Betsy Carpenter, David Sparr, Joanne Lambert and the folks at the Cape, Lynne Kwalwasser, and noted poet Denise Duhamel.

I especially thank the many clients who have taught me about love, commitment, and courage as they share their lives with me and each other in group, couple, and individual therapy.

There are two people I've saved for last because they have been so special to me in working on and through this book. The first is Alexia Dorszynski, whose excellent editorial advice and generous friendship came right when I needed it most. Alexia, you knew exactly what I needed, as always. And last but not least, my husband, Boots Maleson. He knows why.

CONTENTS

Part V Be the Lovers You Were Meant to Be

Part VI Guerilla Mating Tactics: Make Your Relationship a Masterpiece

GUERRILLA MATING TACTICS AND GETTING OVER THE END OF THE HONEYMOON

♥♥

Who started the myth that you fall in love, have a honeymoon, it ends, and – if you're lucky – you have a second honeymoon at some point after retirement? Don't believe this. When the first honeymoon is over, sure, you hit a slump, but the slump should be followed by numerous additional honeymoons. There are honeymoon weekends when you make special plans to go away alone together – not telling his mother or even your needy best friend where you are. There are honeymoon days, which may sometimes go unrecognized because they happen while you are going about your usual routines. And there are honeymoon moments when you are sitting on the couch together, the light catches his face a certain way, and all you can think is, 'This is great. I'm sitting next to the greatest person in the world.'

This is an optimistic relationship manual designed to help you from the day you meet through the first seven years of your marriage (or any serious, committed, long-term relationship), though more seasoned couples will find much to learn here as well. I chose the time frame of the first seven years because this is when most couples need the most help. Statistics show most divorces occur within the first four years of marriage; I've tacked on a few years for late bloomers.

I want to teach you how to extend your honeymoon moments and how to shorten the distance between them. And, most important because this will determine whether or not your relationship lasts, I want to teach you how to come down gracefully and graciously when a honeymoon moment is over, instead of coming down kicking and fighting.

Anyone can be a sweetheart on a honeymoon – it is how we behave *between* honeymoons that is a measure of who we are.

Let me define the word *honeymoon*. A honeymoon is a period of time governed by the profound belief that love will conquer all. And while it's certainly possible for a person to be very happy alone, no one goes on a honeymoon alone. To be on a honeymoon means you are a couple – two persons of any combination, any age – who view your commitment to each other as an occasion for feast and celebration. It does not necessarily mean you've gotten married, although many of us choose to formalize this bliss with rituals. You may go into debt to hire a hall, send invitations to distant cousins you never liked, smash a glass, push cake in each other's faces, get confetti in your hair. Then you go off to a resort where you spend two weeks in a heart-shaped Jacuzzi with a bottle of Veuve Cliquot – great food, better sex, and an inordinate amount of time spent wondering how often they change the water in those Jacuzzis. Or, you may not go through a formal ceremony, but you're there for each other in a deeply committed way, gamely helping each other face the daily slings and arrows of outrageous fortune.

When you go through all that to be together it can only mean you love someone, and when you love someone, you want it to be for life. No one has a honeymoon hoping the relationship won't work out. No one competes to see how fast they can mess up or fall out of love or betray their partner. A couple decides to be a couple because they want, more than anything else, to love each other, to comfort each other, for better, for worse, for ever.

I call my approach to relationships 'Guerrilla Mating Tactics'. It is a four-part approach and each word in this title represents a different part of the approach. Let me explain:

Guerrilla

At first, the word *guerrilla* may bring a grassroots military unit to your mind. However, when I use *guerrilla* I am *not* saying that my approach is warlike (though I do use the metaphor of the soldier). And I am definitely *not* saying that your partner is the enemy. The enemy in Guerrilla Mating Tactics is the harsh words, stupid mistakes, combative impulses, lack of warmth, accusations – the mess that gets between you and your partner when the honeymoon is over. That's the only thing we'll be fighting.

When I use the term *guerrilla*, I refer to the characteristics a guerrilla soldier must possess, rather than the fighting she or he may be engaged in. A guerrilla soldier can work alone as well as she can work with others, remaining focused and keeping her mission in mind. You, too, must not be dissuaded when your partner is not working by your side. Which leads me to another quality of a guerrilla soldier: a guerrilla soldier can hold to her goal fiercely, even when the odds are against her. There will be times when you pick up a newspaper, read about this divorce or that one, and it would be easy to get discouraged. But you won't find a guerrilla soldier getting ambushed by statistics. She knows that a statistic such as '50 per cent of all marriages end in divorce' also means that *50 per cent of all marriages DON'T end in divorce*. She'll find a way to be in the latter group – and to be happy, to boot.

Just as a guerrilla soldier is able to trust his instincts, taking dramatic risks in service of his mission, being in a relationship requires all this bravery and more – you will need to be brave enough, not to launch a sneak attack, but to launch a sneak apology – to surprise your partner by saying you're sorry when she least expects it. In addition, a guerrilla soldier is a master improviser who is successful because he can spot unconventional opportunities and milk them. He may not have high technology and big budget, but he uses whatever is at hand, like that guy on the old television series *MacGyver*. All of these qualities will be invaluable in your relationship as you develop a knack for spotting unconventional opportunities for improvement – opportunities that were previously obscured.

Most important, a guerrilla soldier is not drafted! A guerrilla soldier volunteers because she believes so strongly in her cause. You volunteered to enter your relationship because you believed, as much as anyone believes in anything, that your relationship was worth it. When you fell in love, you thought your relationship was worth dying for. Now, it's worth fighting for.

Mating

Each of us knows what it means to long for someone who loves us and to whom we can return that love with enthusiasm and joy. These days, it is so hard to find that person – to trust, to open up, to believe in lasting love. The point of this book is to honour your commitment to each other by bringing back the incredible pleasures of finding each other, to celebrate the miracles of finding love, loving and feeling loved. Even though the honeymoon is over, what brought the two of you together in the first place deserves to take centre stage again.

You will learn ways to feel more connected to your partner – to feel mated in good times (when it's easy) and bad (when it's not so easy). There is no reason why you can't feel solid about your partnership even when things are rough. Let's face it: relationships do get rough. There are rarely perfect conditions when you are in a relationship, yet many people in relationships keep waiting for perfect conditions to occur so they can connect. You will learn how to give up that practice. Moreover, you will learn how to get started improving your connection with your partner all by yourself if your partner isn't ready to join your efforts. Many of the problems in a relationship are actually the result of misguided solutions – couples trying the wrong things to fix a problem. One or both partners attempt to solve a problem, but they misjudge the problem and/or have a limited repertoire of problem-solving skills. As you build your mating skills, you will also build confidence and self-esteem. This happens because when you feel skilled in a relationship, you abandon the notion of yourself as powerless and begin to understand the potential you have to restructure, repair and make a positive impact on your relationship. Of course, you will have to decide if you're ready to give up the emotional balance sheet of who failed whom for a real shot at being loved to the bone.

Tactics

What you have in your hands, what I call *tactics*, is a system – hundreds of specific strategies for improving your relationship. While what you think and how you feel are important, change in your relationship will occur primarily because of what you do. The emphasis in my approach is based on solutions to problems rather than on an examination of problems. As a psychotherapist I have found that all the understanding in the world doesn't help a person feel better if she doesn't do something different.

Let me tell you where these tactics came from. In the past 30 years an incredible amount of attention has been paid to understanding what makes a couple strong and happy. Love, once the exclusive territory of intense balladeers, fiction writers and poets, has more recently captured the imagination of scientists, philosophers and psychoanalysts who talk about pheromones, hormones and love moans. Love scientists – through interviews, videotapings and research on thousands of couples – know more than ever what it takes for a couple to flourish and stay together. Moreover, with all of the recent studies of men, women and gender differences, significant new information has been added to the pot. Much of that research has been collected here exactly the way the scientists collected it – they watched couples and they listened to what couples had to say. You will benefit from their work because you will be getting the latest research on finding and reaching relationship satisfaction – and without having to read statistics or wade through transcripts.

Many of the tactics you will learn are based on what worked for other couples. I will make you a fly on the wall in other relationships so you can see how others have solved the problems you are having. Why reinvent the wheel? A zillion other couples have had the same problems you are having. Why not find out what worked for them? Other tactics, however, will be invented by you, based on what has worked for you in the past or what you imagine would help your particular situation. No matter what you learn from other couples, you will always bring your own personal touch to these tactics. No one but you understands the nuances of your partner, the inner workings of your relationship, and your own unique self. So, you can take what others have done and fine-tune the tactics to fit your relationship. Still other tactics are invented by me. I'll share with you my personal stories of how I've managed some of the problems you may be having.

Guerrilla Mating Tactics

Put these three words together and you have the fourth part of my approach – the part I consider to be the 'soul' in soul mate, the 'relate' in relationships. It's your wit, your humour, your own charm. In your relationship, how often do you get a big belly laugh? Which of you gets the biggest laughs? Do you have a dry wit or do you slip on banana peels? Did you forget that, in addition to offering a secure tax base, relationships are supposed to be fun – and funny? Hopefully, this book will remind you. Guerrilla Mating Tactics mixes the metaphors of love, war, the military, the jungle, science – putting together things that you wouldn't ordinarily think of together as a way to make you see the humour in your relationship – as a way to make you smile.

What I have found in my relationship and the relationships of all the couples I know and all the couples I've treated, and all the couples I've read about who have remained lovers for life, is that it wouldn't have happened without laughter. Laughter is much more than entertainment. Laughter speeds forgiveness, builds spontaneity, releases old hurts, turns sore spots into high spots, redefines problems, shrinks problems, heals the aching heart, turns pain into belly laughs.

Unfortunately, laughter, like happiness, can't be dictated. You can't order someone to be funny. Laughter happens when you widen your lens, step back, and see the total picture. When you step back, you open your eyes to the dissonance, the silliness, the wackiness of relationships – you surrender. I have used humour throughout the book, and I use it every day in every part of my life. I think it is what makes me a survivor, and I think it is the lifeblood of my marriage. As you read this book, you will be in touch with your own sense of what is funny (you don't have to share mine) and learn how to unleash it in your relationship:

> When anyone tells me they want to get married, the question I always ask first is, 'Does he make you laugh?'

Guerrilla Mating Tactics and Sex

No discussion of your relationship would be complete without an in-depth look at your sex life, and you will find many pages devoted to your hormones here. My approach to your sex life follows closely to the idea of Guerrilla Mating Tactics. You will be exploring your own sexual desires (guerrilla), your ability to communicate them in a way your partner can hear (mating), and how to implement them (tactics). After all, if I am asking you to celebrate the miracle that drew you to each other, chances are that sex had a great deal to do with that. Guerrilla Mating Tactics take the stance that sex, just like love, dies in a relationship because people let it die – *without a bang or a whimper*. Here, you will discover ways in which your sex life can provide you with a glow that can light up the sky (if not a few neighbouring solar systems).

If You're Struggling Now

If you haven't had a honeymoon in months, don't worry. Okay, worry a little – but don't give up. At different points in your relationship it is natural to love your partner, hate your partner, desire your partner, avoid your partner, wish you'd married someone else, marry your partner all over again exactly the same way if you could, solve problems, get new problems, step back in horror as old problems pop up again, fall out of love, and fall back in love numerous times. This is not because we are psychotic or because love is doomed. This is the normal range of marital emotion. It's how you handle these feelings when they occur that is the difference between a golden anniversary and alimony.

Note: I polled many couples who have been married longer than 25 years and who both described themselves as happy. Many of them talked about certain years in their marriage as hard years. At first, I thought they meant that there were hard times during a given year, but I was mistaken. Upon further questioning, they made it clear that they had *hard years*– 12 hard months in a row, broken by days, weeks, moments, but mostly hard times. So if you are in a bad patch, keep reading. Couples can be very resilient, bounce back, and find lasting happiness.

To get back to your future honeymoons, you must keep believing that what you had on your honeymoon mattered. Tune out those cynics who call the honeymoon a trick, an aphrodisiac, or a temporary psychosis. Actually, we have a honeymoon not because we are gullible but because we are human, and we are at our most human when we love.

Your first great leap of faith was falling in love. The universe helped you to do that by giving you someone who seemed perfect. Now it is time to take a second leap of faith:

You must take the leap of faith that allows you to love an imperfect partner.

The truth is that your partner, even if he once seemed like a prince, was never a prince; and your partner, even if he looks like a frog and smells like a frog, is not a frog. Coming down gracefully between honeymoons will entail trusting your partner and yourself when things aren't perfect – it will entail believing in each other, believing that the love you have for each other is real.

You can believe in each other when you realize that what made the honeymoon so perfect wasn't a magic trick. What made the honeymoon perfect was the very real ways in which you treated each other at that time – the ways you were loving each other at that time. It was what you were willing to do for each other at that time. *That was not sleight of hand. That was real. That was you!*

In teaching psychotherapists how to help their clients, one pioneering psychiatrist said that you can only go as far with your clients as you have gone with yourself. The same thing holds true for your relationship. You can only go as far with your partner as you have gone with yourself. Have faith in yourself, have faith in your love – and turn the page.

How to Use This Book:
Quick-Fix Lists

I have done my best to make this book easy for you to refer to over and over again by offering a 'Relationship Quick-Fix Guide' in the beginning of the book followed by more Quick-Fix Lists after most of the chapters. The 'Quick-Fix Guide' cites 53 of the most common relationship complaints, which are divided under various subheadings (fights, sex, etc.) While it's important to read the whole book from beginning to end, it is organized so that you can find your problem in the 'Quick-Fix Guide', flip to the corresponding pages, read that section now or refer to it again and again as you need it. Whether you are getting the silent treatment, or your partner is too demanding or whether you are about to lose hope or hit the roof, the guide will help you find:

Solutions: Strategic moves and tactics you can use that have worked for others before to solve that problem.

Another way to think about the problem: If you've 'already tried that', then you can read about tactics to explore the problem differently, enlarge your ideas about it, redefine the problem, and come at it from an entirely new angle that will to fresh, additional strategies.

An understanding of why this problem is so upsetting for you: Someone else might not be so bothered by what bothers you. Perhaps this problem resonated with your own past and has greater meaning for you. Could it be you've parachuted into this territory before?

The rest of the Quick-Fix Lists constitute a sort of a relationship crib sheet. I've distilled the information in chapters and teased out the central tactics – the actions you need to take to improve a situation. Again, you do need to read the whole book through at least once so you know what

I'm talking about, but after that, when you need help fast, you can look at the Quick-Fix Lists at the end of the chapters – what you need to know will be there. One couple I know tacks them on their refrigerator when they are going through a particular set of problems. Another man I know typed a Quick-Fix List into his computer so he could print it out at a moment's notice.

> Remember: The focus of this book is on how mistakes are corrected rather than on how mistakes are made.

Throughout the book, I have tried to intersperse gender, but most of the techniques work for either gender, not just the gender portrayed there. On occasion, it may seem to you that some of the roles I've portrayed are stereotypes. I've used them because they are true, even though they may not apply to everybody, and even though I wish they were not so often true. Anyway, you may want to modify some of the techniques, feeling that some are not right for you because of your age, religion, or sexual orientation. As I said earlier, all of the tactics will require your own personal touch. In your hands, they will change into techniques with a piece of you in them. Feel free to tinker, to make improvements. If you find something that works especially well, drop me a note – I'd love to learn from you.

Hot Issues

Another phrase you will see throughout this book is *hot issues*. This refers to how your buttons get chronically pushed in a predictable fashion in a relationship. You see this in the guy in the diner who moans, 'My wife doesn't understand me – I just can't please her,' as he eats a big, fat chili dog with the works – knowing he's supposed to be a low-fat diet and that his wife will surely smell the chili. The wife will be upset he broke his diet, she will upset him with how she handles the information, and the only way he knows how to calm himself is to eat. It's also the woman who says, 'My Arnie doesn't communicate – he just yells,' as she buys another expensive dress that will make overburdened Arnie blow up when he sees the bill on their joint credit card. When Arnie blows up, she gets anxious, and when she anxious, she shops. Hot issues are problems that happen in a circular fashion that keep the problem going.

Hot issues are targeted throughout the book, and they are described more fully later. The reason they require so much attention is that, as you can see from the examples above, they happen on more than one level:

SURFACE ISSUE	DEEPER ISSUE
If you picked up your socks...	We're not equal partners.
I burned the toast.	I want you to know I'm mad at you, but I won't just say it.
I spent too much on an item.	I want attention and don't care how I get it.
I'm too tired for sex.	You're not getting any until you help me with the housework.
I ate two chili dogs.	I'm not taking care of myself, and I'm gonna make sure you know it. That'll teach you.

As you read this book you will learn how to think about surface issues and the deeper issues. When you find yourself screaming about socks or burnt toast, you can decide whether that is the real fight – of course, I must say that when you see two adults screaming over such items as toasts or socks, it would seem reasonable to assume that more than toast or socks is at the heart of the fight.

You may decide to focus your energy on the surface issue (the toast or the socks) and go for immediate results. However, when you approach a problem that way, the results can be temporary. If that happens, you may decide to focus on the deeper issue as a way to end the hot issue and solve the problem. It's like the Oxfam saying about how you can feed a person or you can teach that person to be a farmer so she can feed her whole family. As you begin to read more about Guerrilla Mating Tactics you can ask yourself what the hottest issues are in your own relationship. You can then correct them on the surface and see if it seeps down to the core, and if that doesn't work, you can correct them on the level of what is going on beneath the surface.

6, 7, 8, 9, 10 Guerrilla Mating Tactics Solutions

When you read about hot issues, you will also be reading about how to work towards solutions. Throughout the book solutions come in the form of tactics, which are listed and enumerated following the description of the problem. Problems and the people who have them are complex. There is rarely one right solution that works for everyone. You can try the solutions that appeal to you and seem easiest, and if they don't work, you can try others. Just as the hot issues arise on multiple levels, so do the tactics. Some tactics are like plasters, covering a hurt so that time can heal it. Some tactics are more like surgery – dealing with cause rather than symptom. Whichever way you decide to go, you will have many choices and you can try them all to see what works best, and even invent your own.

Guerrilla Success Stories

Don't get the idea that all you will hear are relationship tales of woe. Sprinkled throughout the book you will find numerous vignettes, all true, of happy couples who are truly enjoying each other and their relationship. In some stories, couples have found solutions for ongoing problems; in other stories couples have found ways to protect their time together; and in yet other stories, couples are revealing the silly and sexy things they do behind closed doors. These are stories of playfulness and good will. You'll have a chance to see what a relationship looks like when it is working.

The Epilogue

Another feature of this book is the list of statements you will find if you turn to the Epilogue. Flip here when you need quick support. It is a compilation of key phrases that some might call 'affirmations', some might call 'the moral of the book' and others might simply call 'reminders'. I put these phrases here for when you need a reminder of why working on your relationship is worth the trouble, or for when you need a little booster shot of love. These pages are worth glancing at before you start your day, or during a quiet afternoon, or before you turn off the light and go to sleep.

The Emergency Plan

Last, I am, and always have been, a big believer in having a solid emergency plan. I do not enter a cinema or stay over in a hotel without one, and I definitely wouldn't want to be without one in a relationship. If you have purchased this book during a time when you feel overwhelmed with hopelessness, or your fights escalate out of control, or nothing you try has worked, you can turn immediately to the end of this book and find a lengthy section on how and where to find and how to use a couples' therapist to help you get on track. This section will tell you the warning signs of serious relationship trouble, and it will offer guidance for couples on all income levels. Hold on. There's a lifeline at the back of the book if you need one.

RELATIONSHIP QUICK-FIX GUIDE

53 Relationship Problems and What Page to
Look on for Quick Solutions

My Partner Has Problems That I Want to Change

I Have Problems That I Want to Change

In geo-physics much is known of the dynamics of earthquakes, but no one yet has stopped one; similarly, the science of physical-chemistry is aware of the enormous quantities of energy locked up in a shovelful of sand, but as yet no one has been able to boil an egg with it.

— Smith Ely Jellife

1

THE END OF THE HONEYMOON IS NOT THE END OF THE ROAD: TRAINING FOR THE MISSION

one

YOUR PARTNER IS YOUR ALLY

Marriages are made in heaven, but they are practised on earth.
    – A justice of the peace at my friends Steve and Leslie's wedding.

She climbs into bed ... curling inward like a bent spoon. He flips on his side, away from her, but his breathing tells her he isn't sleeping yet. Still, there is nothing to say. The minor irritations have taken on a life of their own – like a crash on the L.A. freeway, the pile-up is overwhelming. She thinks about the cliché marital advice she's heard about every Tom, Dick and Aunt Harriet over and over about the secret of a happy marriage. 'Never go to bed angry at each other. Always make up before the lights go out.' She'd like to smack Aunt Harriet. It's not the first time this thought has occurred to her.

Who has these relationships, she wonders, these marriages, easy as no-iron sheets? She takes a long, slow breath. She wants to reach over – it's what Aunt Harriet would have done. She wants to, but it's as if her arms have a mind of their own. 'I never wanted this,' she thinks.

His breathing changes. He's sleeping now. She curls her hands against his chest in tiny fists. Dreams come like the noises a blacksmith makes, hammers on anvils, clanking against the night. In the morning, she opens her eyes and she has a thought. It's not a new thought, but she doesn't usually have it in the morning. She fears she may have made a terrible, terrible mistake.

He wakes to find her turned away from him. He remembers a time when they slept holding each other every night. She couldn't get enough of him. He felt the same way about her. He has no idea how to

---

find comfort or sue for peace. She's not my real wife, he tells himself, not the same woman. She's the body double, the changeling. He wonders if they will ever have a civil conversation again.

It is nights like this one that bring couples into my office – nights full of the loneliness that you can feel with your partner right beside you. These are the nights that make couples who truly love each other feel like embattled soldiers. These are the nights that cause couples to begin the long march to a peace maker, a couples' therapist, who can help these two scared people to find their way back to a time when they felt as if they were on the same side. In this case, it was a woman named Maria who called my office to make a first appointment after she and her husband Jack had experienced too many nights like this one. When they entered my office, Maria sat on the couch facing me, while Jack took a chair on the other side of the room, next to the far wall. Maria looked at me pleadingly while Jack remained absorbed with examining a speck on his jacket. When I asked what brought them to see me, Maria reached reflexively for a tissue and started weeping softly and talking at the same time. She said that she was confused about the relationship ... she loved Jack ... but she was so unhappy. Suddenly, her tone changed, and she sounded angry: 'He says I'm not passionate enough.' Then she turned to Jack and fired, 'Why should I be when you treat me like a machine? You treat me like I've got an on/off switch instead of a brain.'

Eventually I asked Jack if what Maria wanted to talk about was the same thing he wanted to talk about. Jack turned to Maria and burst forth with his competing anger: 'Why do you have to have such screwed-up friends who need to talk to you until midnight? When I come home, you're always on the phone. When it's time to go to bed, you disappear.' Jack looked at me and asked, 'How am I supposed to relate to a woman whose lips are permanently attached to a telephone receiver?'

I sat quietly and listened for a few minutes while they fired complaints at each other. The sadness, anger, bitterness, confusion, frustration, exhaustion and hurt were not strangers to me. In fact, I'd heard different versions of the same war stories many times. Just that day another couple had sounded just as angry, just as war-torn, just as bewildered. Linda accused Tony of being a workaholic who purposely avoided her and their four-year-old daughter, while Tony swore Linda would only be happy if they were joined at the hip. Linda felt that the entire burden of their daughter, Lily, was on her shoulders even though they both worked.

Linda was especially angry at how Tony was handling his two solo parenting nights. He had agreed to make dinner twice a week while Linda took a class, but on his solo nights, he served Lily pizza and ice cream. Then he made jokes about these items containing the four food groups. He said that he felt his dinners were fine since Lily would get a proper diet on the other five nights, when Linda cooked.

Linda said their fights were like the Derby – one verbal gunshot and they were off. Grenades were tossed right and left as they flew through their greatest hits: the argument about how little empathy Linda has for what Tony is going through at work, the argument about how Tony can't get his priorities straight. They hit their crescendo with the arguments about Lily, his socks on the floor, her nagging, his inability to hear her feelings. What a tangled mess!

And earlier, another couple, Marcella and Lionel, told their own story of marital unrest. Marcella said that Lionel was irresponsible, that he overspent and made it impossible for them to save money, while Lionel said that Marcella acted like his mother, watching over his every move and waiting for him to screw up. And, speaking of his mother, Marcella said that Lionel's mother was a pain in the neck, calling several times a day at inopportune moments and grilling Marcella to make sure she was doing right by Lionel. This had been going on for years. 'Why can't you tell your mother to naff off?' Marcella sniped in utter frustration.

There Is Hope

These are the kinds of stories that couples tell a marriage counsellor, stories filled with snipers, ambushes, predawn attacks. But no matter how angry they are or how hurt, whether they know it or not, these couples have hope or they never would have called a marriage counsellor in the first place. The same could be said for you. You have hope or you wouldn't have picked up this book. Whether you feel like your relationship is being attacked by sharks or nibbled to death by ducks, a piece of you hopes and believes that if things changed, you'd be happy – or, at the very least, happier. That's why you are here.

So here are my first four pieces of advice:

1 *Don't panic*. There is not a couple alive who has been together for more than two years who has not known the kind of unhappiness and unrest you are feeling. If you want to, you can learn how to keep your relationship above water – even if your partner is resistant. Often, your

partner is just as frustrated as you are and wants things to improve as much as you do, but he or she is unable to make the first move or is trying to improve things in a way that doesn't work (which, unfortunately, can make things seem worse). You can begin to peel away the layers of hurt and futility and make remarkable progress even with a resistant partner – *because you can learn strategies that do work*. The fact that you are trying to understand more about your relationship puts you in an even better position to get through difficult days. Every day, couples do survive.

2 *Remember that happy couples have the same problems as couples whose relationships break up.* All couples argue about the same things – money, sex, child rearing, intrusive relatives and friends, jealousy, shattered expectations, not enough time together, different values – there really are a handful of problems that come up for all of us over and over again. The difference is that couples whose relationships survive and flourish have learned how to resolve some problems, how to accept some problems, how to let go of some problems, how to keep their mouths shut about some problems, how to build on the strengths in their relationship, how to endure some problems, and how to hang in there when that little voice tells them they should find a foxhole and jump in. You and your partner can learn how to do these things and be a happy couple too.

3 *Stay the course.* Fixing your relationship is like starting a diet or an exercise programme – the first few days or weeks are the toughest. People tend to feel deprived when they start a new regime, even when it's good for them. However, if you stick with the programme, you soon start to feel like you are making progress. Because you will be trying new behaviours and new ways of thinking about your relationship, initially, you too may feel deprived. At first, you may not like the feelings you have, nor your partner's responses. Keep turning the pages. Give the new information a chance. No matter what shape your relationship is in and no matter how long it's been that way and no matter how badly things seem to be going, there is a good chance that things can improve. If you don't stick with the programme, you may never know.

4 *Your partner is your ally.* Sure, you may hate the way he is behaving or the way she treats you. You have legitimate gripes, real problems with getting through to your partner, verifiable difficulties with finding mutually satisfying ways to work things out. When one partner is a workaholic or one never serves more than a

pizza to the kids or one constantly complains or the lovemaking has stopped – that is no way for two people to live. Yes, you are pulling out your hair for a reason.

But that doesn' t mean you and your partner are on different, opposing sides.

Even if you feel you and your partner are pitted against each other, your partner is your ally. Remember, the enemy is the harsh words, stupid mistakes, combative impulses, bad habits of interacting, accusations – *not* your partner. The two of you will learn to join forces to combat these unsatisfying ways of relating rather than fighting each other, getting nowhere, and maintaining the not-so-good status quo. It's really quite simple – if fighting with each other hasn't helped things improve between you, if it hasn't brought you what you wanted, then you may as well try fighting something besides each other. The two of you can start fighting for the relationship.

In future chapters you will learn more about the many ways in which your partner is your ally. In Chapter 4 you will learn about the impact of your past on your present. You will see why your partner is the one you have chosen with whom to rework old family relationships. In Chapter 12, you will learn how you can fall in love over and over again with the same person – entering richer, deeper honeymoon moments. I'll say it again: Your partner is your ally.

Why Aren't Relationships Easier?

The end of the honeymoon may frustrate you to the point of thinking that your fate is to spend the rest of your life dangling unsatisfying relationships off the isthmus of your ego. You will be certain you've made a mistake, and you'll be right. In fact, you've made several. It's just that your mistakes probably have less to do with whom you've chosen than with wrongheaded notions of what you thought you were getting when you chose. In fact, thinking that your only mistake is that emotionally paralysed lunkhead you latched on to is probably naive.

On the other hand, sticking around to see what's left after the smoke clears is hard. Some folks never do it. When the relationship hits a storm they jump ship, certain that they chose the wrong person. I appeared on *Sally Jesse Raphael* with a woman who had been in 53 relationships – a woman who never moved beyond the idea that she'd picked the wrong men. Yet, it is only by *not* jumping ship, even when you are certain it's sinking, that new possibilities for your relationship will occur. You can put on your wetsuit, stick around now and take a look, or you can spend the rest of your life experiencing uncontrollable tics every time you flip through the soft rock stations and come upon Joni Mitchell lamenting about only being able to recall love's illusions.

It's your choice. And while you're making it – one more time:

Remember: Your partner is your ally.

You Aren't Unusual If You're Having Problems

If you're having trouble maintaining the goodwill and the passion that brought the two of you together in the first place, you're not alone. The reality is you've probably been taught more about how to floss your teeth than about how to be in a relationship. So it is understandable that when problems arise, you don't know how to handle them.

DARLING, I USED OUR NEST EGG...

Some years ago, Jake and Bonnie were getting married. Jake was a die-hard fan of musician Henny Youngman. He talked Henny much of the time. At their wedding, after the best man's toast and before the meal, Bonnie stood up, took the mike and recited:

Jake, after this we won't have a penny

For our wedding day, I bring you Henny

Bonnie had, unbeknownst to Jake, taken her savings and hired Henny Youngman to come to their wedding and surprise him, and sit at the bridal table with them for the evening. What a sight it was – the three of them sitting at a table having dinner and eating wedding cake.

In addition, contemporary relationships bear great stress that differs radically from the stressors that plagued relationships in the past. For example, it's really only in the past 50 years that couples have begun expecting to find lasting love and lasting self-fulfilment in a marriage. Can you imagine, hundreds of years ago, couples refusing to marry without the promise of self-fulfilment? In those days they were lucky to get a sheep thrown in with the bride or groom.

Today, we have so many choices in how to live and how to love that we have begun to ask more and more from our relationships. We want to be more than happy and more than in love. We want love that knocks us for a loop, love that makes us swoon, makes us feel, makes us glow. We want love like grouting – love that will fill in the holes and smooth us out. We want love-makeovers like in *Cosmopolitan* magazine, where a plain Jane finds her man, becomes a knockout, and never again leaves home without subdued backlighting. Thank God for that first honeymoon, a place where we feel all this and more … temporarily.

Why the Honeymoon Must End

When you look at the fabulous honeymoon feelings, the sexual intensity, the drama, it's no wonder we never want the first honeymoon to end. None the less, you *will* one day wake up listening to him honk into a wad of tissue, your teeth *will* clench when she asks you for the third time when you'll be home that night, you *will* hit the roof when he puts that dripping can of lager on your walnut heirloom:

One day, you will no longer be able to count upon your hormones and your imagination to continue to give your partner the paint job of your dreams.

Something unpleasant will happen, and you will join the ranks of zillions of other people as you hit your forehead and mutter the words, 'What the hell am I doing here?' The turning point starts with three unavoidable changes that we all experience within the first few years of being together.

Loss Number 1: Chasing Versus Winning

Nothing is so exhilarating as the chase. He wines her, dines her, practises his best behaviour, writes sweet notes, thinks about her, strategizes to prove he won't let her down like her last lover, goes all out to win her. For her part, she wears a halter top as if it were nothing special, lazily brushes her finger along his cowlick, becomes immensely interested in his interests, is thrilled to take a day trip with him to his old neighbourhood and meet his drinking pal, 'Stinky' who is still hanging out at the same bar they went to back then.

You both feel electrified as you can feel each other opening up – as you approach this peak experience, winning the heart. It is in the moments when winning each other exists just in front of your face, almost in reach, that your exhilaration is greatest.

After she declares her love, soon your heart won't pound quite as hard. After he declares his love, you'll throw a jumper over the halter top if you're chilly. Most of us feel simultaneously thrilled and let down. We begin to feel more grounded, more stable. The biological and emotional intensity has somewhat lessened. Initially, the stability of love won, even with its vast rewards, is no match for the lush intensity of wooing, the magnificence of a first deep kiss, the days and nights of chasing your beloved.

Loss Number 2: Mystery Versus Knowledge

When we fall in love, the passion vibrates around the fact that our partner is unknown to us. Her sexual energy and his deepest longings are mysteries. The state of not-knowing intensifies the passion, for at any moment a surprise can occur. What will he say if I do that? Does she believe in the G-spot? Does she have a G-spot? Could I find her G-spot? What kinds of noises will he make when he has an orgasm? Obviously, when you win your partner, certain mysteries fade and a piece of the passion fades with it.

Of course, there are deeper mysteries to be discovered, and we'll get to those. You know that you can live with someone for 20 years and feel a sense that you don't really know him. But the deeper mysteries present a different kind of drama. When you fall in love, the mystery exists because your partner is new to you. The diminishment of this type of heart-pounding mystery comes with the territory of winning your beloved.

Loss Number 3: Rosy Light Versus Harsh Light

In the beginning, we are all on our best behaviour. We regulate how we act and react. We work at being scintillating, charming. We shower carefully. We remember to put the loo seat down.

Things just aren't the same when you experience firsthand your partner's bathroom habits or walk in on him wearing his tartan boxer short, all stretched out at the waist, as he hawks phlegm into the toilet.

We all go through these shocks with our partner. Things won't seem the same when she insists on saving 10 years of the magazine *Opera News* and all 10 years end up on, over and under the coffee table. Things won't seem the same when she asks you if she needs to lose five pounds day after day after day after day.

With the unfolding of the routine, we see our partner in a different light – he gives in to his mother, she feels overburdened at work, he wants to take his dog on holiday. As these events permeate the relationship, we see our partner in a harsher light, which shines on a world that we are not the centre of.

These three changes feel momentarily confusing, like the first drops of rain that hit you on a steamy day on a city street. At first, you're concerned because you forgot your umbrella. You're not sure if you're going to ruin your outfit. Then, you're not sure if it's rain at all. You look above you to see if the drops fell from an errant air conditioner. And, in that brief, slightly befuddled, completely unprotected moment of questioning the sky, Hurricane Sally detonates, and the honeymoon is over.

Discovery, Disappointment and Devaluation

As terrible as it feels, the end of the first honeymoon doesn't mean something is wrong with your relationship. Most relationships follow a natural rather than pathological progression – it's natural, but it just isn't pleasant. The progression goes like this:

THE 3-D HONEYMOON

*D*iscovery of your beloved:	He's the best thing that ever happened to me
*D*isappointment in your beloved:	He's not who I thought he was
*D*evaluation of your beloved:	He means less to me

The honeymoon is the discovery phase of love. The disappointment phase begins as you notice your partner's first flaws. In love we are excruciatingly sensitive, like the Princess and the Pea, to the slightest hint that our partner is flawed. You had such exaggerated positive feelings about your partner. So, when you do see a flaw, it becomes amplified, and reamplified, until it vibrates like the megawatt amplifiers of Metallica.

Part of the price we pay for the honeymoon is that, because we exaggerated our partner's perfection, when the flaws appear, they seem bigger.

In the disappointment stage, instead of concentrating on the harmony in your relationship, you concentrate on your partner's flaws. The main quality of the disappointment phase is that you are disillusioned with what your partner *does*, but you give her the benefit of the doubt (If she stopped doing that …, If he cleaned up the bathroom …) If she did things differently, the relationship would work. Thus, disappointment always contains hope.

Devaluation, the third *D*, comes after disappointment and encompasses an actual depreciation of your partner's character. Devaluation means you are disillusioned with who he *is* (rather than with what he does); you think he is worth less as a person. Although most of us experience devaluing our partner when the honeymoon is over, this feeling is stronger and lasts longer for some of us than for others. I wish I could tell you that you will only have to go through the devaluation stage once, but if you've ever been in a long-term relationship, you already know that isn't true. Multiple honeymoons means multiple crashes – multiple devaluations. In relationships, there are many mountains to climb – raising a family, buying a home with a leaky roof, losing a job, illness, an empty nest, expensive dental work, bosses we hate, general crabbiness, dividing housework. With so many experiences, how can our partner always live up to our expectations? These are times when, under stress, we fall back into bad habits, less functional ways of coping. You will gain greater control over future crashes, and eventually you won't devalue your partner. However, whether you devalue each other or not, a person can get pretty sick and tired of spinning her wheels in the same old fights.

If you are wondering if you have devalued your partner, take this brief quiz and find out.

DEVALUATION QUIZ

When my partner comes home from work and I am on the phone, I
A   Hang up because I want to be with him.
B   Wave and keep on talking.
C   Take the phone into the other room because it's rude to complain about him in his presence.

When I haven't seen my partner for more than 10 hours, I
A   Go into a stupor till he comes home.
B   Go about my normal routine but miss him.
C   Go into Manny's Bar and buy a round for the house.

When we crawl into bed at night, I think:
A   I'm the luckiest person alive.
B   We have our ups and downs, but I'm happy.
C   Sleep will come if I lie still long enough.

After we've made love, I
A   Name her genitalia after one of the seven wonders.
B   Name her genitalia after one of the seven dwarfs.
C   Name her genitalia after one of the seven sins.

Three or four a's: You're still in the honeymoon stage.
Three or four b's: The honeymoon is over. You've moved smoothly on to the next stage.
Three or four c's: You've devalued your partner.
Read on.

You may be sceptical as to whether all relationships experience devaluation. Off the top of your head, you may think of a few famous couples whose intense love for each other never abated – Romeo and Juliet, Marc Antony and Cleopatra, Tony and Maria. Yes, it's true! None of these couples reached the devaluation stage of love – and for a good reason. They died before that could happen (except for Marc Antony, who went back to Rome). Their relationships never had to stand the real test of time. Your greatest fantasy of love may be of a love that never got past the first *D*, the 'discovery of the beloved' phase. In the discovery phase, we are all Romeos, all Juliets, and the promise of love is huge.

Devaluation is a turning point. Even if you are committed to your relationship, your impulse may be to cut your losses and run for the nearest foxhole. Sometimes, you may be justified in following the impulse to leave the relationship. If you've discovered truly disturbing character flaws (hanging dirty underwear on doorknobs does *not* fall in this category), leaving him will make life easier for you. On the other hand, if your impulse is to run from a decent mate when you want a relationship, but you feel certain you can't get your needs met, it may be a signal that you are reacting to the end of the honeymoon by devaluing your partner.

The Good News: Devaluation Is Not the End of Love

Devaluing a partner is so scary because it makes us doubt whether we have chosen the right person. We're scared that when the honeymoon is over, the love goes with it. Believe me when I tell you that this isn't true. If you get nothing else from this book, get this:

> Devaluation feels like the end, and it is – but it is the end of the honeymoon, not the end of the love.

It's time to make a transition from Relationship Oz, where love unfolds in Technicolor, to a working union with the two imperfect partners. It's just that you're facing the problem that all couples face:

A transition never feels like a transition, it feels like a crisis.

Let's recap the first three steps of a relationship: You discover your lover, you are disappointed in your lover and, when the honeymoon is over, you devalue your lover. Eventually, each of us must face the end of the first honeymoon and take the all-important fourth step in one of two directions:

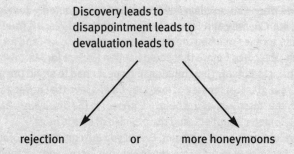

Discovery leads to
disappointment leads to
devaluation leads to

rejection   or   more honeymoons

You probably know how to get from devaluation to rejection. Do you want to learn how to get from devaluation to more honeymoons?

Guerrilla Mating Tactics

Moving on from the honeymoon stage just doesn't sound as romantic as being in the honeymoon stage, and most of us are romantics at heart. None the less, the success of your relationship depends on moving ahead. That's where Guerrilla Mating Tactics come in. Guerrilla Mating Tactics will help you break through to a more solid, enduring love by providing relationship boot camp, basic training for love. You will be supplied with a system of manoeuvres that will help you understand the honeymoon for what it is – a first step towards deep loving:

> The end of the honeymoon is not a wall; it's the next perimeter of human experience, filled with great promise.

In order to get through that perimeter you need the courage and skill of a soldier. This includes a strategic set of goals for how you want your relationship to function, the willingness to risk, a belief that something good will come from this, the faith that you're working towards something worth having, and plenty of *energy*:

When you have the energy to want to throw each other out the window, you also have the energy to make your relationship work.

Or, as the fortune cookie I opened tonight read, 'Discontent is the first step in the progress of a man, of a woman, or of a nation.' (Actually, I added the word *woman*, but I know Confucius would have wanted it that way.)

> **Remember:** *The problem is the place you start working, not the place you stop working.*

WHEN HE FORGETS OUR ANNIVERSARY

Patricia says that the fact that Herb always forgets their anniversary is no longer a problem for her. She's saved the first anniversary card he gave her. When he forgets, she puts that card out on the table and rewrites the present date. She has given that card to herself five times so far. They laugh and laugh every time they look at that ragged card with all the dates crossed out. In the beginning, it made Patricia angry and sad when Herb forgot. But she realized that he's a great guy in a thousand more important ways. These days, she looks forward to Herb's forgetting. It's good for a laugh.

A Wonderful Surprise Will Follow

Hang in there. You have a wonderful surprise in store, even if you don't think so now. The wonderful surprise about love is that love is much stronger, much more resilient than you could ever imagine. Think about it. We all know couples who break up and get back together, or couples who break up because they are miserable and don't get over each other for years to come. That is because the love is so much stronger than they knew – than they ever dreamed it could be. They just didn't know how to massage the love into a happy relationship. So relax – you don't need a princess. Your love is strong enough to see her faults, make it through the devaluation phase, and love her anyway.

You see, the first honeymoon ends because you don't need it anymore. You can trust your partner, yourself and your love without the perfect conditions you required on the honeymoon. Think of the analogy of a parent teaching a child to ride a bicycle. In the beginning, all children use stabilizers. The child requires the peace of mind this extra support offers

– this extra assurance that she won't fall down. But one fine day, the child isn't unsteady on the bike anymore. The child is confident, ready to take up a new challenge. The parent knows that it's time to take the stabilizers off. The child rides off on the bike, a little shaky at first, but riding the bike none the less. The fact is that the child learned how to ride the bike with the stabilizers, then she didn't need them anymore. The first honeymoon is like stabilizers of mature love. And, paradoxically, you will discover that when you let go of a honeymoon and come down gracefully, you develop the spirit and resilience that paves the way to new honeymoons – richer, deeper honeymoons that occur again and again.

Every chapter you read from here on in will be filled with tactics, game plans, tips and strategies on how to work with your partner, how to work on your own if your partner is resistant, and how to help each other. There's a good chance that the best is yet to come. You get to decide if you *want* to try because, while there will be some laughs and high spirits along the way, it won't always be fun or easy. A soldier struggles – she knows what it means to slog through the mud, he knows what it means to feel unprotected and uncertain, she knows how it feels when the sun goes down and she's scared.

But you keep putting one foot in front of the other anyway and you keep your mission of defending your relationship in mind – that's what make a soldier. If you keep going you can reach a resilient, rewarding and enduring alliance, a place you can call home. I'll be your drill instructor. Get in formation. Check the supplies. Don't give up – you've worked too hard and you've invested too much:

> The least you can do is to commit as much sweat to happiness as you've committed to keeping lousy relationships together.

two

RELATIONSHIP BOOT CAMP:
BEGINNING TO INITIATE POSITIVE CHANGE

He's swamped at work with no sign of things easing off. He swears he loves you, yet he makes less and less time for you. No matter how lighthearted your request for attention, he responds as if you are a burden. How can you ask this of him now – when he's emotionally strapped? You're so angry. And just beneath the anger lies the hurt. And just beneath the hurt is something scarier ... the fear that this might not work out.

She is a bottomless well of wants, needs, demands. And after you've adjusted to putting down the loo seat, picking up your wet towels, and calling when you're going to be out late, she's got a new, improved, longer list of demands. Will it ever end, or must you come face to face with the awful truth: You can't please her.

You stare at each other in disbelief. When did this happen? When did you start battling over whether you get to watch a rerun of *Porridge* or she gets to watch a rerun of *Cheers*? It seems as if nothing – absolutely nothing – is too small to argue over.

Atten*shun*!

It's time to leave your comfortable beds and enter relationship boot camp – but unlike military boot camp, in relationship boot camp you get a choice:

> You get a bad haircut, do 20 push-ups with one hand behind your back, march 20 miles and then clean the latrine under the eagle eye of an irascible sergeant from the 'old school',

or

You can make positive changes in your relationship.

For those of you who made the first choice – MARCH!

Now, for those of you who made the second choice, take notes. Today you will take the first lesson in basic training for love. The first lesson is a system for initiating positive changes in your relationship – this will include learning how to deal with, negotiate for, ask for, initiate and even embrace all kinds of changes. Before you do anything else, though, you need to be trained in that obstacle course called 'change'. Then, we'll look at hot issues in a relationship and set up a system of tactics for softening and easing them. You can use the tactics that will be presented to deal with a variety of hot issues, many more than the ones highlighted here.

That's why you signed on, isn't it? Because you want things to change? God knows, you've been trying hard enough. And what you've been trying to do is change things for the better. You've probably tried everything and anything within reason. Because you're ready – ready to help, nudge or elbow your partner into change. You're ready to hurl, boost, even heave your partner into change.

Good. Now that we've got that cleared up, let's move on to you. Are *you* ready to change? More important, are you ready to change first?

But I'm Not the Problem

It's easy to give the order that you want things to change, but much more complicated to do something about it. I'm sure it's true that you've done more than your share of trying to get this relationship back on track: after all, you're the person who purchased this book. But face it, all you've done is increase your frustration. Moreover, even though you've bent over backwards, further than any human before has you has bent over backwards, it just hasn't worked. This brief quiz shows just how double-jointed you are.

If you answered 'true' to even one of these, then our work has to start with exploring your myths about change. If you're anything like the rest of us, you've adopted some rigid and self-defeating myths about change, and these myths aren't harmless. In fact, they're getting in the way of making your life better.

Myths About Change

Myths develop as broad explanations for feelings or events that we do not totally understand. In the best sense, myths spur imagination, but we also use them to avoid dealing with what's real in our lives. If we have pat explanations, there is no need for us to do the work of understanding, changing or figuring out complex feelings.

Myths make us think we've solved the mystery, and you know how we love to solve a good mystery, how we hate loose ends. We are seekers, and we like immediate answers. And, since life and love are full of unanswerables, we create stories that seem to a fit a situation and we tell them as if they were true.

Here are some of the most common myths about change along with some truer ways of thinking about it:

Myth: Change means sacrifice.

Truth: Somehow, we've adopted the idea that in order to change things for the better, someone has to give something up. In truth, change is about *adding* things to your repertoire. It is about having more behaviours, ideas and interventions to choose from. When you have more to choose from, you'll have a better sense of what works, what doesn't, what you can live with and what you can't. That knowledge will help you, and you won't be sacrificing anything.

Myth: The goal is to change things back to how they were.

Truth: You can never go back, but you can move forward – to a better place.

Myth: Change means trying harder and doing more.

Truth: Change means difference; it rarely means working harder to do more of the same. You're probably already trying too hard and doing too much. It's silly to try harder to do what already isn't working. The idea is to uncover new variations, solutions and tactics to tackle ongoing troubles. Difference can actually be easier.

Myth: Deep change is long, slow and painful.

Truth: Change can happen on the spin of a coin. Moreover, it can be full of wonder, adventure and, yes, even fun.

Myth: Change means I have to become the person my partner wants me to be.

Truth: Don't start thinking that this is a wimpy book where we replay the mini-series of your life or encourage your status as a codependent Cinderella who thinks too much. Positive change is not about accommodating, taking total responsibility for, or submitting within the relationship. Positive change is about evolving as an individual and as a couple. Positive change will propel you *out* of unsatisfactory roles, not *into* them.

Myth: If I try hard enough, things will change.

Truth: You can act as an instrument of change, but you cannot maintain ongoing responsibility for the relationship. In the end you need a partner who wants to work with you to be happy. Don't make the mistake of shouldering the whole relationship on an ongoing basis until you are crushed by it. If nothing in this text helps you to move forward, turn to the end of the book, which will tell you how to find a reputable couples' therapist. Some relationship impasses are stickier than others.

Myth: If I can only please her, things will change.

Truth: You are setting yourself up for trouble if you try to invoke change by being a more perfect husband – by agreeing with what she says, by changing your interests to match hers, by viewing change as endless accommodation. This is not change, this is being overly responsible and filled with self-blame. Furthermore, doing so will not make her happy, but it will make you nuts.

Myth: If I take responsibility for changing him, things will get better.

Truth: You must be careful. If your partner is struggling with his issues and you try and jump in to save him, it will be you initiating his changes. If you are the one initiating his changes, HE ISN'T. You could end up stuck in a pattern where you initiate and he responds but never asserts himself. You must learn to model your initiative spirit in a way that leaves room for him to pick up your theme and make it his own. You can't take over his changing. Otherwise, you end up with a passive partner who does what you want, and you end up hating him for it.

Why You're Ready to Change

Change is the essence of life. Our bodies change daily, the world changes daily, we change our minds and our underwear daily. Whether you know it or not, you are always in motion, in change. When your daughter is two, you will be one kind of mother; when your daughter is 15, you will be another kind of mother. When you are president of the bank, you adopt one demeanour; when your puppy wees on your Hermès scarf, you adopt another – demeanour, that is, not puppy. Each way of being requires change and adaptation, and most of us move through our many roles with appropriate finesse.

Moving effectively through change requires personal development, an education as to how you and others have handled change in the past, the ability to take a risk, and a willing heart (it counts if your willing heart is a function of things being so bad that you'll try anything). You have already demonstrated that you have been successful in the past because you take risks all the time. Every time you order seafood, or buy a car, you take a risk. If you can take these risks, you can risk change in your relationship.

You must give up the idea of change as a way to give in.

Consider change as a more effective strategy, one in the long line of strategies you've tried in an attempt to make things better. Consider change as a way to drop old habits in favour of progress. Consider change as a way that you might actually get what you want.

Let's move on and talk about how to change the problems in your relationship.

Problems Form a Circle

If you listen to most couples describe their problems, the explanations are circular, forming a loop:

> *He says:* If she'd stop yelling, I'd stop sulking.
> *She says:* If he'd stop sulking, I'd stop yelling.

Circular explanations are reciprocal, mutually dependent and mutually blaming – 'I react so you act so I react.' Each partner swears that the other 'started it' while he himself is only 'reacting'. For example, he says he is sulking only because she yelled at him the night before. She says she yelled at him the night before only because he avoided her all day. He says he avoided her all day only because two days before that she was highly critical. She says she was critical two days before only because ... and so on and so on. What I want to tell you is that it doesn't matter who is right, whether she catches the blame or he does, whether she started it or he did. What matters is that they are talking in circles and a circle is closed. There is no room for anything to get in or out – no room for new information, no room for compassion, no room for common sense.

The circle of 'who caused what' is closed and thus impossible to change.

Whoever starts it becomes irrelevant when two people are suffering and the relationship is deteriorating.

Breaking the circle and opening the system is what matters most. Fortunately, this you can do alone. Simply stated:

> You do something different, disrupt the circle, and changes will start to take place.

When you get trapped by the idea that *your partner* has to change first, that belief becomes a reflex, a knee-jerk-bad-will reaction. You're cornered. You constrict your range of thinking about issues and your ability to toy with solutions, and you react to what you perceive as bad will with an equal amount of bad will.

Frankly, it may be true that he started it, but even if it is, with all of the times he's started it, if you want your relationship to work, the question you ought to be asking yourself is : *'Have I become more competent at handling it?'*

Dropping a Live Grenade

Guerrilla Mating Tactics for Initiating Positive Change Swiftly

Picture a group of soldiers. They are exploring the inside of a building when they stumble upon a live grenade. One soldier picks it up, panics, tosses it to another soldier, who tosses it to someone else as they all search for an open window. They swiftly toss the grenade back and forth as they try to decide where to throw it so it will do the least harm. All of the energy is invested in getting that bloody grenade out of their hands. No one person wishes to hold on to the grenade for long because it might blow up in his face – so they toss it to each other as they search for a place to let it fly.

Now simply substitute the words *hot issue* for the words *live grenade*. Then, imagine, that the building has no windows! This is how anxiety, troubles and problems generally get handled within the family or couple. Remember that a hot issue is a chronic conflict that doesn't seem to get resolved. It's the drainage system in a couple – it runs underneath the relationship and, from time to time, it backs up. One family member can't hold a hot issue for long; it's too scary. So the issue gets tossed around the family (like a live grenade), with each person trying to get rid of it by tossing it through the air to another person. For example, Dad gets reprimanded at work and feels humiliated, he comes home and says something about his wife watching too much television and this humiliates his wife, she in turn screams at her daughter to clean up her disgusting room, her humiliated daughter swats the cat off the bed. The cat goes into the kitchen and scratches the father's briefcase which has been left on the kitchen chair. Thus, the father's hot issue of humiliation has become a family issue, making the rounds of the family and returning to him. When the father sees his briefcase...

WHEN A PARTNER TRAVELS ALONE FOR BUSINESS

When Jean travels for business, James leaves a note in her suitcase which she will find when she checks in. It may say anything from 'Don't worry honey, I know where you are' to 'I love you. Here's what I've planned for when you come home...'

Dropping the Hot Issue

Now, imagine another scenario. Suppose someone tossed you that hot issue, that live grenade, and *you didn' t catch it*. You let it fall to the ground. It isn't that you didn't care about the person who threw the hot issue. In fact, it's the opposite. It's that you know that catching the person's hot issue will only blow up in your face. And, most important, you know that if you don't catch a hot issue, it fizzles instead of explodes.

Refusing to catch another person's hot issue does not reflect a lack of love. It is not hostility. It is a tactic and, to say it again, a tactic is a strategy for change which acknowledges that keeping that hot issue in the air is not in the best interest of your partner or yourself. Refusing the hot issue breaks the circle, and so, refusing the hot issue initiates change. Refusing the hot issue will teach you how to stop habitually 'reacting'. *Reacting* can be what keeps hot issues, unhelpful interactions, in the air. When you drop the hot issue, prepare to step out of your rut. Let me show you what I mean and how you can use this concept to improve your relationship.

Hot Issue Number 1: She Won't Stop Complaining

Paul says that Annie is chronically negative and never satisfied with his efforts. No matter how hard he has tried to please her, she has a complaint or demand. He wants her to get off his case, and he has tried many ways to get her to stop complaining. Nothing works – not even when he really tries to please her. So Paul doesn't even try to please her anymore. Take, for example, the situation with the dishes. He's agreed to do them half the time, but she isn't satisfied with the way he does them. She finds old egg on them. She has microscope eyes, seeing everything magnified a thousand times. He does the best he can, but it's never good enough. In fact, Paul has got so discouraged that now, he doesn't in fact pay much attention to what he's doing, which makes Annie even madder. Things are no better than when he wouldn't do the dishes at all.

The Hot Issue: If she'd stop complaining, I'd stop doing a second-rate job.

THE SIX-TACTIC SOLUTION
1 Reality-test your partner's reality
2 Reality-test your own reality
3 Try a new way together
4 Use active listening
5 Stop defending yourself
6 Help the complainer complain

Guerrilla Mating Tactic Number 1: Reality-test your partner's reality

When your partner complains, instead of firing a cross-complaint and entering the same old battleground, look for the kernel of truth in her complaint, even when she doesn't have a positive way of getting her point across. Paul ignores Annie's kernel of truth about his skill with the dishes. For example, suppose Annie needed advice on doing something traditionally done by men – something she knew nothing about. Say she got a flat tyre and had never changed one before. Suppose Paul's back was out and he couldn't help her. He would tell her how to change the tyre properly and most likely she would follow his advice exactly, without deviation. What stops the converse from being true? Traditionally, women know more about how to do housework correctly. What stops Paul from seeking Annie's advice on how to do dishes? She seems to know more than he does about how to do it.

Second, we know that women use talk to connect. Annie is not just talking, she's complaining. She wants to connect, yet it seems that building a connection around complaints is all she thinks she can get. Is there some way in which Paul could change the currency of exchange from connection around complaints to connection around warmth? Can Paul jump into the cycle of 'I'd stop complaining if he'd stop doing a second-rate job' and bring about a shift to a more positive, supportive interaction?

Thus, Paul needs to ask himself: If I were willing to listen to Annie and put an end to Annie's criticism, what would we be doing instead of arguing and sulking? Something much scarier than arguing and sulking such as ... er ... real closeness?

Guerrilla Mating Tactic Number 2: Reality-test your own reality

Paul is focused on Annie's complaints, but what about his complaints? Not his complaints about Annie's complaints, but his very own complaints! Does Paul have anger that he does not express directly? Does Paul indirectly show his anger by doing a job halfheartedly? This reminds me of a subtle method of revolt used during the period of slavery in the United States. When ironing, a house slave might burn a big hole in her mistress's favourite yellow dress as a silent protest. Does Paul feel his only recourse is a silent protest, that nothing can be dealt with in a more direct fashion? That was the case for a house slave, but Paul?

Has Paul really tried everything, or has he only tried versions of the same old thing to get Annie to stop complaining? Is it possible that if Paul offered more of himself to Annie, she wouldn't be as provoked by a little egg on her plate? Paul truly needs to investigate *his reality*, the part of himself that may have some investment in keeping Annie as the chronic complainer and keeping himself walking on eggshells. On the smallest level, keeping Annie disgruntled means Paul doesn't have to improve his dishwashing. On the vastly more important level, keeping Annie disgruntled ensures that Paul doesn't have to be in a loving, warm relationship. Is Paul so unfamiliar or so scared of his warm and loving feelings for Annie and hers for him that he is more comfortable with a disgruntled Annie than he is with a satisfied partner? If Annie is disgruntled, Paul doesn't have to do anything different from what he's doing now. On the other hand, if Annie is to be happy, Paul needs to work a little harder at understanding his own anxieties about co-operation and closeness. The following tactics include fairly painless ways for Paul to sort his own reality out.

Guerrilla Mating Tactic Number 3: Try a new way together

Why doesn't Paul invite Annie to join him as he's doing the dishes and ask for comments on his technique? (Or why doesn't Annie offer to join Paul on his turn?) Why not enlist her as the expert and elevate her from a complainant role into the consultant role? This would lift some burden from Paul. He would not have to walk on eggshells, waiting for the bomb to fall. And it would include Annie, give her credit for her expertise (and by the way, Annie is an aerospace engineer; she has expertise in much besides the dishes), and invite her commentary rather than her criticism. It would give her room to communicate positives as well as negatives. And that is what Paul needs to do; he needs to break into the circle of negatives between them and create more space for positives.

In fact, maybe to help her lighten up, Paul could not only invite Annie to watch him do the dishes, he could join her when she does them.

Say: 'Next time I do the dishes, help me out and show me what you want me to do. Also, I'd like your deepest meditations on steel wool.'

This isn't meant to be done in a sarcastic way. It's meant as a pattern change, a rut-buster. If Paul changes his behaviour then he creates new possibilities.

> **Remember:** You are not being asked to pretend things are working when they aren't or to do it all yourself, you're being asked to create a new story in which both of you have responsibility for what isn't working within the relationship. Thus you recognize your own power to improve things. You are no longer a victim, but a co-creator.

Guerrilla Mating Tactic Number 4: Use Active Listening

Most problems the two of you will ever have (and that you will ever have with anyone else as well) can benefit from at least an understanding of active listening techniques. Active listening is a deep listening technique in which you mirror back the heart of your partner's message without adding information, without reacting to what has been said, without interpreting the message:

Annie: The dishes are still dirty. I can't eat off those. I feel like I have to do them all over. What's the point of your doing the dishes if I have to re-do them?

Paul: I didn't get them clean enough, and it's more work for you.

Annie: I'm tired – I was on my feet all day. Now to come home to this when all I want to do is sleep.

Paul: You just can't stand dirty dishes. You feel you won't be able to sleep because of the dishes.

You listen to exactly the words that are spoken, offering no judgment. After you have heard what your partner has to say you repeat or restate back the heart of the message your partner has given you, using many of the same words but trying to capture the essence of her feelings:

Annie: When the dishes are left like this, it pushes my buttons to the max. I want to scream at you.

Paul: You are very upset.

Annie: Don't you have any idea of what this feels like for me?

Paul: You feel I'm oblivious.

Active listening allows you to drop the hot issue by *slowing down your reactions*. You must hear carefully all that is said and that alone slows you down. Poet Naomi Shihab Nye says her favourite line is one from Thailand: 'Life is very short so we must move very slowly.'

Listening is never passive. You can listen hard enough to start sweating. The greatest benefit of active listening is that it helps your partner feel heard. Most of our fights start because we feel we aren't getting through, and this is a way your partner will know she got through. Active listening will help her calm down, will help you calm down, will calm the bubbling emotions down.

In the beginning, you may feel that active listening takes more energy than it's worth because you'll have to learn to think and respond in new ways. I have watched many competent adults struggle through active listening exercises, trying over and over before they get the hang of it. I urge you to sit down together and practise. Keep at it. The benefits will surprise you if you have the discipline to integrate active listening into your lives. And, once, you get the hang of it, it becomes easier.

Warning: Use active listening wisely, *once in a while*. Don't do this all the time or you will start the very common fight known as the 'You're Not My Therapist' fight! This is a fight I am on intimate terms with.

IN CASE OF EMERGENCY

Bob and Carla made a list and put it in a sealed envelope to be broken in case of emergency. They put it in a drawer. On the outside it says, 'In Case of Emergency, Break Open.' Inside it says:

In case of major fight, affair, lasting feud:
1 Do nothing drastic. Allow time to decipher fear, depression, anger.
2 Accept that we can have problems that won't get solved right away.
3 Make no absolutes.
4 We've had great years together. No matter how we screw up, we've got something worth fighting for.

Because active listening is a skill, you can learn it and end up not really paying attention to your partner. Active listening only helps when you put your heart and soul into it.

Guerrilla Mating Tactic Number 5: Stop defending yourself

When someone is a chronic complainer, defending yourself will only increase his opportunities to complain. Instead of defending yourself, put on your high boots and jump into the mess with him.

Beth had a chronically complaining mother who was in a nursing home. Beth was a good daughter, and she visited her mother regularly. But no matter when she came and what she brought, her mother complained about it, saying things such as 'You don't stay long enough ... you come too early ... you come too late.' It is understandable that Beth felt continually on the defensive. I recommended that she stop trying to defend herself and start agreeing with her mother. 'You're right. I came too early. What was I thinking? Where was my brain. I'll leave now because having me around must be irritating to you even though you don't say so.' When Beth began to take this tack, her mother began to rally and defend Beth. As her mother gained perspective on the consequences of

---

her own whinging (Beth might leave, Beth can acknowledge her feelings, Beth is not playing the game anymore), as her mother got in touch with her whinging because the circle was broken and things were happening in a different way, she stopped the complaining once and for all – after 87 years. People can change at any age.

When you feel attacked, it's understandable to want to defend yourself or offer a counterattack. It's understandable, but unproductive. When you did something wrong, say you're sorry – but don't keep defending yourself. Continuing to defend yourself only validates your partner's complaining. *It only keeps the problem going because now you've given your partner licence to continue to talk about it.*

Guerrilla Mating Tactic Number 6: Help the Complainer Complain

The complainer seizes power by asking you to do something and then criticizing how you do it. If you wash the dishes, you didn't use enough hot water; if you choose a restaurant, it's one she already told you she found mediocre. Through a constant stream of criticism, she'll keep you defensive, unbalanced, uncertain. In that way she maintains control. You feel trapped, stepped on, and angry because the efforts you've made are not even noticed, much less appreciated. The complainer feels powerful, you feel small.

Drop the hot issue and initiate positive change by helping the chronic complainer complain, helping them work themselves up.

If he says: It's Sunday morning 6 a.m. The kids have the television turned up too loud.
Say: You're right. It's quite a ruckus.
Don't say: Well, what do you want me to do about it?

If she says: You left a mess in the kitchen.
Say: You're right. I didn't do a good job. I rushed. Show me what I overlooked. Sorry.
Don't say: I did the best I could. I was in a rush because we were going to the movies.
If she says: You never take me anywhere.
Say: It has been a long time since we've gone out.

> *Don't say:* We went bowling last week, what are you complaining about?

Eventually, if you don't play the game, you break the circle. Your partner will need to do something else. If you join the chronic complainer, she may go in one of two directions. The first is that you will liberate her from her complaining role, and she will be free to express positive feelings too, like so:

> *Barbara:* You never take me anywhere
> *Ringo:* It has been a long time since we've gone out.
> *Barbara: (pause)*
> *Ringo:* Yes, we haven't had much fun in a while.
> *Barbara:* Well, we did go bowling a few weeks ago.
> *Ringo:* Right, but not recently. Recently, we haven't gone anywhere or had any fun.
> *Barbara:* But we did have fun that night.
> *Ringo:* I dunno.
> *Barbara:* C'mon. Look at how busy you've been, and me too. We shouldn't be so hard on ourselves. We can still have fun. But we have to set aside time. Let's do that.

The second thing that could happen when you help the complainer complain is that she may feel validated enough to tell you what is beneath the surface hot issue, what is really bothering her.

For example:

> *Barbara:* You never take me anywhere.
> *Ringo:* It has been a long time since we've gone out.
> *Barbara: (pause)*
> *Ringo:* Yes, we haven't had much fun in a while.
> *Barbara:* I guess I've been worried that you didn't want to be around me.
> *Ringo:* Really?
> *Barbara:* Yeah, I thought maybe that you don't love me like you used to – I felt pretty abandoned.

When you help the complainer complain, there is a good chance that something new will happen – that you will break the cycle of complaints.

Hot Issue Number 2: He Never Wants to Talk

Keesha is mystified. She got married to *end* her loneliness. But she's lonelier now than ever. She spends the days teaching third-years, and when she comes home, she is ready to have a more adult conversation with her husband Mike – hah, what a laugh. Even now, as she sits in the living room waiting for Mike to come home, she runs through all the ways to say, 'Let's talk'. First she is Keesha the lighthearted, then Keesha the solemn, then Keesha the African Bitch Queen, then Keesha the casually interested, then Keesha the deeply pained woman. Mike walks through the door, tosses his coat on the dining room table. Keesha approaches him and before she can speak, he scowls, says 'Not now', and walks away.

The Hot Issue: If he'd talk more, I wouldn't be on his case.

THE EIGHT-TACTIC SOLUTION:
1 Reality-test your partner's reality
2 Reality-test your own reality
3 Evaluate your timing
4 Play two hours of sport
5 Schedule short talks
6 Develop yourself
7 Have patience
8 Get additional help when the problem seems more complicated.

Guerrilla Mating Tactic Number 1: Reality-test your partner's reality

We all know that the words 'Let's talk' have different meanings for men and women.

For women, 'Let's talk' means:	Let's be together
	Come closer
	I have so much to tell you

For men, 'Let's talk' means:	Hotel fire
	Code blue
	Man overboard

Women like to talk about:	Paving the way to closeness
	Tenderness
	Connecting feelings
Men like to talk about:	Paving the driveway
	Whether the meat is tender
	Connecting wires

For Keesha, conversation means closeness, and silence means a painful disruption of closeness. But for Mike, conversation with a woman means probing emotional depths that make him feel inept. Mike talks to pass information, not to maintain closeness:

The words 'Let's talk' provide *no* information.

So, you need to start providing more information up front. State what you want to talk about, what you hope to accomplish, and how long this talk will last. Obviously, this is hard to do if you're furious, so wait till you are up to putting your fury aside in favour of positive results. I have personally found that talking goes best when I can provide the most information about what I want to talk about.

Say: Mike, I want to set aside 15 minutes to talk with you in the next day or so about our dishwasher. I think we need a new one, and I've been thinking about how we could afford one. I want to tell you my ideas and hear your ideas before we move ahead on this.

Tip: Don't overwhelm a reluctant talker by asking to discuss more than one thing at a time. Don't say, 'We need to talk about the dishwasher, Little Betty's Brownie trip, and going to my folks for Christmas dinner.'

Tip: When trying to make a sale, a saleswoman never says, 'When can I stop by?' She says, 'Can I stop by Tuesday or would Wednesday be better?' You'll have more success by offering alternatives than you will if you say, 'When can we talk?'

Say: Tom, I want to schedule a short talk because I miss you, and I want to tackle that by making plans for us to get away for a day. Can we talk Tuesday or would Wednesday be better?

As you think about getting your man to talk, always remember that some men, upon hearing these words, fill with primitive, unnamed dread, akin to a Chinese torture version of talk – talk that drops like water on the forehead slowly, forcefully, talk without end. Face it, men have reasons to feel this way. 'Let's talk' can be a veiled assault that really means, 'Let me corner you and tell you what you lack, what I don't get from you, how you hurt me.' After all, we don't usually say 'Let's talk' when we're happy; we say 'Let's talk' when something is wrong.

> **Tip:** Start saying 'Let's talk' when you only want to praise him. Change his belief that 'Let's talk' means something bad will happen.

Guerrilla Mating Tactic Number 2: Reality-test your reality

Keesha takes Mike's silence, compares it to the reasons she thinks that people behave that way (or what it would mean if *she* behaved that way), and makes certain assumptions that fuel her distress:

He'll never want to talk
He doesn't care as much as I care
He takes me for granted
He doesn't respect me
He's self-absorbed
He's bored with me

These conclusions express her hurt and dissatisfaction. They feel true, but are they really true?

In truth, Mike's need to talk may never match Keesha's. None the less, there may be other plausible explanations for Mike's reticence. Perhaps Mike doesn't want to burden her with his problems, perhaps he feels so at ease with her he doesn't need to talk, perhaps he's dealing with his own depression which he does not articulate, perhaps talking is not as enjoyable for him as it is for her.

> **Tip:** Don't leap to conclusions about a behaviour.
> Remember how much better things were when you didn't leap to conclusions:
> You used to think: *He's still mentally at work. How can I help him take his mind off things?*

Now you think: *He'll use anything to avoid me.*

You used to think: *He didn't even notice when I brought the tea. He must be feeling so overwhelmed.*
Now you think: *He didn't even notice when I brought the tea. He's so self-absorbed.*

Tip: Think gentler thoughts, have smaller problems.
Sure, maybe he's quiet, but how do you contribute by making a negative meaning out of his behaviour?

Guerrilla Mating Tactic Number 3: Evaluate your timing

Keesha chronically chooses the worst possible times to engage Mike – after a hard day at work when he's exhausted, when he's about to enter the bathroom, when he's about to go to bed. These are the moments when she typically raises important family business, when she asks him to listen to her recent decisions, when she feels needy. Keesha asks Mike for attention at precisely the moments when he is guaranteed to feel most depleted and least available. She's not doing it on purpose – it's built into their schedules. When Mike comes home exhausted, Keesha is fresh and ready to communicate. Keesha is at 'peak talk', a time of being most interested in talking with her partner, while Mike is at 'ebb talk', a time of being least interested in talking with his partner. Let's all give a big cheer for linguist Deborah Tannen and her great work at bringing much of the information about our talk styles to the general public.

Note: Tannen and others have written much about women placing a high value on harmony while man prefer to debate. Well, of course, men want harmony too. The thing is, women try to preserve harmony through talking while men try to preserve harmony by not talking. Men feel small in the face of women's complaints – they feel like a boy with a huge angry mother scolding. Trained to fight back, men feel easily provoked and when they are provoked they defend themselves. This has been going on for centuries. For a man, avoiding the conversation is also a way of avoiding provocation, defensiveness, unpleasantness – something they know can make their anger spiral out of control. Men want harmony, too – it's just that they have different ideas about how to get it.

One of the best ways to evaluate your timing is to document your peak talk and ebb talk times. Peak talk is the time of day you most want to talk, while ebb talk is the time you are least interested in conversation. For women, peak talk times are frequently after sex, when they come home from from work, after they've seen a good movie. Surprise, surprise – these are often men's ebb talk times.

Note: Women and men peak at different times sexually, so why be surprised that we peak at different times conversationally?

Discovering and documenting you and your partner's peak and ebb talk times can help by:

▶ Illuminating patterns of talk and making them more recognizable
▶ Shedding light on your best time for getting what you want
▶ Clarifying the least likely times for getting what you want
▶ Helping you to anticipate when you might feel the most frustrated so that you can plan for those times as well.

When you know it's going to be hard to talk with him/her, you may find a way not to take it personally!

Take two weeks and document the time, day and date of your partner's and your own peak talk and ebb talk. If you aren't quite sure how to do this, you'll be shown how in the next chapter. So you may want to flip ahead for some guidelines on how to chart your patterns of conversation. If you can't see a pattern emerge in two weeks, try the exercise for a month. Just make notes in your daily date book, and start to notice:

▶ What time of day are you most interested in talking?
▶ How about your partner?
▶ What days of the week are best for you?
▶ Your partner?
▶ What has preceded most interest in talking for both of you?
▶ What has preceded least interest in talking for both of you?
▶ When you both talk, what do you talk about?
▶ What does your partner seem most interested in talking about?
▶ What does your partner seem most comfortable talking about?

Yes, this is work. Did you think that relationships weren't work? Do 50 press-ups and think again.

As you document patterns, you may want to think back to his previous patterns of talk. Is this silence a recent deviation from pattern or an ongoing communicative style? Also, always remember that silence has meaning. It can mean anything from nothing to a bad day to repressed fury. Silence is never just lack of talk, and all silence is not the same. So think about whether there has been a shift in talk patterns or a shift in how you notice them or both.

Tip: Speak his language. If he loves football, try talking in 'halves' or create a time of the day you call 'halftime'. If she loves *NYPD Blue* try 'grilling her' or 'putting her on the stand.' Is there a metaphor, a piece of humour, the words of an eccentric relative, a television character, the language of her favourite sport – anything that can turn talk between you into a whole new ball game?

Guerrilla Mating Tactic Number 4: Play two hours of sport

And, talking of talking his language, there is the old joke that two men will not talk to each other until they have played two hours of sport. The truth is that many men have an easier time talking when they are engaged in an activity. Try it:

- ❯ Walk with him
- ❯ Play tennis with him
- ❯ Hike with him
- ❯ Wash the car with him
- ❯ Exercise at the gym with him
- ❯ Initiate sex with him

Any activity that taxes his body can loosen him up enough to talk.

Note: Do not start the conversation while he is bench-pressing 50 kg or about to go for that lob. Wait until the appropriate moment to talk.

Guerrilla Mating Tactic Number 5: Schedule short talks

In good humour, Keesha tacks a 'sign-up sheet' on the refrigerator. She puts the time and date that she wants to talk. She specifies that the talk will last 5 to 8 minutes. She asks Mike to initial her sign-up sheet to show his consent.

You may not have to resort to a sign-up sheet, but why not schedule talks? You schedule going to the dentist, don't you? Well, if you want to pull teeth, make an appointment. A short talk lasts 5 to 20 minutes – the shorter the better. You may discover that your partner is more receptive to several short talks than one long one. You may discover that with a specified time frame, more gets accomplished because you stay more focused and since he knows when the talk will end, he is not silently praying that the talk will end. Thus, he is more able to listen and respond. This relieves a great deal of the pressure and defensiveness that occurs when one of you is constantly anticipating the other bringing the difficult material up.

Note: If your 'silent partner' is a man and you think this is happening along gender lines, with men generally wanting less talk, then it makes sense to approach the issue with gender in mind. He can be totally happy with his behaviour and not feel the least bit motivated to change. Short talks can make trying out new behaviours easier for both of you.

Guerrilla Mating Tactic Number 6: Develop yourself

Give all the ideas above time to work. And, while you are trying to figure out what works best to get your partner to open up, you ought also to be trying a tactic that reverses the role you've been playing – a totally opposite tactic where you stop trying and:

You are less available to talk
You cut the talks short
You make other plans not in anger, in the hope of positive change

---

GREETINGS AND GOODBYES

Liam and Jenny always greet each other when one of them comes home. They drop whatever they are doing and make sure that they have a proper hello. They've found that whenever they've let this practice go, the bad effect on their relationship is noticeable within a few days. So they never skip it anymore. They never call out 'hello' from the next room. They stand face to face each time. They extend the same courtesy to their goodbyes.

If you've been chasing your partner for talk, stop chasing! Stop working so hard on the relationship. Instead, start working on yourself. Take a pottery class, join a gym, write poetry, get a camcorder and make a movie, take a holiday with a friend … just get busy outside the relationship.

In fact, run the other way, and see what happens. When you stop chasing, he may notice the change – in fact, he may start chasing you. When he starts, run around the corner, STOP, and let him bump into you. Check out how it feels to get that close.

In encouraging you about trying something different, such as you backing off, I am not telling you to give up on trying to enhance communication with your partner, nor am I suggesting you should fill your life with other things as a way of needing less closeness with him, nor am I asking you to let him off the hook of being a real partner to you by your living your life in a fashion such that he doesn't need to relate to you at all because the problem is solely your problem. What I am talking about is expanding your social experiment – increasing your repertoire of responses to the silent treatment and finding out which ones get you more of what you want.

Guerrilla Mating Tactic Number 7: Have patience

When a behavioural therapist tries to help someone get over the fear of flying, she doesn't put him on a transatlantic flight for eight hours his first time out. She desensitizes him slowly. First he looks at picture of planes, then he visits the airport, then he sits on a runway, then he taxis the runway, then he uses the airplane loo ... get the picture? Don't ask for too much too soon. Go slowly.

Guerrilla Mating Tactic Number 8: Get help when the silent treatment seems more complicated

Perhaps the two of you have a tacit arrangement which says that one partner will chase and the other will run. Such situations can breed the rip-roaring, ongoing fights that family therapist Peggy Papp calls the 'Pursuer/Distancer' fight. There are those who chronically withdraw from feelings. They give you the silent treatment, never invite you into their emotional life, never let you know what is going on for them. You feel shut out. Eventually you become exasperated, blow up, name-call, make threats. Then, for a brief period of time, your partner must engage you simply in order to fight back. You fight because it is only at that level of intensity that your partner will engage. It is your valiant effort to get some emotionality from him.

Family therapist Peggy Papp says that after a fight like this the husband should thank the wife for bringing him out of his shell, but you can't count on that. It's true that women often end up expressing the emotional life for the couple, while the husband withdraws. Since couples who can respond directly and actively to each other are more likely to have loving feelings for each other and to regain those feelings more quickly when they have been lost, it makes sense to try the above ideas as a way to engage him. If you still don't get anywhere, you don't have to give up, though. Things can still get better. You can always try a few sessions of couples counselling as a way to get the two of you out of this rut.

Hot Issue Number 3: I Don't Feel Like a Priority

Linda says that all she wants is to feel like she comes first. Is that too much to ask? When she grew up, her mum worked, and she never saw her dad. When she came home from school, she'd find a note on the kitchen table tucked under a plate of biscuits, but no one was around. When she met Tony, the feeling of never being someone's priority dissolved. For the the first time in her life, she felt as if she came first. Then, when Tony opened his own shop and it kept him away from home for long hours, Linda started to panic. When she had to eat alone, she felt like that lonely little girl facing a plate of biscuits.

The Hot Issue: If he spent more time with me, I wouldn't be so needy.

THE EIGHT-TACTIC SOLUTION:
1 Find out how he understands the changes in your relationship
2 Do some soul-searching
3 Set up meetings
4 Don't expect your partner to read your mind
5 Make direct, non-blaming statements
6 Make spending time with you more fun
7 Explore this as a gender issue
8 Define and specify reasonable new behaviours that make you feel like a priority and ask for them

Guerrilla Mating Tactic Number 1: Find out how he understands the changes in your relationship

Unfortunately, your partner can't relate to you forever as he did when he was falling in love, but it may be true that the two of you don't have enough time together: *Find out how he understands the changes in your relationship.*

Start the discussion with a positive statement that you miss him and want to spend more time with him. Then, using your own words, not mine, ask him:

▶ Is he comfortable with the amount of time you have together?
▶ What does he see as the biggest obstacle to your spending more time together? What gets in the way?
▶ You are having trouble carving out couple time – is he?
▶ How does he feel when you ask him for more time together – does he feel pushed?
▶ Does he see this as a temporary situation?
▶ What ideas does he have about finding more time together?

Remember: These conversations require that you *drop that hot issue* and listen calmly to what he has to say. If you can identify the problems, you can solve them. If you get global, defensive, assaulting, vague, and start tossing grenades back and forth, you'll get nowhere. This is a good time to use active listening.

If his response is that he is comfortable with the amount of time you spend together, while you are uncomfortable, don't jump on him. You can still say that while he is comfortable, you need more. Keep reading so you know how to ask for it and negotiate for it. Everybody needs different levels of contact to feel connected. We aren't all cut from the same cloth. It's silly to think that because he needs less contact with you, he has less love for you.

Guerrilla Mating Tactic Number 2: Do some soul-searching

Ask yourself:

▶ *Is he as negligent as you think he is?* Document the amount of time you have together and see what it looks like. If you're anything like most modern couples, the tiny amount of time you have together will be when you get into bed at night. How can you stretch that time or make it so great that you'll both want to get into bed a little earlier and stay up a little later?

▶ *Is your desire to spend more time with him a reasonable request at present?* Remember, the desire to spend more time is always reasonable, but it may not be workable at present!

▶ *If it is a reasonable request, are you handling it in a reasonable fashion?* How are you handling the hot issue? Are you flinging it at him, or can you look at this problem in terms of how to find a solution rather than how to keep tossing the hot issue back and forth?

▶ *Are you superimposing your partner's present behaviour over losses from your past?* Linda raises the subject of wanting more time in the same breath that she talks about having so little time with her mum and dad. Is it possible that this is such a tender issue for Linda because she knows it all too well?

▶ *Could this be negotiated? Can you both bend?* A good relationship requires compromise. The two of you can meet in the middle. Think about compromises that can work.

▶ *Are you looking for perfection in an imperfect world?* It's okay to want perfection; it's just not okay to expect to get it. For everything you want and need from your partner, he has a competing set of wants and needs for you. Given this, plus our imperfect world filled with mortgages, flat tyres, dirty nappies, braces for the kids' teeth and check-ups – all of this set against the fantasy we're handed about the roses around the door and buns for tea – it's just not possible to give each other what we need when we need it on an ongoing basis. A big step forward in your relationship will take place when you develop a repertoire for soothing yourself when your partner isn't available to soothe you.

Exploring these questions requires soul-searching. Dig in.

Guerrilla Mating Tactic Number 3: Set up regular family meetings (or make a date)

Sometimes the hardest part of finding time together is getting two people to sit down long enough to figure out when they can do it. One of the best ways to handle this is to set regular family meetings where you sit down with both your calendars and block out time:

Daisy and Sam came to see me for counselling. They'd been together seven years and were in frequent conflict. I kept trying to figure out why they were so mad at each other. Finally I hit upon asking them when they'd last spent time alone. It turned out that they hadn't had time alone in months – they hadn't shared a meal or even got into bed at the same time. They didn't realize that this lack of time together was having such a negative impact on them as a couple. I had them both pull out their date books and make a date. It took them an hour to do it.

Nadine and Mark came to see me with Mark complaining that they weren't as affectionate as they used to be. I asked them what they thought was different, and they claimed they had no idea what went wrong between them. After asking more questions, I found out that they had a three-year-old daughter, Nadine was working as an accountant, and Mark was about to take his entrance exams for medical school. They were both under a lot of pressure and overwhelmed, yet they did not see the impact that their duties might be having on their personal lives. When they began to look at this and make calendar dates to be together, they were able to join forces against the world and be there for each other.

You can't be there for each other if you can't make time for each other. Saying 'I'm there for you' is not a figure of speech.

Part of our lifestyle today means that no one has time for anything. Mark a time when you can sit down together to make a date and tackle family matters. You'll be surprised at what can be accomplished in 20 minutes when you both put your minds to it.

Note: If your partner is hesitant to find the time to make the time, tell him the story of the couple above. If he puts it off, he will probably have to pay a marriage counsellor just so the two of you can sit together and pull out your date books. Tell your partner that listening to you will save money.

Guerrilla Mating Tactic Number 4: Don't expect your partner to read your mind

Many of us think that because our partners love us they should know what we want. They should be able to read our minds and figure us out.

We take that one step further. If our partner can't read our mind and we have to ask for something, it's not worth having. Your mission, should you decide to accept it, is to learn how to have a conversation about your needs, rather than pouting. Give up the idea that if he loved you, he'd know. He can't read your mind and he doesn't know.

> *Say this:* I get an awful feeling when you work late nights. It's like I'm eight years old and alone in an empty house. It feels as if no one is ever coming home.
> *Not this:* What do you mean you have to work late? You better get your priorities straight.

> *Say this:* I miss you.
> *Not this:* How dare you?

By telling him how you feel in a non-critical fashion, you make room for him to respond to you in a non-critical fashion. You alter the stakes – something new could happen. The above dialogue is categorized as a *disclosure*. Chapter 5 is all about disclosure.

Guerrilla Mating Tactic Number 5: Make direct, non-blaming statements

In addition to speaking about your feelings, make direct statements about your needs so that you can begin to negotiate concrete issues of how the two of you will interact.

> *Say this:* I'm upset you cancelled the holiday. I was counting on it. Can you arrange to have someone cover for you so that we can go? This is very important to me.
> *Not this:* I knew it. I knew you'd cancel. You were never really planning on going. It never changes.

If he can't get away, it is normal to sulk and rage for a while. I am very good at sulking and raging and would not like to lose the chance to excel at my special talent. I have won sulking and raging competitions, and I placed as a national finalist. When I do sulk and rage, I ask my husband to vote on whether I am still fit for competition or whether I have lost my edge and must sulk and rage even more to get back into shape.

Eventually, you'll have to move from that position and state directly what you want.

Say this: Let's pick a date when you can get away. And because I have to wait, I want an even better holiday.

If s/he says this: Next week is bad and the week after is bad and after that is worse...

Say this: Sit down with your calendar when you have a minute and go over it. Then let me know what you figure out.

Guerrilla Mating Tactic Number 6: Making spending time with you more fun

No one says, 'No, Bob, I'll pass on the beer with you because I can't wait to see my brooding, needy wife,' or 'No, Mary, I can't have dinner with you because I'm dying to get home to my depressed, combative husband.' No one says that. So make the time you do have together count. If you greet him with the best of who you are, he may just stop being afraid to come home.

Note: Don't overdo this. On an old episode of *I Love Lucy*, Lucy read a self-help book about how to get your husband interested in you again. The book suggested that the wife recreate the husband's childhood dwelling, a time when the husband felt taken care of and safe. Since Ricky's childhood dwelling was Cuba, Lucy filled their apartment with plastic palm trees, covered the floors with beach sand, dressed like Dorothy Lamour in a Bob Hope – Bing Crosby movie, and adopted a bad Cuban accent. As could be expected, Ricky was flabbergasted, playing to the hilt his *two* basic emotions – surprise and anger. All chaos broke loose.

Guerrilla Mating Tactic Number 7: Consider the impact of gender on this issue

Wanting to spend more time with your partner is natural. It's just that you can't always get it when you need it. As we've seen, Tony wants to build his business. Like so many men, he does not separate what he does from who he is. His identity is bound up in his work. In addition, his work is the perfect hiding place from marital aggravation. He likes it that way. *But:* that doesn't mean this is not open to negotiation or change.

On some mornings when my husband, Boots, and I wake up, we take five minutes to put our favourite song, the theme song from *Beauty and the Beast,* on the tape player. We slow-dance before we go to work.

Special Bulletin: Men, Women and Intimacy

For over 12 years I've led workshops across the US where I've asked groups of women and men to come up with one-sentence definitions for intimacy. Women are quite surprised to know that men's definitions are the same as theirs – intimacy is about two people sharing vulnerable parts of themselves with each other, knowing that it is safe with their partner to do so. While men and women define intimacy the same way, their experience of intimacy is different. Even with the same underlying concerns, what it takes to feel intimate is different for a man from what it is for a woman.

For women, closeness is measured by the amount of time and energy spent together and emotional availability to each other. Women like lots of time together to feel a deep state of connection. For women, intimacy is first experienced with a mother of the same sex. They spend lots of time with her.

Men are usually raised primarily by someone of different sex. At a certain point, to assert that difference, men disconnect from their relationship with their mother (they don't want to be called 'sissy' or 'mama's boy'). Traditionally, fathers, who are often working and unavailable, are not there to offer an alternative model, a male model of intimacy. Traditionally, fathers haven't spent a lot of time with their sons (or daughters). Boys get stuck in a state where they are working hard at being 'not female' (so they aren't spending a lot of time with Mother), but lack a consistent model of how to be male (because they aren't spending much time with Father either). As Deborah Tannen suggests, if you ask a man to recall his most intimate memory with his dad, it is usually when they went to a football match, fixed a car, went fishing. It usually revolves around an activity – something they did together. When boys are with their fathers, they often communicate by doing, rather than by talking.

Boys and men can experience women's request for more talking time in order to feel intimate as a demand, a request to be like a woman. Connection with a woman requires a currency of the intimate exchange of feelings, a length of time for talking together, a way of being that men may have no experience in.

Both genders need to understand that their ideas about intimacy are the same, but what it takes for them to feel intimate is *different and equally valid*. You will never get him to be like you or vice versa. So why not accept these differences as differences rather than deciding they emanate from a lack of love?

The question is not whether this is gender-related. The question is, 'Are Tony and Linda willing to work at this?'

The potential is there for this relationship to offer a great deal of gratification to both of them. He might be open to making changes in his work patterns because he values his relationship. This doesn't happen overnight.

Guerrilla Mating Tactic Number 8: Define specific, reasonable new behaviours that make you feel like a priority, and ask for them

Linda asked Tony to call her from work during the day and speak to her for a minimum of 10 minutes during the day.

Say this: Please call me and talk to me during the day for 10 minutes.
Not this: I get lonely during the day.

Nadine and Mark decided to set the alarm to go off 15 minutes early once a week, so they can lie in each other's arms.

Say this: I want us to set the alarm 15 minutes early so we can cuddle.
Not this: Can't you find more time for me?

Naomi couldn't stand Tim's beeper always intruding on their lives. She settled for his turning it off for two hours an evening.

Say this: It would be great for me to have you turn off the beeper for two hours a night.
Not this: That beeper makes me crazy. Can't you do something about it?

Arnold asked Roberta to rub his feet for 10 minutes a night, and she was not allowed to read a law brief while doing so.

Say this: I'd be in heaven if you'd rub my feet for 10 minutes a day.
Not this: My feet are sore.

Figure out what improvement looks like and ask for that. What specific behaviour could you ask for that would make you feel more special? What specific behaviour could you offer your partner? What deal can you work out to get what you want? A little bit of generosity goes a long way.

Note: Sometimes my husband wants to have long discussions about things when I don't much feel like talking. We worked out an agreement so that, when he feels the urge to talk about something I don't want to hear, he'll give me a back rub while he does it. We both feel satisfied. We worked hard to find a creative solution that appealed to both of us.

A Last-minute Pep Talk

In order for your relationship to deepen and thrive, you must breathe life into and maintain the exploratory nature that came to you so easily when you were falling in love. You must be emotionally in shape, emotionally flexible, emotionally limber. You reach this point emotionally the same way you reach it physically – through exercising, stretching, toning. When you exercise physically, you tune in to your heart rate, you manipulate your body, you focus on how you want to look, and then you push yourself to achieve it. In this process you maintain an ongoing awareness of your muscles and how they feel. You make adjustments, you rest. If you take off too much time you slide back into old habits.

Change is inevitable in your relationship and in your body. If you want to stay physically fit you go to the gym. And if you want to stay fit for love you need an equivalent, a workout for your heart and mind. Call it relationship boot camp. It entails bench-pressing the ceiling off your brain to broaden the themes for your relationship, and trimming the fat off your outlook to see with more clarity. With a little strain and more than a little sweat, you can exercise your relationship skills and keep developing them. You can initiate change in your relationship for the better. You already know it isn't easy. You don't need anyone to tell you that. But chances are you picked up this book because you are ready to separate from bad habits, ready to push yourself forward, ready to 'just do it'. Welcome, welcome, welcome. Drink plenty of liquids. Pace yourself. Wear the right shoes. Don't try to do the whole workout the first time.

Quick-Fix List: Hot Issues

Step Number 1: Define the problem
How does your partner see the problem?
How do you see the problem?
Gather information about the problem

Step Number 2: Get started alone
Evaluate your timing
Document patterns
Try active listening
Practise self-control and drop the hot issue
Stop defending yourself
Help the complainer complain

Step Number 3: Be a little sneaky
Learn to speak his language
Play two hours of sport

Step Number 4: Avoid pitfalls
Don't complain without offering a reasonable solution
Don't expect your partner to read your mind
Be direct – no mixed messages
Make spending time with you more fun
Explore the gender issues
Don't overload a resistant partner
Exhibit self-control

Step Number 5: Try new ways together
Schedule short talks
Allow enough time to work out tricky matters
Provide ample praise when you know your partner is trying
Define and specify reasonable new behaviours each of you want and
ask for them

Emergency Plan: Get professional help if nothing works

three

SCOUTING FOR INFORMATION: DISCOVERING WHAT WORKS AND WHAT DOESN'T

We want to get along with each other. In those times when it is harder to get along, we may try to improve our relationships by focusing on how to do less of what we know irritates our partner and trying to get our partner to do less of what irritates us. In keeping with the idea of initiating positive change by breaking the circle and trying new ways, you may be able to improve your relationship much more quickly if you *stop trying to solve your problems*, and instead, you *change your focus*. Take your focus off problems and what you and your partner should do *less of*, and pay more attention to what you and your partner are already doing right and do *more of* that.

I'm serious. Things are rarely as wonderful *or* as awful as them seem. I mean, if everything stank, you wouldn't still be there, so chances are there are gratifying moments in your relationship. Why not locate those pockets of strength and build up your relationship by trying to build on the strengths rather than by trying to eliminate the weaknesses? Ask yourself how you can get more of those gratifying moments – even if you start off at just one more gratifying moment a week.

Why not become an expert about what makes your relationship work when it is working and do more of that?

Many of us have had years of practice in focusing on what's wrong and little practice in focusing on what's right, so don't expect to be able to shift your attention because I tell you to do it. That's too simple. You need to reprogramme your point of view. The best way to do this is by charting it down – actually writing down what you want 'more of' – in other words, documenting the satisfying part of your relationship for at least two weeks. You will be looking for five positive things:

1 When you feel safe
2 When you laugh
3 When you agree about something
4 When you feel tender
5 When you feel respect

I want you to be more aware of the good things which you often take for granted or overlook. Don't overlook even the smallest positive moments:
   A few good things:

▶ Paying a compliment
▶ Making dinner
▶ Playing with the kids
▶ Shutting the garage door
▶ Putting the seat down
▶ Putting air in the tyres
▶ Picking up dinner
▶ Balancing the chequebook
▶ Doing the laundry when it's not your turn

Note: If your relationship has been struggling for a while and your spirit is flagging, you may decide to read through the whole book and then come back and try the charts.

Getting Started

First, take a look at a blank chart so you can get more familiar with it. You can photocopy this one, so you will have copies. The letters beneath the days represent times of the day: *m* is morning, *a* is afternoon, *e* is evening.

Charting the Positives

	M m a e	T m a e	W m a e	Th m a e	F m a e	S m a e	Su m a e
Safety							
Laughter							
Agreement							
Tenderness							
Respect							

1 Time of Day:
  What We Were Doing:

2 Time of Day:
  What We Were Doing:

3 Time of Day:
  What We Were Doing:

4 Time of Day:
  What We Were Doing:

How to Fill in the Chart

Every time you notice something good in your relationship, every time you have a positive feeling, make a mark on the chart at the appropriate time of day. Then immediately go to the bottom of the chart and write in exactly what you were going when this feeling came up and write the time of day it happened. You may have more than one feeling at a time. If so, mark them all.

The beauty of filling out a chart is that you won't have to rely on your memory to evaluate your relationship. When we are struggling with something, memory can be unreliable, as it becomes what is known as 'selective memory'. This means you remember only events that support your theory of what is happening. If your theory is that your relationship is terribly troubled, your selective memory may remember only your problems. This is a common peril of memory and of theory, and it is why scientists spend decades rigorously testing a hypothesis before calling a theory a fact. In fact, though you think things aren't going well, you may be in for a pleasant surprise.

The Sample Charts of Greta and Jack

Greta and Jack had been married for three years. They felt that their relationship had changed a great deal since the days when they first met – and none of the changes was for the better. As with almost all couples, the characteristics they were originally most attracted to in each other – characteristics they themselves were short on – were exactly the characteristics that began to drive them nuts:

What Greta had loved most about Jack was the fact that he took life one day at a time. He was funny and relaxed; nothing got to him. Greta felt Jack's style was perfect for her because she tended to be frenetic at heart. Then one day Greta began noticing that the Book-of-the-Month Club was sending them books neither of them had ordered because Jack was so relaxed that he failed to return those little 'No Books Wanted' slips they sent them. Not to mention that they received a second notice regarding their car payments. Suddenly one summer, Jack's relaxed style was recast as Jack's lousy, lazy, irresponsible lapses.

When Jack met Greta, he saw as his soul mate, his template. She had energy. She was organized – he knew that the two of them made a great team. In fact, Jack had intensely exaggerated feelings that Greta was perfect. When the fantasy of her perfection waned, the intensity of his feelings remained but the intensity was redirected towards Greta's flaws. Just as Greta's perfection was an unrealistic exaggeration, Greta's flaws were unrealistically exaggerated. Jack experienced a 'feeling crash', a 180-degree shift from a positive exaggeration to a negative exaggeration. It's a twist on the Johnny Mercer song 'Accentuate the Positive', now retitled 'Accentuate the Negative'. Jack began to bristle when Greta clipped a coupon; Jack began to withdraw when Greta woke up in the morning and tried to make the bed – with him still in it!

Greta and Jack came to see me, and while it certainly sounded as if they were having trouble, I had many questions about specifics and much curiosity about exactly what was going on. I knew a lot about when their relationship didn't work, and I was curious to find out more about when it did work. I thought a chart might offer specifics. At first, Greta didn't want to try the chart because she said things in the marriage had changed too much. She felt discouraged, and she thought she didn't have time.

But time really wasn't the issue for Greta. No one has time, but when something is important enough, we make time. The real issue was that Greta was sceptical about charting – afraid of what she might discover. Her scepticism is understandable. When things are going badly in a relationship, it's hard to believe and scary to hope that the relationship could get better – what if you hope and it doesn't work and you are let down twice as hard? Eventually Greta was ready to try the charts, and when she did them, she did them begrudgingly. As did Jack. And, as many a therapist has said to many a couple – you don't have to like it, you just have to do it!

Greta's Chart
Charting the Positives

	M			T			W			Th			F			S			Su		
	m	a	e	m	a	e	m	a	e	m	a	e	m	a	e	m	a	e	m	a	e
Safety	X	X	X										X								
Laughter	X	X	X										X								
Agreement	X																				
Tenderness	X	X	X										X	X							
Respect	X	X											X								

1 Time of Day: Monday morning
   What We Were Doing: breakfast, talking about having sex that night

2 Time of Day: Monday evening
   What We Were Doing: having sex

3 Time of Day: Tuesday morning
   What We Were Doing: having breakfast together

4 Time of Day: Friday morning
   What We Were Doing: having breakfast together

5 Time of Day: Friday afternoon
   What We Were Doing: Jack called at work just to say hello

6 Time of Day: Friday evening
   What We Were Doing: having sex, cuddling

Greta's Interpretation

When Greta read her chart, she realized that although she and Jack seemed to fall easily into chronic bickering these days, they still had some of the old spark. Basically, she found that times they got along best seemed to start with their having breakfast together. Unfortunately, they were usually in too much of a rush to do that. That seemed to change her mood and Jack's mood. Plus, Greta noticed that when they had breakfast together they often had sex that night, holding on to their good feelings.

Greta also noticed that they did well in the morning and in the later evening and not so well in the day or in the early evening around dinner time. However, on the day Jack called her at work, she felt positive about the relationship. Greta and Jack both had high-stress jobs, and they seemed to have trouble winding down when they came home. She concluded that *daily stressors had a bad effect on their relationship* and she should give less credence to the time they didn't get along, because the problem wasn't them – it was the world they lived in. She noticed that she did not have one positive feeling about Jack all weekend and she knew this was because she played golf all weekend and hardly saw Jack at all. Maybe a change there would help. Greta began to concentrate the following week on how to get 'more of' the good times. Greta got up a little earlier to prepare breakfast, since that seemed to get them off to a good start. She cut back golf to one weekend day. She invited Jack to spend a weekend away with her. Instead of arguing over the bills and whether Jack was or wasn't responsible, she took over paying a few of them and eliminated the problem entirely. *And*, she made a recommendation to Jack that, no matter what was happening in their lives, they eat breakfast together at least four times a week.

Jack's Chart
Charting the Positives

	M			T			W			Th			F			S			Su		
	m	a	e	m	a	e	m	a	e	m	a	e	m	a	e	m	a	e	m	a	e
Safety	X												X								
Laughter	X			X										X							
Agreement	X			X									X								X
Tenderness	X			X									X	X							
Respect	X												X								

1 Time of Day: Monday evening
 What We Were Doing: having sex

2 Time of Day: Tuesday evening
 What We Were Doing: watching some television together

3 Time of Day: Friday morning
 What We Were Doing: good-bye kissing

4 Time of Day: Friday evening
 What We Were Doing: Greta was happy when I came home

5 Time of Day: Friday evening
 What We Were Doing: having sex and renting a movie

6 Time of Day: Sunday evening
 What We Were Doing: ordering dinner in

Jack completed a chart that was fairly close to Greta's, but he seemed to think things were going better than Greta did. She'd thought he was more dissatisfied than he was and so was surprised to see his chart. Funny thing was, so did he. The chart let them talk about the events of the week and look at what behaviours they might change. Jack was glad when she gave up a day of golf because he told her it had made him resentful. Greta was surprised because she thought he wanted her out of the house. They found they agreed that the good times seemed to be more present when they had sex. Greta hadn't realized how important the breakfast time was to Jack, nor how much he appreciated it when she greeted him when he arrived home. When Jack saw his good feelings on paper, he felt like being more tolerant towards Greta. He felt like doing the dishes more often, too.

Here are charts for you and your partner to use.

Charting the Positives

	M	T	W	Th	F	S	Su
	m a e	m a e	m a e	m a e	m a e	m a e	m a e
Safety							
Laughter							
Agreement							
Tenderness							
Respect							

1 Time of Day:
   What We Were Doing:

2 Time of Day:
   What We Were Doing:

3 Time of Day:
   What We Were Doing:

4 Time of Day:
   What We Were Doing:

5 Time of Day:
   What We Were Doing:

6 Time of Day:
   What We Were Doing:

Charting the Positives

	M	T	W	Th	F	S	Su
	m a e	m a e	m a e	m a e	m a e	m a e	m a e
Safety							
Laughter							
Agreement							
Tenderness							
Respect							

1 Time of Day:
   What We Were Doing:

2 Time of Day:
   What We Were Doing:

3 Time of Day:
   What We Were Doing:

4 Time of Day:
   What We Were Doing:

5 Time of Day:
   What We Were Doing:

6 Time of Day:
   What We Were Doing:

Report the Positives to Your Partner

After you've done this for two weeks, take a look at what you've found. Were there times when the relationship felt fine? Are there certain times of day when you get along better than others? Based on this, can you predict when your rough spots will be and act accordingly? Does this change your perceptions about your relationship or how the relationship feels to you? Tell your partner the good news. After all, she may be under the impression that you two aren't getting along as well as you are. She too may have a tendency to exaggerate the bad. Tell your partner you decided to try an exercise that points out the strong times in a relationship. You decided to remind yourself about what was good and when those times happened. Point out what you appreciate about her. Tell her you'd love to hear the same kind of good news about yourself, and hand her a few charts.

Do a Joint Chart and Report the Results to Each Other

Although you can always chart alone, it's interesting for couples to each do a chart and report back together on the same week. Did you notice the same things? Were the same times good times for both of you? Were you both able to do the assignment? It can be a rich experience to find out when your partner felt safe and tender and compare it to when you felt safe and tender.

Note: Men may feel resistant to charting the word 'safety', since the opposite of safety is unsafe and men don't want to say that about themselves. So he may want to use another concept that the two of you can come up with together and agree on.

Note: Charting is also helpful to learn more about each other's sexual desire. You may add, if you like, charting in when you felt sexual stirring. You and your partner completing such a chart may help you tune in to times when you both feel eager to make love. You may learn something about each other. (Don't be surprised if one of you doesn't have enough room on the chart for all his/her X's.)

When Karen and Mal did a joint chart, they were struck by the fact that Mal was getting a lot more enjoyment out of the relationship than Karen was. Together they identified her as the more dissatisfied one. Mal's first impulse was to call it 'Karen's problem', but he knew that it would be more beneficial to work together to discover what might make her more comfortable. Before doing the chart, Mal had just assumed she was in the same place he was, and it was only when he saw it in black and white that he realized they needed to get to work on their relationship.

When Martha and Bill did their charts, they turned them into the same kind of competition they had on the tennis courts. Each tried to make things good for the other so the chart would fill up. Rather than seeing the limitations of such a competition, they considered the benefits – both of them felt they wanted to 'score', so they both competed to be more considerate with each other.

Charting Rough Times

In addition to charting the good times, couples can benefit when they chart the bad times too, as long as they use the exercise to look at *when the bad times occur* rather than how many there are or what they are. After all, it can be helpful to know that you have patterns there which, if you recognized them, you might actually be able to avoid.

When you chart bad times you are looking for patterns, so I won't have you say anything for now about content. That's why it says 'conflict' instead of 'mother-in-law'.

Charting the Rough Spots

	M			T			W			Th			F			S			Su		
	m	a	e	m	a	e	m	a	e	m	a	e	m	a	e	m	a	e	m	a	e
Conflict																					

1 Time of Day:
   What We Were Doing:

2 Time of Day:
   What We Were Doing:

3 Time of Day:
   What We Were Doing:

4 Time of Day:
   What We Were Doing:

5 Time of Day:

What We Were Doing:

6 Time of Day:

What We Were Doing:

Alexis's Chart

Alexis was upset because she and her new husband Kevin seemed to bicker frequently. She decided to try a chart to see if she could figure out what kept setting the two of them off.

Charting the Rough Spots

	M	T	W	Th	F	S	Su
	m a e	m a e	m a e	m a e	m a e	m a e	m a e
Conflict	X	X X		X	X	X	

1 Time of Day: Monday morning

What We Were Doing: waking up

2 Time of Day: Tuesday morning

What We Were Doing: getting dressed

3 Time of Day: Tuesday evening

What We Were Doing: having supper

4 Time of Day: Thursday morning

What We Were Doing: waking up

5 Time of Day: Friday morning

What We Were Doing: who got to use the loo first

6 Time of Day: Saturday morning

What We Were Doing: talking about weekend plans

Results

After Alexis filled out this chart she discovered that Kevin should be banished to the pantry before breakfast. He is surly and cranky till he's had his coffee. The problem was that before she realized this was chronically true, the morning scuffles had already set the tone for the day to come. Now Alexis ignores Kevin's remarks and puts the kettle on first thing. After coffee, they speak.

Here's what other couples found out after charting the rough times:

Nan and Johnathan were surprised to find out that they had their most frequent and lengthiest arguments around dinner time. They realized that neither of them had wound down from the day yet and were taking professional problems out on each other. They decided that no matter how cranky or rushed they felt they would gaze into each other's eyes for 60 seconds before uttering a word. They discovered that by the end of the 60 seconds they were often laughing or at least feeling connected and empathic towards each other. After beginning this tactic, their six o'clock flights decreased by almost 80 per cent.

I found an interesting thing about my own life. My husband is a musician, and for a while he was playing a Broadway show. The show let out at 10.40 p.m. That meant that by the time he got home, I was ready for bed but not quite sleeping. When he came home, he made too much noise coming in, he asked a question, the phone bill was unpaid, he told me I left a shoe on the floor. He wanted to spend time together, and I wanted to sleep. So he'd create something to talk to me about, even if it meant we started bickering. Our spats always occurred when I was in bed and he'd just come home. Our chart pointed that out. So I started staying up later so we could be together, and getting up later in the morning. Almost immediately, the conflicts stopped.

Is there a time of day when you two are most apt to fight or disagree? In later chapters we'll talk about the content of your fights, but, for now, try to look at the 'when' of it, rather than the 'why' of it. Does knowing when you feel cranky or misunderstood help you to think of ways to avoid a fight?

Warning: If you are fighting a lot, don't jump to conclusions about your relationship. Read the second part of this chapter, and read the chapters about fighting. Fighting can often be a misguided attempt to stay connected. There are many tactics for breaking the fighting cycles, and you will learn them all.

Note: If you feel like there is nothing positive in your relationship, then try charting when things are less awful. Even when things are truly horrible, there are times when they are a little less horrible. What is happening when they are 'less horrible'? If you can figure out when that happens, it can be a first step in creating more 'less horrible' times, and then you can search for times 'less horrible' than that.

Stimulate His Curiosity: Reporting Negatives to Your Partner

Reporting what isn't working to your partner has to be done differently. Never say:

> We can't get along when...
> Things don't work when...
> Things are worse...

Don' t start off presenting negatives. Instead, invite curiosity about the patterns.

What you might say to your partner is: 'I was wondering if there was a pattern, like a time of day when we were more prone to argue with each other than other times, so I wrote down those times this week to see. The results were pretty interesting. Want to see them?'

Or: 'I wish we were closer. I noticed that trouble seems to happen around the same time of day – always around dinnertime. I was trying to think of how we could make that time better for us and here are the ideas I came up with.'

- ▶ Skip dinner
- ▶ Spend 20 minutes unwinding with a glass of wine or just talking
- ▶ Taking a bath together before dinner
- ▶ Promising each other to try harder
- ▶ Waiting until after dinner to talk
- ▶ Eat dinner separately for a week so we can start to miss each other
- ▶ Go out to dinner because it's harder to yell in public

Then ask, 'What do you think might help us?'

If you speak carefully, so you never sound patronizing or sarcastic when you say these things, if you display patience and are willing to get started by yourself, if you show curiosity about how your relationship could be better, if you muster up a pioneering spirit, you may find that your partner would love to join forces with you and try to work together. Together you can co-operate to bring your relationship into a happier place on the chart.

What to Do If:

Your partner won't chart
You don't feel like charting either
Improvement takes longer than you thought it would
You've charted and it didn't work
You've charted and you still feel discouraged

I want to spend a moment with those who have read the first two chapters and who still feel discouraged. If that means you, then hear this:

Sometimes things have to get worse before they get better.

Don't give up if progress doesn't happen as quickly as you hoped for or change doesn't come as easily as you'd thought it would. Sometimes it takes longer, and sometimes things get worse before they get better. You see, you can swiftly modify your behaviour – what you do on the outside – but in some cases, it can take longer to change how you feel on the inside.

Let me explain. You have a mental mini-series in your head about your relationship, a story that you tell yourself and others. If your friend Edna asks, 'How is it going with you-know-who?' you tell Edna your mental mini-series, scene by painful scene. When you lie in bed at night, you watch it on the wide-screen TV of your mind. In order for you to improve your relationship, you need to change the channel to a different mental mini-series. To do that, you need to separate from the story you now have in your head – clearing your head to make room for the new story.

The previous two chapters tried to help you separate from your old story by working from the outside in: *You were asked to change what you do, which would then change how you feel.* If that didn't work, then we have to try to do the opposite – separating from the inside out: *You will be asked to change how you feel in order to change what you do.* Changing from the inside out is a more complex process, a process that stirs the psyche up more because it entails separating from long-held beliefs, conscious and unconscious feelings. When you work at separating from deep feelings, even when they are unpleasant and you don't want to feel them, this process can evoke thunderstorms in the landscape of your heart. We're not all cut from the same cloth, so it's natural that there would be differences in how we are most effective in working at improving our relationship. If for you nothing has helped yet, or if even trying has made you anxious and angry, please read on and learn about separation anxiety since it may explain why you are having trouble in your attempts to improve your relationship.

HELPING YOUR PARTNER GRIEVE

Greta had some unresolved issues with her father, who had died nine years before she met her husband, Jack. Jack suggested that they pay a visit to the gravesite because he thought it would help Greta. They drove six hours to get there, and when they did, Greta cried for hours. She said that the fact that Jack thought of that, and wanted so deeply to help her with it, in itself provided her with great healing.

Separation Anxiety

To understand separation anxiety, let's go back to childhood and take a look. Have you ever witnessed a three-year-old being introduced to the baby-sitter? Three-year-old Richard does not share even one bit of the pleasure that his parents enjoy about their Oasis tickets – instead, he experiences a profound loss of love, a total catastrophe of huge magnitude. When his parents leave the house, Richard's feeling of being loved goes with them. This is true regardless of whether his parents treat him like a genius or like a little burden. For Richard, physical absence and the absence of love are exactly the same. Separation is the difference between having his most fundamental needs met or not met – a terrifying feeling. Thus, many a three-year-old will not allow himself to be soothed. Many a parent gets paged at an event to come home. Many a baby-sitter decides to take a computer course and change careers.

Actually, the saga of Little Richard and the Separation Response (not to be confused with a fifties rock group) goes way beyond being left with the baby-sitter. Little Richard feels abandoned whenever his parents can't offer him perfect love. The phone rings and Dad talks on it, Mum spends half an hour in the lavatory – and Little Richard feels insignificant, unimportant, bereft while his parents grow huge, powerful, cruel.

A Pandora's box of angry feelings is born inside of Richard. Little Richard's anger gets channelled into the shapes of monsters in a cupboard, snakes in the cellar. When Little Richard calls his mother in to check under the bed, what he is really saying is, 'How can you do this to me – leaving me in danger, only thinking of yourself?' Little Richard projects his anger into lurking beasts because he cannot bear the conflicted feelings aroused by those he loves most.

Mum checks the cupboard, Dad leaves the night-light on, and eventually Little Richard struggles through puberty. Today, except for the patent leather pompadour, he may look a lot like you. Unhappy in his relationship, he decides to change – maybe do a chart. He clings to the old relationship patterns and unpleasant arguments for dear life, and thus he ensures that the charts won't help and change is impossible.

On one level he's ready, willing and able to try something new. On another level, he's struggling to separate from his own negative mini-series of his relationship. He's trying, but trying reawakens some of the same feelings he had about separation when he was three years old.

The Consequences of Changing

Family therapist Peggy Papp has done groundbreaking work in understanding what happens when people change. The first consequence of change is that it may elicit terrors of separation, *even when change is for the good*. This may be felt in many ways – smaller ones such as apprehension, scepticism, misgivings, or exaggerated discomfort – or it may feel bigger, like a depression, a desertion, a paralysing force. The depression has its roots in your abandoning of your familiar old story and patterns in favour of an unknown. It's awful; it's common; it's a consequence of change; it's temporary.

As people struggle to find new stories, new ways of doing, they frequently do feel worse – actually depressed – before they feel better. It takes courage and resilience to keep moving forward, to refuse to surrender to defensive motifs of blaming and withdrawing and relying on old patterns that don't work. The depression mirrors the abandonment depression you felt at three when your mum and dad, unable to soothe you, walked out, closed and then locked the door.

Note: If you are a man, even more may be asked of you. You will be dealing with more than separation anxiety. For men, familiar patterns are synonymous with greater prestige and power. Initially, it's hard to let the power go, even if what you get in its place is a sense of connection and a happier relationship.

A second consequence of change is that you change and not get results for a while. This is particularly difficult when you know you've done things in the best possible way – you've done the charts faithfully, you've tried to tackle hot issues calmly, and all your partner can do is freak out. We don't take changes lightly. Some of us have eaten the same things for breakfast every day since 1962. One measure of the changes in you will be in your ability to hang on to things you know are for the good of the relationship in the face of a partner who is yelling, as psychologist Harriet Goldhor Lerner says, 'Change back, change back.' Change takes time to sink in – people don't know what to make of it. You'll have to keep at it.

A third consequence of change is that it may rock the relationship boat. The two of you, in the honeymoon stage, may have implicitly contracted for the relationship as is (we don't talk about problems, we don't air bad feelings). You will have to renegotiate certain things to change the relationship so that you don't throw the baby (the relationship) out with the bathwater (what you want to do differently). We'll talk more about this in Chapter 13, where we will focus on how to solve problems when the two of you change at incompatible rates.

So, if you have not been able to get yourself to try anything you have read about so far, to initiate positive change or to develop a 'more of' point of view, you may be a person who needs more time to get started, or you may be a person for whom things will get a little worse before they get better, or you may be a person who will have to work through separation anxiety. Time may be all you need, so the first thing you can do is simply to wait longer and keep trying. However, if time doesn't help, some sessions of couples counselling could be just what you need to get started. Or, there is one more option...

The Freedom of Not Changing

As Papp says, the idea of making change should never be taken lightly. There are always consequences to change. With that in mind, it's clear that not changing may offer certain freedoms. Let's talk about the benefits of not changing. You don't have to learn any new behaviours, you don't have to deal with separation anxiety or master new skills – you don't have to muddle through the charts. There certainly is a level of comfort in keeping the status quo, a certain reliability in waking up to the same old reveille. Sometimes we want something, but we aren't really sure what it is. So we focus on our partner and try to make changes in the relationship. As long as we get resistance, we can focus on the changes we aren't getting as the thing that is making us miserable. But, if we successfully invoke change, we can discover that we feel exactly the same way we did before. That we really needed something else. For example:

> Helen wanted Sam to be tidier. She fought with Sam over this matter for years without realizing that Sam's mess allowed Helen to be more relaxed about her own mess. When Sam cleaned up, Helen's mess screamed for notice. Sam now wanted Helen to clean up and Helen began to see that there was some comfort in the way Sam had been, in keeping Sam's status as the messy one.
>
> Sarah wanted Eli to lose weight. She fought with him over this for years. Eventually he decided to lose weight and he lost two stone. He then began to eat only special low-fat meals, he no longer delighted in going to most restaurants, he jogged during the time he'd once spent with Sarah. Sarah, more than once, wanted the old Eli back – potbelly and all.

Note: Ask yourself what change would mean for your life – and what would it mean not to change?

You have the freedom to change, and that means you also have the freedom to decide that things aren't so bad, that you like having something to whine about, that you may use your freedom to decide you don't need 'more of' anything and you do not want to change. You may decide not to change the relationship and instead to get a pet reptile or dye your hair blue.

Making Change Work for You

You can decide to use a 'more of' point of view to see what you are already doing right, or you can change your relationship or change your view of your relationship, or a little of all three. You can work at it from the outside in by modifying behaviours, or work at it from the inside out by exploring feelings, or both. On some days, change may come more easily; on some days, change may come hard. Some issues will fall into place, others will be a long, slow haul. You have choices about how to work at this, and here is how you can make them:

- Ask yourself what's worked for you in the past and do more of that.
- Look at which strategies have brought you success and try more of those.
- Think about what kinds of strategies you've meant to try, and give those a shot.
- Imagine the ways you want to feel, and notice specifically what is happening when you get closest to having those feelings.
- Ask friends, family, and couples on the bus (if you are brave enough) what works for them and how they got more of what they wanted in their relationships.
- Become a scout, a reconnaissance man who dares to go first, entering the unknown, testing your mettle, pioneering in new territory – even though you're scared.
- Seek professional help if you feel stuck.

Whatever choices and changes you make (or changes you don't make), there's good news. You aren't three years old anymore. You have, just by virtue of lasting this long, developed strength, resilience, courage and the capacity for reason that you didn't have at three. In the next chapter, we'll look at the influence of family history on your relationship. This will offer yet another lens to understanding your relationship and making improvement – another step toward more honeymoons.

By the way, Greta and Jack just celebrated their fifth anniversary. From time to time, they still do a chart or two when they need a reminder of what is going right for them.

Quick-Fix List: How to Get 'More Of'

A quick checklist for getting 'more of' the good things that brought you together in the first place.

Step Number 1: Change your focus
Stop trying to solve your problems
Focus on what is already going right

Step Number 2: Develop a 'more of' outlook
Think about what you want 'more of' in your relationship
Put aside thoughts about what you want 'less of'

Step Number 3: Chart what works
Document what works for you
Have your partner document what works for him or her
When you know what works, resolve to do more of it

Step Number 4: Report positives to your partner
Discuss the results of your chart
Stimulate your partner's curiosity
Join forces with your partner

Step Number 5: Accept that things can get worse before they get better
If nothing works, flip your strategy and try working from the inside out
Look at your reactions to separation
Consider not changing your relationship and instead learning how to
    appreciate what you already have
Finish reading the whole book and come back to this chapter later

11

RELATIONSHIP RATIONS:
STOCKING THE RIGHT SUPPLIES

four

UNLOADING BAGGAGE: DON'T BE YOUR PARENTS/DON'T BE A CHILD

Stan was a doctor who fell for Kyra when she brought her ill aunt into Casualty. He loved Kyra's sweet nature, her devotion, her unselfishness. But a few months into their marriage, he began to feel that Kyra was so devoted to others that she was not there for him. When he needed her, she was taking care of someone else's needs. One morning, he had an 'aha' experience – this was an echo of his relationship with his mother. When he was growing up, his mother was a school governor and an elder at their church. She was so busy organizing others that he occasionally went to school without lunch money and had to get food from friends. And just as he felt towards his mother, Stan was resentful towards Kyra. 'How did this happen?' he muttered out loud. But Kyra never heard him – it was her day to volunteer at the children's hospital.

Margie, who grew up on the East Coast, moved to Los Angeles as soon as she graduated college –partly so she could get away from her overbearing mother, who had actually been known to go through Margie's desk drawers and open and read her mail. So imagine Margie's shock one year into her marriage to Ted, when Ted started opening all the mail – even mail that was clearly meant for her.

Caroline's father was irresponsible and was constantly being fired from his jobs. Caroline would come home from school to discover he hadn't even got out of bed yet. When Caroline married, it was to Dave, a stable, hardworking printer who had never missed a day of work in the entire time they dated. Then, Dave was laid off from work. Two months after that, he was still collecting unemployment and watching soap operas all day.

It's been said that you will pick a partner who mirrors the most neurotic qualities of your parents. But this is a limited view: you will pick a partner who also mirrors the finest qualities of your parents. The father who was rarely home was also the father with great charm. How lucky you were to find a mate who appreciates your charm in the way your mother appreciated your father's charm. The mother who opened your mail was also the mother whose sense of humour brought delight to all she knew; hmmm, only your husband creates such worthy puns. The father who yelled so loud when he was angry was also the father who told the elaborately creative bedtime stories; how familiar when you watch your wife telling equally zany stories to your children. The mother who had an affair you later found out about was the same mother who walked into the High Street shops, memorized the latest styles, then came home, created patterns, and sewed them for you because there was little money for new clothes. When your husband cheers you on as you hammer and nail – you, a woman with no talent for home repair, who is none the less struggling to build a playroom for your kids because the two of you can't afford a playroom any other way – it is an old, familiar, family feeling.

Yes, you have experienced – and picked up – the best and the worst of your parents. And you will bring aspects helpful and unhelpful from your childhood into your adult relationships as well. These aren't conscious choices. They are behaviours and beliefs that are almost automatic because you grew up with them. Moreover, your connection to your parents and your past is probably so strong that, even if you manage to locate a partner who is the opposite of your parents, *you will turn him into your parents* within a short time. Or you will become your parents. You will create, project, and interpret behaviour in the same way you felt your parents were behaving towards you.

Why should this surprise you? You spent the first 18 years of your life learning about relationships from the people who raised you. You learned how people are supposed to love each other and treat each other by experiencing how your parents treated you, and you learned how partners treat each other by watching how your parents treated each other. To understand more about this legacy, let's go back to childhood and take a look at your earliest lessons about relationships.

Welcome to Your Childhood

Stroll with me through that Dependency Training Ground where, in a few short years, you learned enough about relationships to confuse you for decades – because your first instruction in how to have a relationship was in how to be totally dependent. As a child, you were totally dependent on your parents for your survival. You arrived in your family unable to survive on your own, and you remained that way for years. Your family provided for you. In return, you offered total devotion and love – at least that's how it started out. When you think about it, it sounds like a cult – although eventually the cult leaders let you down.

For example, your first and most immediate longing in life was for food. A baby longs for a mummy with a nipple. At first, the baby thinks that hunger and feeding automatically occur together – being hungry is synonymous with being fed. But no matter how loving the mother is, the infant will come to know what it means to have lunch withheld, what it means to be disillusioned with Mummy. After all, the mother must drop the research she was doing for her Ph.D. dissertation, walk upstairs to get the baby from the cot, walk back down to the living room, sit in a chair, unbutton a tricky blouse, and turn on 'The World at One' before she can feed the baby. During all this time, the infant does not feel, 'Oh, she will get to me soon enough.' The infant feels, 'There is no her, no world, no food ... I am all alone, and I am dying.' If you have watched a squalling, red-faced baby, its arms and legs thrumming in the air as if to a John Philip Sousa march, you see the intense upset, the horrifying belief of the baby that all is lost. Waiting is not a tolerable experience for an infant – it can't be processed. After all, Mother is life. From this early experience of waiting to be fed, a child may develop the belief that mothers can be unresponsive, so *all people must be unresponsive*. You can't trust people to be available, you cannot hold on to love, there is no security, you never know when they'll let you down. Unresponsiveness from others feels like a given fact, a fact that can haunt future relationships – a fact that acts as the 'pocket organizer' of relationships.

As a child grows a bit older, she feels a rumbling of independence and she wants to take over what her parents once did for her. Most parents encourage independence, knowing in their hearts that the child isn't capable of much more than sucking a bit of toast on her own. Parents let us learn how to get frustrated because they think we can handle it. Other parents don't handle our emerging independence very well. Some can't wait to get rid of us; some won't let us go. And, in addition to dealing with our feelings about being more self-sufficient, we are dealing with our parents' responses to our independence as well. In short, growing up is a seesaw struggle, filled with frustration. We assess the struggle of growing up with the mental brainpower of a toddler. We figure it out – our parents failed us ... again. We now realize that parents have more than the power to nurture and love us, they also have the power to abandon us – to not want us. This realization fills children with hurt and grief. As children, we turn to dolls and bears and blankets, and we make them beloved companions with the ability to soothe us when our parents will not. Bereft, we weep into a tattered blanky, feeling unwanted or adopted or confused, and rage is born. Rage beyond soothing, rage beyond words, rage beyond explanation. The love for our parents is huge, the rage at our parents is huge. When we feel loving towards our parents, we get our parents' approval. When we feel rage towards our parents, we can get terrified by our own anger. And so children can stuff the rage deep inside – and twist the arm off little Paddington Bear.

A lot happens between this time and the time we grow up, but:

> The belief in the enormous power another can have to love us or hurt us stays with us.

We store this belief until we are adults and ready to tackle it. As kids and teens, we're too young to seek resolution of such complex emotions – but as adults, we're ready to tackle them now.

Note: We don't always sort this out with our parents because it is hard to re-meet them on equal ground. They are always parents. We are always their children – there's so much history between us. One day, however, if we are lucky, we develop authentic empathy for our parents. We stop spouting platitudes such as 'They did the best they could' and instead we feel their lives. We realize that, while they had their deficits, life with us (and life in general) was also no picnic.

In addition to experiencing how we are raised as individuals, we watch how our parents experience our siblings, each other, and their own parents. These observations constitute a huge root system, a multiplicity of familial and cultural influences spanning generations. Yet, when we look at the tree, it is easy to forget about the root system – after all, we don't see it. If you are having troubles that don't get better when you deal with them directly, then respect the root system and check that out – even if that means doing some digging, getting soil on your hands.

Keep in mind that, for most of us, the difficulties and deprivations of our childhood should not be used as an excuse for our current behaviour, but rather as a way to expand our range of understanding. What the past can offer you is a valuable overview of your family root system. An overview is knowledge of the way members of your family intertwine and interact. As you begin to make connections between events in the past and in the present, you take a step back and view yourself through a wider lens, and you understand yourself better. But it's essential to keep in mind that just understanding ourselves better doesn't help us to feel better about ourselves or change our ways. For that, we need to take action. Also, although there is something to learn in putting the past under a microscope, it's not a good idea to get stuck on an archaeological dig. This happens when people get captured by their pasts. The past becomes their excuse, and they spend their time sifting through ancient details over and over. It is quite unfortunate to see – or to be – one of those people who directs all of her energy into unravelling the past at the expense of solving her problems in the present.

How to Know When You Are Imposing Your Past on Your Present

In talking about difficulties in growing up, let me repeat that I don't mean to say that your upbringing was bad – although it could have been bad, and most assuredly it was imperfect. None the less, much of what you saw and learned growing up in your house, from the way you tell a joke to the way you stretch a pound, is worth keeping, and you will carry these things with you for ever. However, there are other carryovers from childhood such as:

Unexpressed anger
Inappropriately expressed anger
Conflicts about being dependent on your partner that are a carryover from conflicts about being dependent on your parents
Feelings about how your parents took care of you that connect with feelings about how your partner takes care of you
Rebellion against your parents that may never have been resolved

These carryovers are worth a second look. Here are a few ways to consider the extent to which your relationship difficulties today stem from the root system:

◗ When you examine your reactions to your partner, you find that sometimes they don't make much sense, and you're not sure what you were responding to.
◗ You have the same fights that your parents had about the same sorts of things.
◗ You fell like you married your mother and/or father, or you've turned into your mother and/or father.
◗ You grew up in a stormy family with problems, and now you have a stormy relationship with problems.
◗ You find yourself repeating the same phrases to your partner that your parents spoke to each other.
◗ You already know that you have unfinished business from your past which affects you.

If you're lugging emotional baggage, then you ought to know that you'll carry it everywhere. It will show up in all your relationships. However, if you can spot your baggage, you can also choose to 'check it' rather than to 'carry it on.'

How to Turn This Around

Here is an eight-tactic turnaround for sorting through family matters. These suggestions are for you and your partner to talk about together. They can help each of you understand where your behaviours come from as you gain more realistic views of each other. In fact, I don't think two people should be allowed to apply for a marriage licence without having checked off each of these tactics and done the work they suggest:

GUERRILLA MATING TACTICS

1 Draw a family tree with your partner so you can explore the impact of your past on your present.
2 Take your current differences back a generation. When you have a problem with your partner, ask yourself how your parents would have handled that same problem.
3 Look at your childhood role in your parents' problems.
4 Talk about and explore major family events, including milestones and mishaps.
5 Talk with your parents and/or siblings to find out how they understand the family dynamics.
6 Ask yourself which family role you are still loyal to.
7 Don't be a child.
8 See the possibilities in finding a partner who is 'just like' your parent.

Guerrilla Mating Tactic Number 1: Draw a family tree

Get a very large piece of artist's paper and actually draw a tiny tree with a very large root system. Give roots to all significant family members, including grandparents, siblings, aunts, uncles, or anyone else who spent a great deal of time in your home. Give couples side-by-side roots and put their children in, as little roots coming out of them. If a couple got divorced, note the year and put a single line through them. Put a shaky line wherever a relationship was shaky. If a person died, note the year and draw an X through that root.

Yes, that root systems looks mutant! No one needs to see or understand it but you and your partner. At the bottom of the page, jot down your impressions or questions about your family tree.

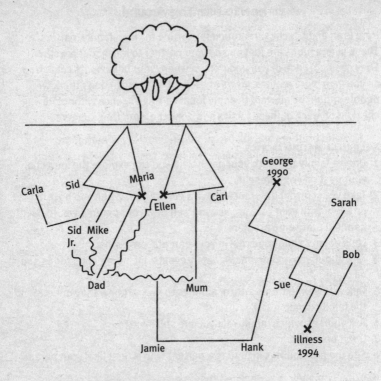

Hank's niece died, 1994.
Both my grandmother's sisters died very young.
My father had no family here at all.
Why doesn't my father have contact with his brothers?

The root system that you are looking at belongs to a woman named Jamie, and I'd like to tell you what she learned about her family when she used this exercise. But first, here are the questions that spurred Jamie's thinking and that you can answer too, because your understanding of how your family solved problems (or never solved them) can teach you about how you handle problems in your own relationship – and with your own children:

How did your parents and grandparents get along as couples and as a family unit?
What stories did they tell you about their relationships?

What were the stories told about them when they weren't there?

What was their role in the community?

What was their status with each other?

What happened in the family when a member got sick?

What happened in the family when a member died?

How did they handle money, affection, child rearing, in-laws, practical matters?

What were holidays like – who planned them?

How did brothers and sisters, aunts and uncles get along?

Was the parenting for all of the children consistent?

What kinds of parenting skills existed? (Who disciplined you, changed your nappy, chose your clothes, made your dinner, taught you right from wrong, told you a bedtime story, etc.)

Today, what do you find most striking about your family?

Note: Don't get hung up in blanket statements such as 'My parents never had time for me' or 'They were always angry.' Look at specific relationships. Don't try to blame your parents and take the easy way out.

Jamie decided to draw a family tree to gain more understanding of her relationship with her husband, Hank. Jamie's major issue with Hank was that she felt she couldn't trust him. She believed that if she had a big crisis, Hank would not be there for her. And, in the minor crises of day-to-day life, Jamie felt that Hank left the burden to her. Now Hank had an emotional legacy of his own childhood that he was working out, but was also a solid guy. The impact of Jamie's mistrust was eating away at their relationship because she was on guard and questioning his constantly.

After completing the family tree, here's what Jamie realized (of course, in reality, Jamie and Hank spent much more time talking about their backgrounds – you are getting the abridged version):

Jamie was an only child whose parents and maternal grandparents lived in the same road. Jamie's father's family lived in Italy, and she only met them twice, so they had little influence in her life. As a child, Jamie thought that her family got along well, although her father frequently complained that her mother's main loyalty was to her own mother rather than to her husband. Jamie remembers her grandmother telling her that men come and go, but your mother is your mother for life. And Jamie's grandmother frequently told Jamie that her father was not good enough for her mother. Jamie was unable to remember spending much time with her dad at all; her mum and her grandmother basically raised her.

When Jamie's grandmother took ill, Jamie's mother moved in to care for her mother 24 hours a day. This lasted for months. Her father made it clear that he resented this, and that her mother should get her grandmother a nurse and come home at night. When Jamie's grandmother died, Jamie's father felt he would be getting his wife back. His wife resented that he was less than devastated by her mother's death, and their relationship changed for the worse after she lost her mother.

What Jamie found most striking when looking at her family tree was the real turn for the worse her parents took after her grandmother died. She hadn't really thought about how that was the turning point in their marriage. Soon after her grandmother's death her parents were sleeping in separate bedrooms, although they never got divorced.

What Jamie came to realize was that her mother spoke to her about how her father deserted her after her grandmother's death. Now she realized that story wasn't exactly true. She realized that somehow her grandmother had been the glue, the piece of the puzzle that let her mother and father manage their relationship decently, and when her grandmother was gone, the glue was gone. Her mother and father fought about her grandmother instead of dealing with the problems they had with each other in their marriage. Also, Jamie realized that she was missing an important piece of understanding as to why her mother's allegiance to her grandmother superseded her allegiance to her own husband. She realized it might be connected to the fact that her grandmother lost both her sisters at a young age.

Jamie recognized that her belief as a child that her father deserted her mother tracked her into her relationship with Hank. Because she expected that what happened in her family would happen to her, she saw it happening, even when it was not happening. And, she realized that even if her father had deserted her mother, it had nothing to do with her and Hank.

Guerrilla Mating Tactic Number 2: Take your current problems back a generation – ask yourself how your parents would have handled that same problem

Recall your parents' relationship and talk with your partner about it. This questionnaire should help jog your memory.

Parental Patterns

When my parents were unhappy with something:
>   They threatened divorce
>   It was business as usual
>   They withdrew from each other
>   They would work it out
>   They would take it out on me
>   I rarely saw my parents disagree

My parents' communication style was
>   Loving
>   Civil
>   Contemptuous
>   Threatening
>   Distant

My parents argued about:
>   The same things over and over
>   Different things all the time
>   Everything they discussed
>   Little
>   I never knew what they argued about

My parents were able to resolve differences:
>   During a conversation
>   Within hours
>   They stayed resentful
>   They stopped speaking
>   They yelled at the kids

My parents fought:
    Rarely
    Sometimes
    Frequently
    All the time

My parents' arguments seemed:
    Mild
    Reasonable
    Intense
    Greatly overblown

Rate the following statements as to how true you think they were for your parents. One would mean that these things were not true for your parents, and 10 would mean that they were always true for your parents. (If you put a 10 next to every statement, enjoy the fairy tale. I hope it never ends.)

____ My parents respected each other.
____ My parents co-operated around important matters.
____ My parents communicated in a positive fashion.
____ My parents were not bound by gender stereotypes.
____ My parents felt their relationship was fair.
____ My parents worked at their relationship.
____ My parents showed affection for each other.
____ My parents made an effort not to draw me into their fights.

After you've finished this, talk about your responses. Then try to complete the same questions about your grandparents. See if you can locate how your parents responded to your grandparents, when and why your parents made the choices they made because of their own upbringing.

Did you make promises to yourself about how you would behave in your own relationship as a response to how your parents behaved in theirs? Did you promise yourself you'd never swear at your partner or storm out of the door? Did you keep those promises? How are you like your parents? How are you different? What have you learned from them? Do you fight like them? In what way is your fighting style similar and in what way is it different?

When Marla thought about how her parents fought, it was painful. They really went at each other, and there was frequent name-calling. She decided that when she was a mother, her kids would never have to listen to what she had to listen to as a child. So she held her anger in, thinking she was doing her children a favour. Meanwhile, her children had little idea of how two adults resolve differences, and they would take this lack of information into their own marriages. In addition, she held in so much that, from time to time when she did express anger, it was inappropriately hostile and defensive.

Caroline had been totally puzzled about the intensity of her own anger with Joe until she realized that she was parroting the fights that her parents had, escalating them, making major threats and standoffs.

Manny thought about how his father had treated his mother. He recalled that his father had completely tuned his mother out. It was as if his father went into a trance. That was how his father avoided his mother's feelings. Manny had those trancelike manoeuvres down to a tee.

But My Parents Had the Greatest Marriage I Ever Saw

Elaine came into couples' counselling with her husband Henry because they had fallen into a pattern of chronic bickering. Part of our work included looking at the root system of both families. Elaine was adamant that all she wanted was to have a relationship just like her parents'. That's why she came into therapy – because she knew how good a relationship could be from watching her parents. She saw her parents' relationship as perfect, and when she held her own two-year marriage up to their marriage for comparison, she felt that he and Henry fell short. Elaine said her parents were a great couple, and that she and Henry just didn't have the same spark.

I pointed out that in her parents, Elaine and Henry had a remarkable resource, and that they might be able to teach her and Henry a few things about getting along. I said they were really shortchanging themselves if they didn't grill her parents to learn their secrets. In fact, I wanted to know them, too!

When Elaine and Henry returned the next week, Elaine said that she had learned a lot and that she was a bit shocked – she had been both right and wrong in her picture of her parents. She was right in thinking her parents were really happy together. She was wrong in thinking that it was a bed of roses. Elaine and Henry had sat down with her parents for a long talk. Elaine told them that she and Henry were struggling now, and that she feared she would never be as happy in her marriage as her parents were in theirs. Elaine's parents laughed and told Elaine and Henry the story of their relationship. They told them that they worked on their relationship for years when Elaine was too little to know what was going on, that there were a few points when they almost called it quits. Elaine's mother turned to her father and said, 'Remember the year we moved to Long Island so you could start that new job? We spent a month camped in different sections of the house because we couldn't stand each other.' Elaine's father countered with, 'I remember. I never thought we would get through that year, and I'm still not sure how we did it.' Elaine's parents told them about good years, bad years, doubts, and that, through all these times, they both used the strategies of talking about it, working at it, and, when all else failed, waiting it out. They explained that the first seven years were the hardest, and after that, it seemed that every year things got better and better. Elaine left this conversation with a new understanding of her parents and herself.

Tip: If you know a great couple, ask them how they do it. If they give you vague answers like 'we communicate', just keep repeating, 'What do you mean?' until you know what they are specifically talking about.

Guerrilla Mating Tactic Number 3: Look at your role in your parents' relationship

In addition to the way your parents related to each other, what was your role in their relationship? Were you kept out of their difficulties? Did they discuss their problems with you? Were you drawn into their disputes? Did you feel helpless? Responsible?

> When Irene's mum and dad fought, it was usually because her dad came home late (and usually drunk). Her dad used to threaten to leave her mum. Her mother, in a state of desperation, would wake up Irene and send her in to her dad. It was Irene's job to beg her dad to stay. Of course, it was a terrible thing to do to a child, but Irene's mother felt desperate. Today, when Calvin is late, Irene feels desperate.
>
> When her parents fought, Marla would collect her younger brothers and sisters into her bed and mother them. When they fell asleep, Marla would silently cry herself to sleep. Today when Marla's husband gets angry, she gets sleepy. She leaves the room and crawls into bed, which infuriates her husband even more.
>
> Manny felt like he had to be a husband to his mother. Since his father wouldn't listen to her, Manny kind of felt he had to. It had been tough when he met Molly and married her because he felt as if he were deserting Mum for another woman.

Guerrilla Mating Tactic Number 4: Talk about and explore major family events

> After 13 years of marriage, Alan, a businessman, decided to leave his wife. They had a daughter who was 12 and a son who was 7. He began an affair with a woman who lived in London. He entered therapy and after two sessions, he realized that when he was 12 his mother had left his father and taken up with a man who lived in London. Although Alan didn't understand why this was happening to him, this knowledge allowed Alan to slow himself down enough to look more carefully at the events and refuse to be a willing partner to them.

> Marianne's dad had died when she was 15. When her own daughter turned 15, Marianne had an irresistible urge to leave her husband. She realized at some point that she would be doing to her daughter exactly what happened to her.

Couples do repeat traumatic family events, reliving a past that was left unfinished. These events are known as repetition compulsions. You repeat something that happened to you or a way you felt at an earlier time in your life. You are not repeating the event because you want to hurt yourself or others or because you like doing it. You are repeating the event in the hopes of creating a satisfactory resolution.

Look at your family tree. Always take an inventory of when truly traumatic childhood events – death, divorce, major illness – occurred. You may find that you get depressed, angry, lonely, or more volatile during the months these things occurred or during the year you reach the age your parents were at the time of the event. The following story is my own:

> My father died when he was 41. When I turned 41 I had a rough year. Then I thought I was over it *until my husband, who is younger than I am, turned 41.* Then I made sure he had a terrible year.

Guerrilla Mating Tactic Number 5: Talk with your parents and/or siblings to find out how they understand the family dynamics

Many of us cling selectively to ideas about our childhood: ideas of deprivation, isolation, abandonment. We forget the many sacrifices our parents made for us. We forget that our parents may have been struggling with problems of their own such as the deaths of their own parents, illness, and frustration. This might be a time to talk to your parents about their lives and find out how they see their lives, their own childhoods, their relationships. Nancy had never known that her father had declared bankruptcy when she was two, which was why her mother had suddenly taken a job and left her daily with an aunt she couldn't stand. Rick had never known that his father's younger brother had committed suicide, and that that was why his father had gone into a terrible depression when Rick was 11. Tony had never realized that his dad was never home because he took two jobs in order to send four children to university. And you can see in the story about Elaine that talking with her parents about their relationship was very helpful to her. Remember that many of the ideas you have about your parents were formed when you were a kid and you could only relate to the world in terms of yourself as the centre of it. By talking to them now, you may gain a new perspective, a new respect, and a new understanding of the complexity of your family root system.

THE SWEETEST SOUNDS

Rachel and Joe were getting married. Rachel's grandfather Samuel was a Holocaust survivor. He had been a cellist in Germany and had many times told the story of being transported to a camp and having to leave his beloved cello behind. Joe and Rachel had made a trip to Germany on holiday. While there, Joe, without telling Rachel, went to Samuel's old address. After some searching he found the families who lived in the building during that time. He traced the cello and found that one of the families had kept the cello as a remembrance of their friend. They did not even know he was still alive. Joe secretly had the cello transported to England and to the wedding. At the wedding, he surprised everyone by returning the cello to Samuel. When Samuel played the cello, there was not a dry eye in the room.

If your parents are no longer living or if they are not able to talk with you for whatever reason, it might be helpful to talk to siblings, aunts, uncles and other relatives to get a fuller picture of your parents and your childhood. Other family members may have information that illuminates the past. I turn to my 88-year-old cousin Dora for family lore. She doesn't care what anyone thinks about her anymore, so she's always willing to tell the truth. You'd be surprised at what you find out.

Guerrilla Mating Tactic Number 6: Ask yourself which family role you are still loyal to

As you grew up, you soaked up a family identity which may continue to track you: the troublemaker, the joker, the black sheep, the baiter, the flirt, the favourite son, the scapegoat. Families assign roles which we adopt in the service of keeping our family structure intact and controlling emotions. For example, a child may get the role of the 'sickly one', developing one illness after another in order to keep his parents from fighting with each other. If the parents focus on his illness, they have less time to fight with each other, plus they are joined in a common concern. As long as the boy stays ill, they get along. If the boy gets better, then

---

they have to deal with each other again. On some level, the boy understands this dynamic very early on. A daughter who is berated for her decisions may decide to become the 'helpless one', pretending she is stupid in order to keep from being criticized over the decisions she makes for herself. Such roles get carried into adulthood. For example, the boy who was the 'sickly one' may find he got a lot of attention for that. He may carry the role into his other adult relationships in his bid for attention or to prevent another kind of conflict. He may get headaches when his wife wants to have a good fight. She may never get to vent her feelings for fear it will make him feel worse. His family role (or your family role), which kept his family together, may now work to obstruct a valuable part of the relationship.

Take a look at your old behaviours and notice which ones you are still loyal to – perhaps you were the oldest child, so you got the role of 'caretaker', and you're still doing it. Perhaps you were the 'troublemaker', always the one to provoke others because they weren't in touch with their emotions – are you still that provocative? And, if you are, how does your behaviour help your relationship and how does your behaviour hurt your relationship? Do you still need your childhood role, or is there a better way to get your point across?

Guerrilla Mating Tactic Number 7: Don't be a child

A parent can be loving, but the child is never an equal. Though we all need to have our partner take over and be our parent sometimes, you want to be an equal most of the time. But a person who acts like a child *usually gets better at being treated like a child* – they get more and more dependent.

> I treated a couple, Margie and Billy, where Margie felt she could never win the power struggle, let alone compete – so she never even tried. One day she called to ask me what time our next appointment was. She said, 'Billy didn't remember when our meeting was.' Since she was present when we made the appointment, I asked her if she remembered. She said, 'Oh, no, Billy is supposed to remember. When you said when we were going to meet, I was thinking about something else. Billy is the one who is supposed to remember. You told him, not me.' Margie's main complaint was that Billy tried to control her. Maybe he did, but this conversation led me to think she might be a willing partner.

Another way of acting like a child occurs when, instead of recognizing and validating your partner's complaint, you act as though you are defence-less and beset by a cruel world.

> *Jan*: We agreed you'd tip the postman for Christmas. I relied on you to do it, and you didn't.
> *Al*: Why are you always picking on me? I can't remember everything.

> *Jan*: I stood waiting for you in front of the theatre for 30 minutes. We're late now.
> *Al*: I did the best I could.

The problem with this behaviour is that you constantly offer yourself up as inferior – you are weak, defenceless, so you can't meet your partner as an equal; you can only meet her as an inferior. When you act inferior, it is impossible to stay off the defensive because you've taken a defensive stance. You don't say, 'I did it', you say things are beyond you, being responsible is beyond you. Your partner has to either treat you like a child or attack your stance. Is that what you want?

Guerrilla Mating Tactic Number 8: See the possibilities in a partner who is 'just like' your parent

Years ago I did a television show in Los Angeles where one of the other guests was a very funny comedienne. As part of her routine, she identi-fied herself as a woman who wanted to find a mate, but feared that she'd end up with someone like her father. Later, as we sat on the panel talking, I pointed out to her that if she was spending her dates weeding out men like her father, she was missing the point: finding a man like her father would be her real opportunity to work this stuff out once and for all so that 'not ending up with someone like her father' could cease to be the focus of her relationships.

No matter how strongly you discover your partner evokes unpleasant memories of your childhood, think of the possibilities of such a union. Look at how this happened to Caroline:

I always knew that I made my father uneasy. Once he had to take me to the doctor. I was six. We parked the car, and I got out and walked around to him. I took his hand, and he pulled it away. 'You're too big for that,' he said. I felt so pushed away. I did not get close to someone until I knew that he was emotionally available – to the point of being a touchy-feely kind of guy. That was the one thing you could definitely say about Manny ... in the beginning. He called me daily from work, he couldn't last four hours without a love fix. In fact, sometimes he was too loving. But all in all, I was so glad not to be pushed away that I married him. We were as close as two people could be. About six months into the marriage, he went back to night school and was gone two nights a week. Soon I started feeling that he was unavailable, that he was not there for me. I began to seek out more and more contact, to try to seduce him into skipping a class or meeting me for dinner at 9.30 when his classes were done. He began to back off. I realized that I had not escaped my upbringing, I'd re-created it with Manny. He was my father, and I was a littler me.

In this case Caroline takes an old hurt of not feeling wanted and brings it into her present relationship. She doesn't do this consciously. She never set out to seek the ways Manny could hurt her that reminded her of how her father hurt her. She never chose how to make her life harder, and neither did you. But when her husband feels unavailable to her, it automatically evokes an earlier time when her dad acted distant and pushed her away.

> This is one of the gifts that a committed relationship offers – the chance to complete unfinished business from the past in the present with a loving partner.

Caroline reconnected with the feeling she had with her father, the feeling which, as a child, she had few resources to manage. Now, as an adult, she is at a point in her life where she and Manny can work this out. Today Caroline can *mend*. She can:

Monitor herself, since she knows she's sensitive to this, and work hard to recognize it when it happens and call it what it is
Enlist Manny to help her work this out, so that she can let go of this terrible feeling which has tracked her life and her relationships once and for all

Nip her words and stop it when she acts like a little girl responding to a daddy, and remind herself that she is a grown woman responding to an equal partner

Disclose and discuss her family history and feelings from the past to help Manny understand what a tender issue this is for her

(The next chapter is all about disclosure, and you will see that making honest disclosures often draws on your knowledge of your past.)

Your Wisdom in Choosing a Partner

You too probably ended up with a partner who has the unique ability to push all your buttons at once. Well, as Freud said – coincidences happen to those who need them most. Part of the way you chose your partner was based on a set of conscious decisions: he had the right warmth, humour, look, style, availability, and reciprocal interest in you to make pursuing him worthwhile. Yet, chances are that there are others who possessed these attributes, others whom you passed over, feeling that the chemistry was not right. The person you ended up with had many things to recommend him ... and then a little more.

You may not feel clear about what 'little more' was, but it is the part of you that honours your upbringing, understands exactly what unfinished business you need to complete, and will custom-design your relationship to help you do it. It is the part of you that knows that only certain people can move you by tapping into your emotional life in powerful, powerful ways, and that, if you want to deal with the legacy of your family, you have to choose a partner who gives you access to your family issues.

Love Heals Old Sorrows

Each one of us has leftover pain from childhood that follows us. It hurts like hell, and we'd do anything to get rid of it. It's always there. It doesn't leak, it doesn't move, it doesn't give – it's kind of like a breast implant, but it's a pain implant. The pain encompasses all the things you fear will happen to you, all the things that did happen to you, all the love you didn't get, the fact that it's just so hard to feel safe.

The honeymoon stage of love makes us believe that the pain is gone, but one day a realization hits with all the force of an Evander Holyfield right hook: The pain is still there. The hurts of childhood are still there.

The relationship didn't make them go away. In fact, the relationship intensified them:

> It's human nature, not human folly, which mobilizes us to re-create that original glimpse of love. Here's your chance to confront the past and re-do love with a happier outcome.

To re-do love with a happier outcome, you must borrow your partner to finish your parents' job. That is why, when the honeymoon is over, all that old hurt comes back double-time. Only when you love do you let someone get close enough to your heart to reawaken all the dependent feelings you had in the first hopeless love affair with your parents. When he rushes to get you a can of Coke before you know you're thirsty, a biscuit before you asked, a tissue before you even know you need one, it's a familiar feeling – a feeling of re-finding something very treasured, very old, lost.

And when all that old hurt comes back, it's important to know that this doesn't necessarily happen because your parents did a lousy job – it doesn't necessarily happen because your parents didn't give you the kind of love you needed. Though psychology books tell us that we are fully formed human beings by the time we hit our teens – that becoming well adjusted is something that is supposed to happen to us by the time we are in the sixth form – I don't think this is true. Our parents aren't meant to finish the job of helping us develop. We are meant to become fully formed human beings in our adult relationships with others. We finish the work of growing up and growing into our true personalities in our relationships. We pick up the past and work it out in the present with our partners.

Your relationship with your partner is your chance to re-find the sorrows of childhood and heal them. A relationship provides a way to undo childhood hurt, childhood rage. It's your chance to be soothed for all those times you needed soothing and didn't get it. Yes, love heals. The hard part is that it never seems to heal all we count on it to heal. Love refuses to be a magic wand. The other hard part is that, in order for your relationship to do its work of healing, you've got to re-experience the pain. That's why you picked the person who could take you there. You did it not to frustrate yourself, but to help yourself let go of the past and to continue developing yourself as a person in the present – in a relationship. So go back to the eight tactics above – go through all of them, and as you do, recognize how far you have come, how far you have to go, and how uncanny your eye is for 'whom' you need to get there. You sure know how to pick 'em.

Quick-Fix List: Understanding Family Matters

Guerrilla Mating Tactic Number 1:
Draw a family tree with your partner so you can explore the impact of your past on your present.

Guerrilla Mating Tactic Number 2:
Take your current differences back a generation. When you have a problem with your partner, ask yourself how your parents would have handled that same problem.

Guerrilla Mating Tactic Number 3:
Look at your childhood role in your parents' problems.

Guerrilla Mating Tactic Number 4:
Talk about and explore major family events, including milestones and mishaps.

Guerrilla Mating Tactic Number 5:
Talk with your parents and/or siblings to find out how they understand the family dynamics.

Guerrilla Mating Tactic Number 6:
Ask yourself which family role you are still loyal to.

Guerrilla Mating Tactic Number 7:
Don't be a child.

Guerrilla Mating Tactic Number 8:
See the possibilities in finding a partner who is 'just like' your parent.

five

OUTWITTING EMOTIONAL MISERS: HOW TO GET YOUR NEEDS MET

Maria meets her three friends at the gym, as she has done every Thursday night for the past two years. They waddle and groan through a step aerobics class that has yet to produce the desired results. It's a mystery how you can sweat so hard and not lose weight. Each week all four of them try to solve it over a few beers.

One friend is giving a wart-by-wart debriefing of her most recent blind date when suddenly, they all turn simultaneously, glare at Maria and say in singsong voices, 'Maria doesn't have to deal with this anymore. She's in a relationship.'

Maria remains silent. She knows if she utters one word they'll hate her. But she's worried. The pounding in her heart has turned to pounding in her head.

She wants to tell her friends that things aren't going so well – that her relationship, once characterized by an easy generosity, seems to have fallen into a tight-lipped race to see who will screw it up first. But she's afraid to talk to them, to Bill, to face it herself. In fact, she doesn't know what to say to anyone...

When the honeymoon is over and you rise from the ashes of your love coma, you face the challenge of starting to build a new relationship with the same person. In the fifties, reaching this phase took seven years, and we called the resulting crisis the 'seven-year itch.' But the world has sped up considerably since Marilyn Monroe flashed her magical thighs over a New York subway grate (to the delight of the hormonally rampant Tom Ewell). With inflation, the seven-year itch has shrunk to four years.

If Hollywood were to portray how scary this realization can be, they would edit the trailer of *Alien 3* to keep Sigourney Weaver's bald-faced terror, but replace the 'alternative life form' with your husband of four years.

Okay. I'm exaggerating. But our staggering divorce rate suggests that the responses to the end of the honeymoon aren't always pretty. The most dramatic of us quit, whine, cheat. But just as often relationships get whittled away by resentment, confusion and apathy. Unprepared for the provocative work of building a new relationship with the same person, we respond by shutting down the system, removing our true selves one emotion at a time. And, *replacing* our true selves is, yes, you guessed it: the alternative life form – up to no good and emotionally mean, mean, mean.

Financial Misers and Emotional Misers

When it comes to cash, you don't have to look far to find a tightwad. We all know one. He rarely picks up the tab, no matter how many times you've treated him. When paying for herself, she undertips. He argues about the cost of everything – acting as if the world is trying to pull one over on him.

The *Random House Dictionary* defines a miser as a person who 'lives in wretched circumstances in order to save and hoard money.' To this day we uncover stories of people suffering in dilapidated houses with a million pounds in cash stuffed under the refrigerator.

Suppose we take this discussion and substitute the word *feelings* for the word *money*. Without ever intending to present themselves in a miserly fashion, people hoard feelings, withhold emotions, and storehouse warmth. Did you realize that you can be just as stingy with who you are as a miser can be about what she spends?

You have millions at your disposal – millions of sensations, that is – a rich emotional life that runs the gamut from remarkable tenderness to unbearable beastliness. You're quite powerful, but perhaps you're uncomfortable with that idea. Many of us are afraid of our powerful feelings, particularly when it comes to love. After all, relationships are so unpredictable. What if you parted with your true colours, showed your true feelings, and met with disaster? We find it so hard to open up to the one we love most.

However, being hesitant or afraid to show your feelings isn't what makes you an emotional miser. That only happens when *you are afraid to say you are afraid*. Or when you don't even know you're afraid – when your emotional life is as mysterious to you as it is to your partner.

Are You an Emotional Miser?

Before we venture into the world of emotional misers, you may want to know if this chapter has relevance for you. Here's a test you can take to assess your own tendencies to withhold who you are from your partner.

Scale: 1 to 5
1 = You never have these feelings
2 = You rarely have these feelings
3 = These things cross your mind occasionally
4 = This dilemma troubles you
5 = This stuff plagues you

Keep in mind: Miserly behaviour is not a wish to be cruel. It's a misguided attempt to manage the anxiety that fear of closeness causes.

The Emotional Miser Index

_____ I keep a mental check and balance sheet of who did what in the relationship. I make sure that each of us holds up our end of the bargain.

_____ I'm careful not to show too much of myself to my partner. I don't want him to think I care more than he does because he'll walk all over me.

_____ I don't allow myself to get too excited or too upset. I'm uncomfortable with displays.

_____ I'm always aware of what I put into the relationship because I only have so much to give. I don't want to deplete myself.

_____ I hold back because I have misgivings about my partner. If only he'd make a few changes, I could let myself love him completely.

Tally your score. If you scored:

5–7   Apply directly for the Florence Nightingale Chair at your local charitable association. You're too good to be true. In fact, you need a nap in order to rest from the burden of your goodness.

8–13   If you're in a new relationship, you're realistically cautious about letting go. You protect yourself as you learn to trust someone. The more you trust, the more you let your guard down. If you're in a long-term relationship, you still have work to do.

14–19   Intimacy makes you anxious. You've been hurt – join the club. You could benefit from extra support right now because it's hard for you to enjoy another person without feeling worried.

20–25   Your fears about getting closer make you hold your feelings in instead of spreading them around. But there's hope. This chapter was written just for you.

Fears That Make Us Mean

People erect fortresses around their emotional lives because it's the only way they've learned to protect themselves. Getting closer presents an array of risks that we may feel yet not understand, such as:

- Fear of putting out more than you get back
- Fear of giving up control of your life to the other
- Fear of your own feelings
- Fear of running out of feelings
- Fear of the unknown
- Fear of conflict
- Fear of repeating bad relationships
- Fear that your partner will stop loving you
- Fear that your partner isn't who he says he is
- Fear that you can't have a perfect union
- Fear that you don't come first
- Fear that you can't count on her to be there
- Fear that you won't get your needs met

or, the most common

- Fear of all these fears

These fears are understandable. We've all lost a friendship, a partnership or a relationship with someone who couldn't be bothered with hearing our true feelings or who couldn't handle them. In addition, most of us have been disappointed in, cheated on by, abandoned by, unjustly accused by and manipulated by a partner at some point. Trying to hide or ignore the fears requires a huge expenditure of energy. The energy you use to suppress what you're afraid of compromises the amount of energy remaining to petition for positive changes. Resentment grows instead of love.

Each tentacle of fear can be pulled away to reveal the common central fear: fear of loss. The underlying fear is that the love will be withdrawn, either by you or by your partner. Without good relationship tactics, we adopt a miserly posture to protect ourselves. Unfortunately, it doesn't help and it doesn't work.

TYING THE PAST TO THE PRESENT

For Tim's birthday, Kayla bought him a first edition of his favourite childhood book, *Tom's Midnight Garden*.

But if hiding the fear doesn't work, neither does overloading your partner with it. After all, if you needle your wife with 'Honey, would you leave me for Bono?' and she says, 'No. Don't tell me you're gonna start that again,' do you feel reassured for longer than five minutes? Probably not.

Disclosure: A Bridge to Generosity

What *can* help, and one of the building blocks of a satisfying relationship, is learning the appropriate tactic for expressing an uncomfortable feeling. It's called a *disclosure*. A disclosure is an 'I' statement that paints a picture of your internal experience. Since it never blames, it is never a 'you' statement. A disclosure is a way to be generous rather than mean in your relationship because it shows trust. While disclosures contain an element of risk, at least they give the two of you something to work through. Disclosures can be low-risk, medium-risk, or high-risk – small talk or a way to bare your heart and soul.

Low-Risk Disclosures

A low-risk disclosure reveals a small part of you that has little impact on the person you tell. With a low-risk disclosure, you share your troubles, memories, worries and joys, and your general experience of *yourself* as an individual. Let's look at a low-risk disclosure in action.

When someone gives you flowers

> No disclosure: Roses – how pretty. Thank you.
> Low-risk disclosure: I love roses. As a girl, I used to keep dried rose petals in my night table just for the smell. Thank you.

A disclosure such as the one above, which seems to be simply adding details, actually permits someone to know more about your inner life – in short, to know you better. Here's another example.

At the movies

No disclosure: What a bomb! Let's get a pizza
Low-risk disclosure: I didn't like that movie. The ending made me feel creepy.

Since any new skill requires a few practice runs, why not practise low-risk disclosures with people other than your partner? When you flub it, you can still learn something. Imagine what the accompanying disclosure would have been and how it might be different from what you actually said.

To the musicians at your friend's wedding

What you said: Can't you play something I like?
What you could have said: I'm terrible at slow dancing, and I want to impress my date. I'd love to hear you play 'In the Mood'.

When shopping for your wife in the lingerie department

What you said: Do you have the item in the window in stock in a big size ... like one that would almost fit me? You don't? Oh, well.
What you could have said: My wife just had our first baby a couple of weeks ago. She's been a little down about her weight gain. I wanted to buy her something that would let her know how gorgeous I find her. Can you help?

When you get a disclosure right, you may notice people responding to you with more warmth and co-operation. Even if there is no immediate gratification, give it time until it feels right. Then start practising slightly higher-level disclosures with more important people in your life. You'll soon see just how much disclosure can change the nature of the conversation.

Medium-risk Disclosures

A medium-risk disclosure is one step up in sharing your feelings. It is still an 'I' statement about yourself as an individual, but it is likely to have more impact on your partner. What differentiates a low-risk disclosure from a medium-risk disclosure is that you are talking about something that is of medium importance to you (probably not the weather), and you are making the disclosure to someone who is important to you (probably not the musician at your friend's wedding). In a medium-risk disclosure, the way you express yourself can be the difference between a comment that encourages empathy and communication or a comment that turns your partner into your opponent. Like this:

You realize it was your father-in-law's birthday – last week

> Say this: I feel bad ... I forgot your father's birthday, and I forgot to remind you to send a birthday card.

> Not this: Hey, why didn't you remember it was your father's birthday last week?

You go to the beach hating your body when you notice your partner looking at you

> Say this: I wish *I* didn't have this cellulite.

> Not this: I wish *you'd* stop staring at my cellulite.

Raising the subject of your new haircut

> Say this: I have mixed feelings about this new haircut.

> Not this: You don't like my hair.

Confronting the professor who graded your paper

> Say this: A C? I'm disappointed, and it would help me to understand your thinking about this.

> Not this: A C? I don't deserve it.

Commenting on the project your boss just handed you

> Say this: This is a big task. I'm not certain I can finish it by the end of the day.

> Not this: What am I, a machine? Look at all this. You don't expect it today, do you?

When you get a medium-risk disclosure right, you are likely to notice more warmth in your relationship and more co-operation from your partner.

High-Risk Disclosures

High-risk disclosures resonate the heart of our internal landscapes. They reveal *your experience of yourself within the context of your relationship during a difficult encounter*. What you say will have real impact on the pulse of the listener. Rule one of a high-risk disclosure (as with all disclosures) is that it never blames. If you turn your fears and conflicts into blame, you're likely to start that same old battle that no one wins. A disclosure provides a hidden opportunity, not present in blame, to feel better. Again, the disclosure needs to be clearly framed in 'I's'.

> Say this: I get scared so I hold back.
> Not this: You make me afraid to talk.

> Say this: I feel alone right now.
> Not this: You're not there for me.

Before you start making high-risk disclosures to your partner, one of the safest and most productive ways to practise them is in your head. Think of any situation in which your partner ruffles your feathers. Got it? Now, imagine what the accompanying disclosure would be. No matter how provoked you feel, see what your complaint sounds like when it's framed as a disclosure, instead of an attack. Here are a few examples:

> Uncomfortable situation: Sometimes when the two of you are having sex, your partner rushes ahead, immensely excited. He doesn't seem to notice that you haven't even started breathing heavily.
> Attack: You don't care about my satisfaction.
> Imagined disclosure: I love it when we make love nice and slow. I get very turned on by that, and it's easier for me to have an orgasm.

Uncomfortable situation:	When your partner leaves for work, he often forgets to lock the door. This has happened a few times.
Attack:	You don't care if I'm murdered.
Imagined disclosure:	I get worried – even scared – when I come home and find the door unlocked. I'm afraid that when I go inside, I'll discover we were robbed – or worse, the robber will be there. I want to feel safer when I come home.

Practising in your head is a proven technique for improving your 'game'. I read a story about a prisoner of war in Vietnam who, upon his release, asked to be taken to an 18-hole golf course. In spite of the fact that he'd not seen a golf course in years, he played an almost perfect game. When astonished onlookers asked how this could be, he explained that he'd been playing this game, several times a day, for years and years in his head.

Are you ready to start making high-risk disclosures instead of practising in your head? Here are two examples:

Raising the subject of marriage

Say this: I want to talk about marriage. I've been thinking more and more about it.

Not this: You never bring up the subject of marriage.

Raising the subject of loneliness

Say this: I miss you. Let's make plans to spend some time together as soon as possible.

Not this: You're never around. Why do you have to work such long hours?

Warning: You cannot take a 'blame' statement such as 'You're not there for me' and try to disguise it as a disclosure by adding an 'I feel' qualifier to it (as in, 'I feel you're not there for me'). A disclosure must reflect your experience of *yourself*, not of your partner.

The Silas Marner Syndrome

There is a curious phenomenon that almost always occurs when you feel but do not disclose your emotions. The emotions you try to withhold – such as hurt, anger, frustration – are the very emotions you will create in your partner. I call it 'The Silas Marner Syndrome', and I'll dissect the following case studies to show how it happens. You'll see:

> *The Fear:* What the person is trying to hide.
> *The Symptom:* How the fear gets expressed.
> *Guerrilla Mating Tactic:* How to use disclosure for a less conflictual, more satisfying outcome.

The 'Let Me Suffer Alone' Miser

As Jan was moving a large plant from one part of the living room to another, she dropped it on her foot and screamed out in pain. Her husband, Mitch, ran to help her, but Jan darted into the bathroom and locked the door, alternately crying and running a tub to soak her foot. Mitch called to her through the bathroom door, asking her to let him in or least tell him what happened. She yelled back, 'Leave me alone.' He repeated his request. She repeated her answer. He stood by the bathroom door, feeling his neck turn red.

Jan cut Mitch out. Whether this is her style of handling pain or whether she's angry at Mitch for not having moved the plant when she first asked him to two weeks ago is of less importance than how Jan handles the interaction. She handles it in a way that culminates in Mitch feeling cut off and mad that he was yelled at. Mitch will sulk or yell back, and a cycle of hurt feelings begins. Since he doesn't *know* why Jan has cut him off, he will *imagine* why Jan has cut him off, and who knows what he'll think up? The feelings Jan withholds (pain, confusion, anger) are the very feelings she evokes in Mitch.

The Fear:	Sharing pain and/or painful feelings.
The Symptom:	When you are troubled, upset, sick, or when something unpleasant happens, you withhold and/or yell.
Guerrilla Mating Tactic:	The next time you're tempted to shut your partner out, try disclosure instead of withdrawal. Remember, a disclosure is a snapshot of what's happening inside of you. In this type of situation, here are a few of the things that Jan could have said after the commotion died down:

I shut you out because that's what I'm used to doing. I'll work on it because I realize you don't deserve that. Please, tell me when you see me doing that.

I wanted you to move the plant. Instead of asking you again, I let the resentment build up. I'm angry.

I worry that my feelings are a big turnoff. That makes it hard to tell you what's going on.

When I get angry, I automatically retreat because I hate conflict, and I don't want to start a fight. I realize that swallowing my anger is no good for our relationship.

With disclosure, Jan makes room in her emotional life for Mitch to join her. She can use it as a way to enlist Mitch and turn him into her ally. Certainly, if Jan says she's angry, Mitch may respond in anger, but at least they both come clean. Disclosure may even offer her the hidden opportunity to be comforted by Mitch. By running from her anger, if that is what she feels, Jan creates resentment that will show up in other places and create more problems.

The 'Clipboard and Whistle' Miser

Whenever Mark asks Ellen to do something, he prefaces it by telling her what comparable task he's recently completed – like this:

I took out the garbage, so would you do the dishes?
I took the dog to the vet, so would you wash the car?
I hoovered the hall, so would you hoover the stairs?

Mark is afraid of ending up on the short end of the relationship stick, so he operates on the point system. Maybe Mark's parents did it this way, or maybe Mark has a legitimate gripe and he really does more than Ellen. Or perhaps, Mark feels safer in the relationship if the energy spent can be quantified. He counts good deeds to mask his anxiety of how unpredictable relationships really are. Unfortunately, Mark ends up invested in counting symbols of co-operation rather than in real co-operation. Mark's style of interaction leaves Ellen feeling as if Mark has 'relationship scales' in his head. She's so frustrated that she's starting to shut down. As soon as he begins to utter the familiar sentence, she shudders. Like Jan, Mark elicits the very behaviour he is working so hard to guard against.

The Fear:	Putting out more than you get.
The Symptom:	You march around with a debit/credit list of who-does-what for 'the relationship'.
Guerrilla Mating Tactic:	If you're obsessed with who-does-what, dump the qualifying phrases, stop the miserly cycle, and offer direct disclosures of your needs, wishes, and fears:

It would make me feel great if you did the dishes tonight.

I don't want to be in a relationship like my parent's relationship, but sometimes, I feel as if they're shadowing me.

I can't get past the idea that everything has to be 50/50. I keep thinking that I'm not going to get my share of something. Can we talk about it?

I think I'm acting so fussy because something is bothering
me. Could we talk about it?

With disclosure, Mark invites Ellen to participate in understanding his
quirks instead of making her the object of them. However he decides to
handle it, he creates a scenario in which his behaviour is not so loaded.

The 'He Done Me Wrong' Miser

Early on in their relationship, Beatrice and Johnny indulged in a spree
of reckless nights, one of which included her taking him to the office
Christmas party. After a fourth mai tai, Johnny disappeared with Beatrice's
soon-to-be-ex-secretary, Trudy. Under the usual circumstances, we'd say,
'end of party/end of story', because Johnny wasn't the guy that Beatrice
thought he was.

But Beatrice and Johnny screamed (then talked) it through, agreed
they were partying too much, agreed to try again, and agreed to settle
into a less intoxicated existence. Time passed, they married, all was fine
– except Beatrice could not stop herself from rifling Johnny's briefcase,
credit card bills and desk drawer.

Although Johnny has devoted years of helping her forget his adulter-
ous slip, Beatrice has been unable to find it in her heart to trust him
again. She says nothing, but feels a constant suspicion, going as far as
sneak-checking his pockets for motel matchbooks. Johnny wonders how
long he will have to pay for his mistake.

Maybe Beatrice thinks that her constant vigil is necessary to keep
Johnny true blue, maybe this incident has never properly been resolved,
and maybe the local jazz radio station keeps playing Billie Holiday's
greatest hits, constantly reminding her of how low-down a man can be.
Whatever the case, Beatrice's suspicion diverts her from exploring her
own issues about getting closer. After all, out of all the men in the world,
she chose Johnny, a man who had betrayed her. Beatrice needs to explore
her investment in keeping Johnny in the position of being a husband she
can't trust. And she'd better get to work, because Beatrice's style of
interaction is driving Johnny away. She risks a self-fulfilling prophecy,
unaware of the way in which she orchestrates it.

The Fear:	Your partner will cheat on you.
The Symptom:	You're always suspicious.
Guerrilla Mating Tactic:	If you've lost trust, in spite of your partner's efforts, then learning to trust again begins with disclosing instead of accusing:

After all this time, I still haven't put this problem to rest. Maybe I need help to do that.

I want to trust you, but I can't get myself to do it. How can we work on this?

What happened with that woman still scares me. It's so hard to let go of the past, even though I know how hard you've tried to help me do it.

If you can enlist your partner in helping to put the past behind, working with him instead of against him, you can begin to minimize and eventually put an end to these fact-finding missions.

Note: If this doesn't work for you, then go back to Chapter 3. Do a chart on when you are *more able* to let go of the past. Look at what is happening in your life when you are able to get off your position of mistrust and more able to feel trusting and loved. Then, do more of whatever you were doing at that time.

The 'Make Me the Sun, the Moon, and the Stars' Miser

Angelique was dating Larry, and he wanted to marry her. He was kind and thoughtful, and Angelique, at 38, wanted to be married. But Angelique felt that there was a problem with this union that could not be overcome. Larry had a 12-year-old son from a previous marriage. Larry and his son were close and visited at least twice a week. Angelique believed that marrying Larry would bring too many problems into her life because of his relationship with his son. She'd made a similar decision to break up with Greg, a salesman, who had had to entertain clients a few nights a week. Angelique felt it presented Greg with too many temptations while it presented her with too many lonely nights.

Harriet said that her husband approached her out of the blue and said, 'Happy anniversary.' She responded that their anniversary wasn't for another 10 months. He replied, 'I know, but today is the anniversary of the day we met.'

This was an issue with scope that went beyond Larry and his son and Greg and his clients. In fact, no matter what relationships Angelique looked at in her life, it always came down the same thing: no one was quite suitable for her because no one could offer enough of what she needed. Angelique feels as if there's not enough love coming her way.

Angelique might explore her idea that she has to compete with Larry's son for Larry's time. Or maybe she fears that if she truly commits to an intimate relationship, she'll ultimately be alone. To avoid dealing with the fear, however, she cuts herself off from deep involvement. She rejects her suitors before they abandon her.

Angelique's style of interaction includes her hopping on the dating treadmill like a hamster on his fourth cup of espresso, with no end in sight. Angelique isolates herself – before any man gets the chance. Thus, the very thing she is trying so hard to avoid is what she draws into her life.

The Fear: There's not enough love coming your way.

The Symptom: You can't connect comfortably with anyone because you require a bottomless well of attention.

Guerrilla Mating Tactic: When a part of you wants to bolt and you're in the business of creating distance, instead open a dialogue about it. At least then your ambivalence can be discussed:

As we get closer, I get the urge to run. It scares me.

I'm worried about taking on a step-parenting role. I'm not sure how to get started.

I feel insecure about us. I'm having trouble handling it.

I worry that I'm always going to come in second.

Angelique needs to start looking at whether her demands are reasonable. Maybe the same can be said about you? What is reasonable to expect from another person? Disclosure will get that inquiry off the ground.

In each of these miserly cases, disclosure is the first step towards opening a dialogue in which our fears, worries and discomforts can be explored. So now comes the hard part:

If it's so simple, why don't we do it?

As we've already discussed, we are partly motivated by a central fear of abandonment or loss. From that first night we sought milk and Mummy was unavailable (because she was in the operating theatre performing delicate brain surgery), from that first night we ran to Daddy and found him unflinchingly absorbed with Alf Garnett's latest scheme, each of us knew, in our heart of hearts, that sustaining the feeling of being unconditionally loved was going to be a difficult task.

Most of us were eventually able to incorporate the feeling of being loved, even when a parent wasn't available. We learned how to carry the feeling of being loved *inside of us*. Even so, for the rest of our lives we lose and find that feeling depending on life's circumstances.

For example, when I was 15 and my boyfriend left me at my door, I felt that I'd never see him again. I feared that he no longer loved me. I only felt loved by him when he was in front of my face, lipping a Silk Cut and calling me 'Baby Doll'. My hormones and my life stage made it hard for me to hold on to the feeling of being loved when my mother removed him from the porch and sent him home. So I called him 20 times a day (and hung up when he answered 19 of those times – thank goodness there was no '1471' facility in those days!).

As adults we still totter between the fear of abandonment and its opposite: the fear of getting too close, or engulfment. We worry in one moment that our beloved will leave us, and in the next that he'll take over:

ABANDONMENT	ENGULFMENT
He'll leave me	He'll swallow me whole
There'll be no him left	There'll be no me left
He won't be there	I won't get a minute alone

People say things like,

> I'm not a person anymore, I'm his wife.
> She expects me to be there for her all the time, It's too much to ask.

Note: Did you ever wonder why your partner could go out of town for two days and you couldn't wait to see him, and then he walks in the door and you kiss him deeply, and 10 minutes later you wish he'd go away again? Well, you are waffling between fear that he'll never come back and fear that he takes up too much space.

We enter an ongoing mental negotiation between the two extremes. And we try to defend ourselves from feelings that get stirred up by focusing on our partner rather than on ourselves. We deftly create smoke screens to throw us off the trail of our real worries. Mark projects the anxiety onto household tasks, Beatrice uses Johnny's old injustice, and Jan hides her pain – not because they are deficient people, but because it's so hard to stop and look at our own behaviour.

You Couldn't Be More Normal: Intimacy Versus Isolation

The fear that collects in your gut like tainted chow mein is not only normal, it is so common that psychologists have called in the developmental task of all adults. Psychologist Erik Erikson teaches that we go through stages in our lives. In each stage, from infancy to death, we have tasks that must be resolved in order for us to move ahead successfully to the next stage. If we resolve one task, we move to the next. If we do not successfully resolve the task, we have what Erikson calls a developmental crisis. That means an emotional piece of us gets stuck in that spot.

For example, the developmental task of a two-year-old is to learn self-control. This paves the way for being potty-trained and learning how to do things for herself. It also puts an end to the terrible twos, which impel her to run around supermarkets screaming, pulling canned peas off the shelf, and smacking other toddlers in the aisles. If she learns self-control, she completes this task in her crusade for autonomy. However, some children, instead of meeting with praise for their successes, meet instead with ongoing criticism of their slips. Say Sally's mummy greets all of Sally's actions with 'You idiot. Now, look what you've done.' Little Sally will experience a developmental crisis filled with the echo of messing this, messing that, messing up – stuck in a world of shame and doubt. As she grows older she will be filled with low self-esteem and little confidence. In fact, Little Sally runs the risk of marrying a guy who agrees with Mummy's assessment of her because it's so familiar. The feeling is, 'If the people who are supposed to praise you and love you don't do it, why would anyone else?'

As adults, our developmental task is establishing intimacy with other adults by learning how to be generous, tender, supportive, loving, open and respectful. The accompanying crisis is that if we can't get close, then we'll feel isolated. It feels more terrible than the terrible twos because, in the early stages, it's much harder to tell if you are intimate than it is to tell if you are potty-trained.

A HAPPY BIRTHDAY

Alice says that every year for her birthday her husband asks her, 'What is something I can give you that money can't buy?' That has meant so much to her, whether he takes the kids for a weekend or writes her a sonnet.

We establish that intimate connection through deep disclosure – that means we work towards engaging in free, open exchanges with our partner, we work towards gaining the courage to reveal the parts of ourselves that we fear will be unacceptable to others (unprotected feelings, unexpurgated thoughts, unshaven legs). Through disclosure we gauge whether others can be intimate with us, whether they can hear and respond to us. Our disclosures are intimate invitations to enter our inner life. Thus, disclosure is always a risk, but without this risk, intimacy cannot grow. Disclosure constitutes our effort to invite intimacy and fend off isolation.

How Emotional Misers Handle the Task of Intimacy Versus Isolation

What an emotional miser does is different:

By withholding disclosures, an emotional miser invites isolation and fends off intimacy.

This is not because he does not long for intimacy, but because he does not trust that he will be able to struggle through disclosures successfully to reach a satisfying outcome. Fearful that he will not be able to achieve intimacy, the emotional miser withholds disclosures, thus creating a situation in which his isolation is the only natural outcome of the relationship. Even though the miser's partner is right there beside him, she doesn't know what he feels or thinks or wants or needs. He's lonely, and all he can do is get lonelier by the minute. Chances are that in your relationship you don't avoid disclosure all the time, or your relationship probably wouldn't have lasted this long. We tend to do more avoiding when we are upset, angry and stressed, but as in the examples we've seen, when you avoid disclosure, you tend to evoke in your partner the very feelings you have avoided expressing.

Relationships That Go Nowhere

Barney has been in three longish relationships that have had one thing in common: all three went nowhere. Barney cited lack of chemistry, lack of timing and lack of sexual compatibility. The truth was different. Barney, worried that he'd screw things up, held back his true feelings by not making any disclosures or revealing anything that might threaten or change the nature of the relationship. His misguided effort to protect the relationship by 'keeping it light' (after many, many get-togethers) was actually a way to stay underdisclosed, thus strangling any potential for real intimacy.

If you have dated someone who insists on keeping it light, understand that you are being asked to minimize disclosures. That's why the relationship becomes so frustrating. Without disclosures, you can date someone 20 times and not know them any better than you knew them on the first date. If you have been the one who tries to 'keep it light', thus entering a series of relationships that start marvellously but go nowhere, consider lack of disclosure as a prime suspect. Are you choosing the crisis instead of the task?

Relationships without mutual disclosure are difficult to sustain. However, occasionally you see long-term relationships in which both parties have entered into a tacit agreement to remain underdisclosed. Neither partner shares, reveals or has a deeper sense of knowing the other. Often, these couples have an impaired sense of themselves. They make a great investment in the fantasy of being a couple without knowing how to do the hard work of being a couple.

Choosing Intimacy Instead of Isolation

Disclosures are a cornerstone of intimacy. In studies that followed couples who were falling *out* of love, lack of self-disclosure was cited among the primary causes for the disintegration of the relationship. Of course, disclosures aren't cure-alls. They are emotional truths that represent precursors to important conversations, *which you then need to have*. Obviously, you'll want to choose your spots. If you disclose for each little thing, your relationship risks sounding like a fifties sitcom rerun:

> Emily: Hi, Bob.
> Carol: Hi, Bob.
> Jerry: Hi, Bob.
> Bob: I need you all to stop saying,
> 'Hi, Bob.'
> Emily, Carol, and Jerry: What, Bob?

Note: Countless studies have proved that people who practise disclosing experience more healthy mental states, less disease, and better outlooks over all. Nowhere is there a better example of this than in a study done for a US television science programme called *Healing and the Mind*. Patients with heart disease and cancer were put into groups where they disclosed feelings about their family relationships with regard to their diagnoses. Getting their feelings off their chest was a step towards healing their minds, and in some cases, their bodies. It created an atmosphere of intimacy that was unprecedented for many of these people.

Five Great Reasons to Disclose

If it's difficult in the beginning to frame your disclosures, you're on the right track. It *should* be difficult. Here are five reasons to keep working at it:

1 You allow your partner to know you as you are, and give up on the idea of him knowing you as you present yourself. This relieves resentment that builds up when you feel you have to act in a certain way to be loved.

2 Your interactions feel more authentic, and as such, more satisfying.
3 You have the chance to work through difficulties instead of swallowing them.
4 You don't waste your time hoping that your partner will read your mind and do the right thing.
5 You take responsibility for your feelings and actions, rather than blaming your partner.

Six Cautions about Disclosures

Keep these caveats in mind as you integrate disclosures and build trust:

1 The point of disclosure is not to tell your partner everything that is going on inside of you all the time – that would be flooding the relationship with your feelings. Flooding with feelings is the same as flooding with water – good people drown. What you want is to be able to convey important information in a positive, non-blaming way. Don't mistake disclosure for a directive to tell your partner *everything*. Good relationships depend on *your not doing that*. Relationships thrive on partners who know when to keep their mouths shut.
2 If disclosures are new to you, then your partner doesn't expect them. A change in your behaviour may not immediately be recognized, let alone appreciated. Give her time to adapt and absorb the fact that something new is happening in your interactions.
3 When relationships are starting out, disclosures need to come slowly. Pay attention to whether, as you begin to disclose, she shares at about the same rate. If she continues to hold back, you eventually need to comment on it:

◗ I notice that you seem quiet when I talk about my ex/kids/dog/job.
◗ I've shared a few secrets with you. Am I overdoing it?

If you don't maintain balance in disclosure so that you are both disclosing with some equanimity during the early stages of a relationship, you risk overwhelming her with your emotional life.

Don't overdisclose: It makes you sound too needy and throws the balance of the interaction off.

4 Be careful about slipping into blame statements. Remember: A true disclosure uses the 'I' pronoun.
5 As we've discussed earlier in this chapter, you may be in a relationship that depends on secrets to survive. Both of you have formed an alliance that includes a pact of silence and a tacit agreement on roles. If so, disclosures are risky. You must be committed to the evolution of the relationship in order to be willing to experiment with new ways of being together.
6 Sometimes disclosures don't work. There's a fight that needs to happen. There's an impasse that needs to go on for a while. There are bad feelings that need to erupt like blisters in the Arizona sun. Be realistic enough to accept this. Then flip forward to the next chapter.

Final Thoughts on Emotional Misers

We can become pretty adept at making disclosures when we're falling in love because it's easy then. We're floating, floating, swept away in a tidal wave of love. However, when the tidal wave parts to reveal the humans scurrying across the ocean floor, we often stop disclosing and start withholding.

So, if you're feeling that the love hasn't died but it could use a little resuscitating, disclosure is the skill that will help you remember why you fell in love in the first place. It's a troubleshooter that helps to ensure that misunderstandings don't snowball. It's a way to get closer. It's the stairway to a honeymoon moment. And it's a method useful in helping you get your needs met.

Remember: If Silas Marner parts with his money, his money will be gone. If you part with yourself through disclosure, that won't be true. You can get enough love back to fill your heart and replenish you. Rather than depleting the well, disclosing is a way to keep the well full.

Quick-Fix List: Proper Disclosures

A disclosure

▶ Is an 'I' statement that paints a picture of your internal experience
▶ Never blames
▶ Is never a 'you' statement

Low-Risk Disclosures

A low-risk disclosure reveals a small part of you that has little impact on the person you tell. You share your troubles, worries and joys and your general experience of *yourself as an individual*.

When someone gives you flowers

> Low-risk disclosure: I love roses. As a girl, I used to keep dried rose petals in my night table just for the smell. Thank you.
> No disclosure: Roses – how pretty. Thank you.

Medium-Risk Disclosures

In a medium-risk disclosure, the way you express yourself can be the difference between a comment that encourages empathy and communication and a comment that turns your partner into your opponent. Like this:

You realize it was your father-in-law's birthday – last week

> Say this: I feel bad ... I forgot your father's birthday, and I forgot to remind you to send a birthday card.
> Not this: Hey, why didn't you remember it was your father's birthday last week?

High-Risk Disclosures

High-risk disclosures reveal *your experience of yourself within the context of your relationship*.

> Say this: I feel alone today.
> Not this: You're not there for me.

III

THE BOMB SQUAD:
HOW TO DISARM CONFLICTS

six

FRIENDLY FIRE: HOW TO ACTUALLY LIKE THE WAY YOU FIGHT

You hate to fight – most people do. However, often the real problem with fighting is that you hate the person you become and the person your partner becomes when you fight. You hate the way you argue, the depths you'll sink to, the *modus operandi* of your attack, the things that are said about you and to you, the viciousness of your thoughts, the way your fights make you feel. This chapter is filled with tactics for how not to hate yourself in a fight and how not to hate your partner either.

A worthy life goal would be to actually learn to like the way you fight.

Liking the way you fight would include:

- Feeling proud of your ability to confront a difficult matter
- Making sure your point is heard without cruelty or defensiveness
- Arguing in a fashion that makes room for differences to be resolved
- Understanding that differences do not need to divide a couple and can actually strengthen the relationship

But Why Do We Have to Fight?

You'll be together for decades – for life! So face it – you can't always be in sync. Differences can range from tiny irritations such as 'he leaves the loo seat up', or 'she keeps the volume on the television too loud', to heated disputes, such as 'I can't believe you voted for them', or 'I refuse to invite your friend Stinky to our house', to a humongous parting of ways such as 'I will leave you if you stay out all night again', or 'This time I mean it – I want separate beds.'

What I find interesting is that couples fight almost as often when they have *no* real disagreement on their hands as when they have a *valid* disagreement. Couples fight with each other for many, many reasons, including boredom, foreplay, loneliness, debating practice, contrariness, headaches, caffeine overdose, not-getting-the-cheque-in-the-mail-you-expected-to-get. Couples fight because it is an *available form of involvement*, along with loving, joking , sex, silliness and mud wrestling. No disagreement is necessary.

In addition, the range of our angry feelings is so complex and enormous that when I started looking up words that describe anger, I discovered that angry words could have a dictionary all to themselves. Here are just some of the words I came up with:

Irritation	Tension
Exasperation	Torment
Distress	Harassment
Nuisance	Indignation
Displeasure	Abuse
Aggravation	Persecution
Provocation	Disparagement
Annoyance	Animosity
Conflict	Ire
Strife	Outrage
Friction	Wrath
Struggle	Acrimony
Clash	Hatred
Dispute	Hostility
Quarrel	Malice
Squabble	Rancour
Anger	Fury
Resentment	Bitterness

Believe me, I'm talking the tip of the iceberg here. It is clear that anger is an important part of our lives. And it's not going anyplace without you, so you may as well learn all you can about how to manage it.

But I Know a Couple Who Never Fights

About now you may be saying, 'But I know a couple who never fights. I want to be like them.' Everyone has heard about that couple. They have discussions, not arguments, they agree on all matters from child rearing to sexual frequency to how money should be spent. I want to go on record here as saying – these people have some nerve. If things really are as wonderful as they say they are, they ought to have the decency to shut up about it. *P.S. You will never find a relationship like that, so don't waste your time looking.*

Besides, who knows what goes on behind closed doors? I remember one woman who came to see me – alone. She had been one half of a couple who never fought, a perfect couple, adored by all. After 20 years together, with absolutely no warning or major incident, she ran off with a man she met in the supermarket checkout queue.

Anger Myths

Part of the reason we struggle with accepting anger and the need to fight well is that we've been raised with myths about it – myths that have followed us all our lives. These are myths such as:

Myth: Couples who fight are much more likely to get divorced.
The Reality Behind the Myth: The number of fights you have is not a predictor of divorce. Rather, it is the way couples resolve their fights that indicates whether they will have a troubled or a stable marriage.

What is true is that partners with poor conflict skills erode the goodwill in their relationships. What partners need to resolve tense issues is to find a fighting style that is acceptable and that works for both of them.

Myth: The more compatible you are, the less you fight.
The Reality Behind the Myth: Although there is no one right way to interact in a relationship, *healthy* couples have *healthy* disagreements, no necessarily *no* disagreements. Healthy disagreements that are expressed properly make a relationship stronger, not weaker. Studies have shown that couples who within the first few years of their marriages feel discontented and incompatible and learn how to express that discontent in healthy ways do better over the long haul. Discontent and compatibility are not mutually exclusive. Joining two

lives requires a great deal of work – especially in early years – and relationships require a great capacity for tolerating conflict and discontent.

Don't shortchange your relationship by jumping to negative conclusions.

Myth: Fighting never solves anything.
The Reality Behind the Myth: Sometimes people choose fights that can't be solved. Not every fight you have is meant to solve something. Sometimes people fight just to let off steam. When you understand your own fighting patterns and cycles better, you'll know whether you are fighting to solve a real difference or fighting for another reason.

Myth: If your partner starts a fight, he is angry at you.
The Reality Behind the Myth: People fight when they need contact and they are afraid to ask for it. Some people fight out of habit, like smoking. When your partner starts a fight that comes out of nowhere, the message behind the anger may read, 'I'm lonely', 'I'm sad', 'Don't you want to have sex with me?', or 'Please give me more attention.'

Or it can be style. I know one man (and we know how men love to debate) with whom if I say 'black' he says 'white'. I argued with him for years yelling 'black, black, black' until one afternoon as an experiment, I said, 'White, you've finally convinced me that the answer is white.' To which he replied, 'You never listened carefully. I never actually said it was white. I said it was *closer* to white.' I realized then that we'd never been fighting, we'd been playing. His contrariness was his sport; the way other men play rugby or tennis, he took verbal sides in a game.

Fighting Cycles

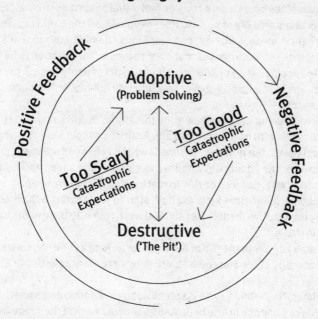

Most couples have fighting cycles – periods where they fight less, periods when they are in high conflict. You may have already used the charts in Chapter 3 to learn more about your fighting cycles. According to couples therapist Bill Pinsoff, couples have a startlingly clear circular pattern of fighting:

THE FIGHTING CYCLE

1 At the top of the circle the couple feels good. They solve differences with affection and goodwill.
2 Feeling this good leads to catastrophic expectations, such as 'we'll never disagree on anything of importance,' or 'she'll never let me down,' or 'things will always be this good.' People get greedy, and they want even more. Or one partner begins to feel taken advantage of – the closeness starts to breed contempt.
3 Couples begin to focus on negative feedback, becoming crabby and argumentative. Feeling close has led to fear-of-feeling-too-close, which has led to conflict as a defence against feeling so vulnerable.

4 Now couples fall into what Bill Pinsoff labels 'The Pit' – the cold, dark bottom of the circle where couples feel pitted against each other, and anger takes on a life of its own. Here people fly off the handle easily and fight in mean, sarcastic, contemptuous, blaming ways that are beneath them. Occurrences that once caused minor irritation (when the loo seat is left up or when you find 12 pairs of panty hose in the sink when you're in a rush to shave) now turn into full-blown, histrionic arguments.

5 Instead of being upset by how good things are, couples scare themselves with how bad things are. Again the couple has catastrophic expectations, but now they are about what will happen if things stay this awful. The Pit arouses primitive aggression and anger, and it soon gets terrifying. Couples decide to reach out and try to make up.

6 Somebody apologizes first. You both start to show caring behaviours and offer positive feedback again. You work your way back to the top of the circle.

7 You stay happily in the top of the circle for as long as you can tolerate the intensity of the closeness – until things get scary again.

Sometimes, the fighting cycle is spread out over months, and sometimes, all of this can happen in one hour. And as couples work at their relationships, their times in the Pit become less and less frequent. In addition, the Pit becomes a less cruel place.

Conflict Precedes a Relationship Breakthrough

When you realize that conflicts happen in a circular fashion, you can heave a sigh of relief knowing that your relationship will enter periods of high conflict – but it doesn't *stay* there. High-conflict times are those times when your relationship is stuck in 'the Pit'. High conflict doesn't necessarily mean that something is wrong, in spite of how awful it feels. However, it's time to work on how you behave when you are in the Pit, so that you can have healthy disagreements instead of damaging fights.

SHARING MEALS

At one point Jason realized that he hadn't seen his kids in a month. They grabbed a bite before he got home from work or they came to the table with headphones and ate while Jason read the paper and his wife, Sandy, watched the news on television. Sandy and Jason decided to institute a new policy regarding meals so that all of that stopped and

---

the family spent dinner time talking about the day and catching up on the latest news in their lives. The first week, everyone was irritable, and it was awkward. It made Sandy and Jason realize how far apart they'd all grown. By the third week, they felt that they were actually getting to know each other. The positive results were amazing.

Remember: Healthy couples have healthy disagreements, not *no* disagreements.

In fact, disagreements may mean that the two of you are in for positive developments. Let me explain: Think back to any major change you have made in your life. Whether you decided to go back to school, buy a house, marry someone, play the stock market, chances are that on the way to accomplishing any of these things, you experienced extensive internal conflict – you shifted positions back and forth, you wondered how you'd manage, you felt insecure, angry, worried, upset. Major positive changes in an individual often come after there is significant ongoing internal conflict that lasts a long, long time:

Major breakthroughs in the relationship between two people can take place in the same way, after much conflict.

If you are in a high-conflict stage in your relationship, it may mean that one of you or both of you wants something in the relationship to change. Of course, some people get scared of real change and they spend most of their lives in the Pit – they never break through. Some couples get scared to really join their lives, to experience each other's reality and each other's differences, and they live their lives in the Pit too, defining each other as the enemy. They never learn how to join forces in conflict, appreciate conflict and prosper from it. But not you!

First Steps in Appreciating Conflict

Here is an exercise to help you begin to appreciate conflict by discovering your conflict style. This two-step exercise takes 10 minutes and must be done with your partner. Once you begin the exercise you *must* complete it. You cannot stop halfway through, so, before you start, you must promise not to answer the phone, get a soda, or do anything else to interfere with the progress of the exercise.

What to Do When Your Partner Calls You an Animal

Step 1: Figure out what type of animal each of you is by taking the following quiz:

THE 'NAME MY SPECIES' QUIZ

When we fight, I
A Yell louder
B Let her yell
C Leave the room
D Feel my heart pound madly

If the fight lasts a long time, I
A Have no problem continuing and I usually win
B Give in because it's easier
C Try to ignore her because all I want to do is get out
D Feel hurt and shock that we're fighting

When my partner starts a fight I hadn't expected, I
A Take my position and hold it
B Let him have his way
C Tune out or walk out
D Freeze and hope it will pass quickly

If you answered with a's, your anger style is to *Attack:*
You're a lion, singlemindedly attacking to hold on to your position in the pride.
You yell with minimal provocation. It's hard to hear what your partner has to say because you're roaring so loud.
If you answered with b's, your anger style is to *Submit:*
You're a prairie dog looking up the snout of a coyote. You're too weak to take him on. You let yourself be bullied and badgered. You blame yourself.
If you answered with c's, your anger style is to *Flee:*
You are a mountain goat racing to higher ground. You leave the room, stomp out, refuse to participate, forget what you just said. You can't take the tension and the anxiety – you don't want to face the issue.

> If you answered with d's, your anger style is to *Freeze:*
>
> > You are a deer caught in the headlamps. You can't respond. You're frightened of the anger. Conflict throws you into shock. Your heart pounds wildly. You stumble over your words.
>
> If your answers are mixed, your anger style is to *Freeze* prior to *Attacking* after which you will feel terrible and *Submit* after which you will *Attack* again before you *Flee:*
>
> > You are a chimpanzee – closest to a human being. You're a complex creature who can beat your chest in one moment, hightail it for the hills in the next, and then change your mind and come back.

Okay, now that you know how far you've climbed up Maslow's hierarchy, you are ready to move on.

Step 2: Face each other and make noises appropriate to your species. Insist your partner do the same. See how far you can get when you're howling and she's braying. Do this in the future instead of yelling.

Note: Do not imitate Cheetah in the *Tarzan* movies, since Cheetah is a paid actor. He had the benefit of directional choices, rehearsals, and subdued backlighting. His howling is affected.

Note: Dr J Rosen, a New York City couples therapist, actually prescribes that couples make the sounds of monkeys to each other. He instructs them to move like apes and talk like Tarzan, omitting the 'I' and using only the 'me' pronoun. For sex, he has them saying, 'Me want your banana' or 'Me want your petunia.' For food, he has them say, 'Me want yummy.' Most couples, feeling quite ridiculous, tend to improve rapidly so they can stop therapy.

Five Favourite Blowups and How to Solve Them

Let's move on to typical fighting patterns and how to change them. Here are five favourite fighting themes – available in stereo everywhere. Can be purchased separately. Batteries not included, but solutions are.

Blowup Number 1: We don't want the same things

Christmas is just around the corner. Mary is hoping that she and Zack can both go to her parents' house, while Zack is assuming they will go to his mother's house.

Rita lives with her lover, Al. Rita has decided to go on holiday for two weeks in August, and she is dying to hit Lanzarote. Al has his heart set on a phoneless little cabin in the Lakes.

Aisha and James need a new sofa. Aisha has her sights on an over-stuffed off-white tea room type of thing, while James wants something leather, preferably brown, right out of the private room of a men's club that didn't want him as a member.

The Problem:	There are real differences to negotiate. A mutually acceptable choice needs to be made.
The Blowup:	The couple doesn't co-operate. One bullies the other. One makes plans without consulting the other. One whinges. One never gets her way.
Guerrilla Mating Tactic:	Learn to negotiate.

In Relationships, Winning Is Not Victory

If Mary coerces Zack into going to her parents', Mary can hope to experience Zack's resentment in spades. Getting Zack to go to her parents' may not feel like a victory as Zack goes off into the living room, turns on the telly, and proceeds to ignore everyone. If Aisha and James end up in a fight about the sofa, she could get the sofa she wants, but she may never get to enjoy it.

Here is how the blowup starts:

I Want a New Sofa
Aisha: Our sofa is ratty.
James: It's not that bad.
Aisha: Yes, it is. I want a new sofa.
James: You want a lot of things.

Aisha: What's that supposed to mean?
James: Whatever you think it means.
Aisha: Why can't you just come out and say what you mean?
James: Why are you putting pressure on me on my day off?

Aisha makes an indirect complaint. James' intention in saying it's not that bad is to help Aisha feel better about the sofa; plus, it's possible that he may not want to be bothered with thinking about the sofa. Aisha's wish for a new sofa is experienced by James as a criticism that he is not a good provider. They lose focus, they make the issue personal, they take opposite sides of the issue, and they end up in a completely unproductive blowup.

*SUPER Negotiation: A Model for Negotiating Differences

This type of fight can be solved with a tactic for negotiating a legitimate difference, a model based on openly airing the dilemma and working it through from start to finish. I use the acronym 'SUPER' here to help you remember the steps of the negotiation. (Of course no fight is super. They all stink. I'm being patronizing when I use this acronym. I can't help myself. Please forgive me.)
SUPER works like this:

Situation: Air initial positions and obstacles
Underlying concerns: Acknowledge deeper and/or core feelings
Persuasion: Attempt to persuade partner to give in to your position
Empathy: Validate the position of the other (this needs to happen not at one spot, but throughout the negotiation)
Resolution: Find mutually acceptable compromise

Here is a fight using the tactic of SUPER negotiation.

Situation: Air Initial Positions and Obstacles
Aisha and James *lay out the territory* of what they will be discussing. Empathy, which you will read more about later, is demonstrated in the words of James that are italicized. He doesn't dismiss Aisha by ignoring, minimizing or arguing her position about the sofa. He hears her feelings about it without getting defensive.

* Based on Heitler's conflict model.

I Want a New Sofa: Replay

Aisha: Our sofa is ratty.

James: It is getting bad. I think we can wait before replacing it, though.

Aisha: I'm not comfortable waiting. I love it when people drop by and that huge stain is embarrassing.

James: When people drop by they drop by to see us. If they're dropping by to see our sofa, then they should wait till spring when we get a new one.

Aisha: I saw an advert in the paper for a sofa on sale ... down stuffed ... off white ... it would look so great here.

James: I don't like that look. I want something that won't stain – like I used to see in those movies of men smoking at the club. Those big brown leather sofas.

Aisha: That's not my taste at all.

James: That's what I want if we get a sofa...

Underlying Concerns: Acknowledge Deeper/Core Feelings

James and Aisha enter the next level of discussion – telling each other why what they want is important to them. They explain their positions without defending them, without acting defensive. Again, when you see italicized words, this is a moment of empathy. We're getting to that.

James: The sofa you describe doesn't sound comfortable to me. I have a bad back, and it doesn't sound like a sofa I can be a true couch potato on.

Aisha: Um hmmm.

James: Also, I grew up in a house where the sofas were always covered in plastic. Someone had to die for us to be allowed in the living room. I don't want that kind of living room.

Aisha: I see what you're saying, and I've had this dream of a formal living room in my head since I was a little girl. I always thought that when I was settled, I could have a living room with this certain look.

James: Yeah. I have to say that a formal living room makes me nervous.

Aisha: I can't explain to you how badly I want it and what it means to get it. It really means a lot to me. Plus, the kind of sofa you describe reminds me of poker games and cigar smoke ... so masculine.

More About Underlying Concerns

Many fights between couples are about just what it looks like they're about – socks on the floor, lateness, in-laws. However, some fights tap into core feelings. Core feelings are deeper feelings underneath the surface that show up over and over again in fights that we repeat over and over again. Whenever you are fighting the same fight over and over and you get nowhere, it is reasonable to suspect that a core feeling is behind it. The most common core feelings that run thematically through many different kinds of fights are:

> I get no respect
> I'm treated like a servant
> I'm not a priority
> People walk all over me
> Nobody hears my side
> Things aren't fair

Always be listening for these feelings, which run deeper and are the cause of many escalations of feeling.

Persuasion: Attempt to Persuade Partner to your Position
Aisha and James attempt to change each other's mind. They barter and negotiate, saying what they will give if they get their way.

> *James:* Think about it. The sofa I want never gets dirty. You wipe it off – no stains, no rips.
> *Aisha:* Still, I'd be unhappy with it. If you agree to my choice, I'll tell you what. I won't ever put plastic on it. If it gets dirty, we'll clean it.
> *James:* Well, if we get the leather sofa, you can choose anything else you want in the living room. I just want that.
> *Aisha: Yes, and* that will make the rest of our decor look strange. That would dominate the living room. It wouldn't go.
> *James: You think it wouldn't go and I* think it would go fine. I really do.
> *Aisha:* Well, if you go with my choice, I'll pick Derek up from football training all summer. And ... I'll cook your favourite meal once a week for six weeks.
> *James:* Six months.
> *Aisha:* Three.

Empathy

This is the process of tuning in to each other and validating the other – this happens not at one spot, but throughout the negotiation.

As I said, the empathy is in the dialogue, and it occurs all the way through the process. Every time you see words above in italics, you're seeing empathy in action. James and Aisha are listening to each other without being defensive, without trying to prove that their position is the correct position, without derogatory remarks about the other's choices. Empathy makes it clear that they can tune in to each other's position, even if they don't agree with it. Here is a breakdown of empathic responses:

Back Channelling: Saying '*Umm hmm*' and '*yeah*' as a verbal acknowledgement when your partner pauses is called back channelling. When you make these verbal utterances as your partner is talking, you are demonstrating that you are listening. Frequently in a disagreement, when our partners are speaking, we don't hear what they actually say because we are too busy searching for our retort. Back channelling helps the speaker feel heard. It lets the speaker know that you are following the conversation. This is a particularly important point for men to add to their listening repertoires. Men often listen in silence as they are trained to do. Women often take total silence as disinterest.

Active Listening: See Chapter 2 for a complete description of active listening. Active listening or reflecting back part of your partner's phrase has always been an important part of showing empathy for your partner's position. With active listening you never change the meaning, interpret, or judge. Active listening lets your partner know that you have understood him.

Yes, and is different from 'yes, but'. We'll talk more about this in Chapter 8, but for now, keep in mind that saying 'yes and' acknowledges that the two of you hold different positions and you aren't trying to invalidate each other's position.

Gentle Tones: Neither Aisha nor James is escalating the conversation by raising their voices or rushing their words. You can only negotiate a point when you are in control of your volume and tones. The discipline of a well-modulated voice keeps the discussion grounded. Again, this takes practice.

Recognition of Intentions: You assume that your partner's intentions are not to hurt you and that you are both operating with goodwill. Thus, no matter what you thought he said, you check it out before reacting. Remember James and Aisha's fight about the sofa? In the first snippet of conversation between them, there was lots of bad will. Here is a piece of that conversation to remind you:

Aisha: Our sofa is ratty.
James: It's not that bad.
Aisha: Yes, it is. I want a new sofa.
James: You want a lot of things.
Aisha: What's that supposed to mean?
James: Whatever you think it means.

When Aisha said that she wanted a new sofa, James thought she was intentionally criticizing him as a provider. When James snapped back at her, Aisha didn't realize that he had felt attacked. Aisha assumed that James was attacking her. Thus, Aisha and James argued because they thought the other had bad intentions and meant to hurt. When you speak in a fashion that lets your partner know that your intentions are honourable, you will fight less.

Resolution: Find a Compromise

Is the sofa as important to James as it is to Aisha as long as he can put his feet up on it?

> *James:* Maybe we should go the sofa store this Sunday. Maybe there is a third sofa we'd both like.
>
> *Aisha:* That sounds good. What I was thinking was that maybe the sofa I want would look good in other colours. It doesn't have to be white. It could be blue or gold.
>
> *James:* I still like leather, and so I was thinking that if we put a leather sofa in the study, I could have my leather sofa.
>
> *Aisha:* That could work for me, although I'm not sure we could afford two sofas right now. Could you live with that if we got the leather couch next year?
>
> *James:* Maybe. Maybe if that sale is good enough, we could buy two. If we can't, I'll go along with your plan if we choose a different colour, and if you promise never to cover it in plastic.
>
> *Aisha:* Thanks.

But We Could Never Do This

In the beginning, it's a lot to remember, and I don't expect the SUPER tactic model to go this smoothly the first time through. Like any new skill, it takes practice and maybe a chart to pull out when you need it – even when your intentions are good. But things can go this smoothly – if you stick with the issue and refuse to get sidetracked into a fight. While you are acclimatizing yourself to SUPER, be patient. If you remember only two things from this chapter, let them be:

1 *Focus*. Don't go off on a tangent. Stick with the issue at hand. To do so takes discipline – the discipline not to get sucked into a stupid battle that goes nowhere, the discipline not to lose all the gains with a single caustic remark, the discipline not to be dragged down into the pit, the discipline not to make that clever little sniping remark that just came into your head, even if it is really fitting. If your partner isn't as disciplined as you are yet, you need the discipline to move forward anyway.

2 *There is rarely a single solution to any problem.* Almost all problems have multiple solutions, many options. Fixating on a sole solution means you have a major fight on your hands, the 'My way or the highway' fight.

Blowup Number 2: He Wants to Control Me

People who know Franny love to tell the story of how she took her graduate studies finals while breast-feeding her new son. She had to get special permission to leave the room for 20 minutes to feed her baby. Her mother was waiting outside with the baby. Franny graduated with honours and has her Ph.D. Yet, when Franny's husband Trevor brought her to a function, he introduced her by saying, 'This is Franny, the mother of my children.' Franny asked Trevor to go into the other room with her for a moment, and then ... she let him have it, both barrels. Why was it she never got credit for anything but carrying *his* children in *her* womb while he went on and on telling the party guests about his many recent accomplishments? Why didn't he see motherhood – raising two children well – as an accomplishment that long outlasts one of his merger deals at work?

The Problem:	The couple has a psychological tug of war, a power struggle over: Who has the power Who is the boss Who has control Who's on top Who deserves the spotlight Who should step aside for the other
The Blowup:	The couple can't share the spotlight. One feels he can only appear accomplished at the other's expense. One tries to dominate the spotlight, but when he feels dominant, the other feels victimized.
Guerrilla Mating Tactic:	Balancing power by taking turns, sharing and putting your partner's needs first for the good of the relationship from time to time.

The Biology of a Couple

A couple is like an organism, seeking homeostasis – internal balance to feel right. Balance in a couple is achieved in two ways. One way balance is achieved is when things are equal between two people. Welcome to fantasy land! Usually, balance is achieved because one gets less of something that her partner gets more of. Like so: she likes to chase, he likes to be chased; or he likes to be the star, she hates the spotlight; or she likes to be taken care of, he likes to take care. When one gets more of something, the other one gets less of it, and when this is acceptable to the couple, it all works out fine.

The problem is that *sometimes we both want more of something at the same time* – we both want to be chased, coddled, supported, made to feel special – we both want the same thing at the same time and we can't both have it. The more you want something and the less you get it, the more out of control and upset you feel about it. Then you try to get what you want by pulling rank on your partner, bullying your partner, whinging to your partner, subtly exerting pressure over your partner, purposely obstructing your partner.

The blowup starts when one partner starts to feel out of control because he wants more than he is getting. His not being able to get what he wants turns into the struggle for power. We use power to get back in control. We feel bad so we push our partner around.

How to Know If the Shoe Fits

You put your partner down.

You minimize or underplay your partner's accomplishments or you claim that you are responsible for them.

When you feel insecure and depressed, power struggles escalate.

You have strongly mixed emotions when something good happens for your partner.

When you aren't on top of a situation you become more critical and attacking of your partner.

Note: Real power never needs to be proved – ask a Zen martial arts expert. Concentrate your efforts on how to feel power from the inside out rather than how to manipulate your partner so you can feel it.

What to Do When This Describes You

Hey ... we all have our moments. Here are tactics to try when you have one of yours. These tactics reflect a commitment to change your fighting habits by exploring your inner world as well as changing your behaviour.

Guerrilla Mating Tactic Number 1: Try to increase your understanding of the problem

Ask yourself the following questions:

- Why is having control so important to you?
- What is it about not having control that is so disturbing to you?
- What would happen if your partner was on top or more in control of the relationship for a while?
- What needs to happen for you to feel more comfortable sharing the power?
- Do you see her accomplishments as detracting from yours?
- How can you take turns meeting each other's needs, and what can you do when one needs more or takes more than the other?

In the beginning, it makes sense to start by exploring the problem more fully. These questions offer fertile ground for more understanding of the problem.

Guerrilla Mating Tactic Number 2: Try to become more sporting

Ask yourself how the power struggle can be friendlier, less destructive, more sporting, less hurtful. Perhaps you can turn it into something besides a power struggle:

> Paul and Mina run Sunday night wrestling matches on their living room floor. They use these to make their power struggle and other struggles more playful and more concentrated so they don't spill into their weekly activities.
>
> Susie and Bill play odds/evens to see who gets to be the star of the day.

Flo and Eddie schedule two power struggles a day. In the morning, it is Flo's turn to argue over being the boss. In the evening, Eddie offers all the reasons why it should be him. (Eventually they got tired of doing this twice a day and decided that learning how to co-operate would be simpler.)

Guerrilla Mating Tactic Number 3: Learn to be a good loser

One of my favourite quotes on losing comes from a book about the eight worst teams in baseball:

> The best hitter in baseball fails nearly 70 per cent of the time; the best team in baseball loses between 40 and 60 games during a season. At the end of the day, as Earl Weaver sagely observed, 'We gotta go out and do this again tomorrow.' ... Life is like baseball at least this much: It isn't about winning, it's about learning to live with losing.
> George Robinson and Charles Salzberg, *On a Clear Day They Could See Seventh Place: Baseball's Worst Teams*

You've got to learn how to make the best of the times when you don't get what you want.

Guerrilla Mating Tactic Number 4: Find a nurturing team

Decide to connect with people outside the marriage who make you feel good. Exercise at the gym, join a support group, take up an old passion such as pottery, poetry, or ping-pong. The better your support system, the better you will feel about yourself and the less inviting a power struggle will seem. You may think that this advice has nothing to do with working on the power struggles in your relationship, but you couldn't be more wrong. I cannot recommend this tactic highly enough, having watched couples benefit remarkably from taking this step. Taking this step can be as simple as making plans to have dinner with a friend. Know how to pick a good support system that can act as a nurturing team:

A good nurturing team:

Listens
Supports
Points out things you may have left out

Does not tell you what to do

Does not overreact when you've had a bad fight at home

When you tell your nurturing team, 'I had another bad fight with Marvin':

A GOOD NURTURING TEAM SAYS	A BAD NURTURING TEAM SAYS
I'm sorry, sweetie. Want to tell me about it?	Leave him; I told you to leave him.
You two can sure go at it, but you always seem to come out the other side.	You should give him an ultimatum.
Want to come over and have some tea and sympathy?	Want to move in with me? I'm looking for a roommate.

It may be wise not to try to make a nurturing team out of overprotective, highly reactive family members who lack objectivity. You will not be helping your marriage if you tell your overprotective father that Mark screamed at you, and his advice is, 'Move home, move home. I told you he was a lout.' Look for a nurturing team that soothes you and helps you to think a matter through, not people who want to make your decisions for you and inflame you further, or work you into a frenzy.

Guerrilla Mating Tactic Number 5: Ask yourself how you contribute to this power struggle

One-way power struggles don't occur. You may be struggling because you haven't thought much about how roles are divided up in the relationship on a daily basis – i.e., who handles the chequebook, does the laundry, arranges social events:

> Cheryl met Brian in a laundrette. She introduced herself, offering to help him sort his clothes. Two years later, he still expects her to do his laundry *and* he criticizes how she folds the shirts.

Brian gives up the power over his shirts, but then he seizes it back by criticizing how Cheryl does it. A variation of this struggle is when I let my husband drive, then criticize him for driving too fast. We tell our partners to do something and then we are only satisfied if they do it our way.

The real issue is not how to fold a shirt or drive safely; the real issue is power, power, power!!!

So take a look at your own contribution, fold your own shirts, and stop expecting your partner to get in the driver's seat if you don't like being a passenger with him:

> Years ago I saw a couple where the woman's complaint was that the man was too controlling. At our fourth meeting they were 30 minutes late. She got unbelievably upset because he'd dawdled. She spent the session complaining about his being late. I asked her why, when she realized he'd be late, she didn't arrange her own transport so she could be on time. It never occurred to her that she had a contribution here. The following week she took her own car.

Note: If you have a controlling partner, don't ask, 'Why is he like that?' The real question is 'How do you contribute to helping him stay that way?'

> ### IN SICKNESS AND IN HEALTH
> Alan went out of town to a wedding with his wife, Theresa. It was her friend and the wedding was important to her. While they were there, Alan started to come down with something. He felt awful. Theresa put him in the car, drove to the nearest hotel and checked them in. She put Alan to bed. He felt so lucky to be with this woman, knowing that she could just take over when he felt out of it.

Guerrilla Mating Tactic Number 6: Consider the impact of gender

Men and women tend to think about love and power differently. Women tend to seek romantic love, and they achieve power through love. Men tend to seek heroic love, and feel they have power over love. Men are raised with issues of power close to their hearts. For example, as linguist Deborah Tannen and others have suggested, men are often the more involved with power struggles because men are taught in their boyhood games to compete for power. Their favourite methods are domination, coercion, and/or manipulation. Women use other methods to obtain and hold power which include exerting control through sex (well, we've got to have something) and/or caretaking. Lastly, little boys' childhood games focus on winning and losing. Many little girls' games are based on taking turns and sharing. So understand that competitive urges within the relationship may flood men more quickly and easily, and men may operate in a relationship in terms of how to be on top of the hierarchy. For example, you pick your partner up at work, he jumps in the car and changes the radio station you were listening to; or, if you get to pick the movie and he doesn't like the movie, he sulks rather than taking it gracefully. It has been said that when men meet other men, among their first thoughts are how to situate themselves hierarchically (Which one of us has more status?). They organize relationships by deciding who's on top. After all, they developed organizational charts, didn't they?

What to Do When This Describes Your Partner

Guerrilla Mating Tactic Number 1: Get a crown and crown him king for a day

Provide him with a wand (make one out of a yardstick, chopstick, or dipstick) and a few loyal subjects (your dog is often happiest to volunteer). Encourage him to be a benevolent dictator rather than instituting a reign of terror. If you can put him in touch with his own sense of humour (and find your sense of humour too), take two steps forward.

Variation: There is an old song from the forties called 'If I Ruled the World.' I rewrote the words to this song, and my husband and I sing it when we feel a power struggle coming on:

If I ruled the world
You would do everything that I say
You would never let your needs get in the way
If I ruled the world

If I ruled the world
You would throw yourself down at my feet
You would kiss each toe
and then kiss my seat
If I ruled the world

The words change every time we sing it. Breaking into song helps us.

Note: I once saw TV journalist Barbara Walters interview legendary news reporter Walter Cronkite. She asked him the secret of the longevity of his marriage. He said that it had to do with the fact that his wife had a great sense of humour. Where's your sense of humour? Go find it.

Guerrilla Mating Tactic Number 2: Initiate a conversation about how to take turns regarding whose needs get met

You can't both be rulers at the same time, so go back to the section on negotiating real difference and negotiate to take turns about who's on top. Oftentimes power struggles occur when partners' needs bump up against each other. See if you can't find something that feels reasonable to you both.

Suggestion Box: Alternate by days or weeks.

You can take turns by alternating days or weeks. Decide that on Monday, Wednesday and Friday your partner rules. On Tuesday, Thursday and Saturday, you are the boss. On Sundays, you both take a rest (and you'll need one). On the days your needs get met first and you rule the roost, notice how your partner reacts and how you react. On the days his needs get met first and he rules the roost, notice again how he reacts and how you react. What are you learning about each other with this exercise that could be helpful in struggling less?

Note: Alternating days or weeks works well when you are struggling over child care, too. If the two of you cannot agree on how to raise your child, take turns making major parental decisions. Notice how reactions differ and tensions lessen when there is no longer a reason to fight over who decides what when. If you find that you cannot even agree on who takes Tuesday and who takes Wednesday, consider getting professional counselling. Don't keep banging your heads against the wall.

Guerrilla Mating Tactic Number 3: Develop a crisis plan

It is wise to be flexible enough to develop an intelligent crisis plan in which you give up your time for your partner if the crisis is hers. However, couples with real PS (power struggles) on their hands do tend to have multiple crises that are ongoing. If you find that none of these suggestions is helpful for you, then, as always, a few sessions of counselling may be in order.

Warning: You may be someone who is in a constant crisis state – that is his *modus operandi:*

> Kelly wanted Grant to try the alternate day plan for 'who's on top', but Grant constantly cited one crisis after another as a reason not to partici- pate. He was overloaded at work, he had just taken on a new consulting job at night, he needed four new crowns on his teeth. Kelly waited patiently until he got through this. Then, when this was finished, Grant tore a ligament in his knee jogging, got transferred to a new department at work, and took a part-time teaching job that was so far from his office that he barely made it in time. Every day was a day he 'might not get through' – nothing more could be asked of him.

When this is the case, your crisis plan won't work. You need to have a different understanding of this problem. Your partner will protest that he didn't invite this and he doesn't know 'how this happened' to him. In truth, give your partner two days without a crisis and he'll take a third job, lose his car keys, decide to take up Chartered Accountancy – he'll find a crisis.

If, when he is in crisis, he becomes more productive and get things done, they you may have to go back to Chapter 2, reread how to 'drop a hot issue' so you don't make his crisis your crisis, and then solidly negotiate for a more reasonable balance. You'll have to see his crisis mode as part of his style and focus on ways to integrate your two styles so you can have more harmony.

If, on the other hand, his crises do not make him more productive, he has deadlines up the ying yang, and he chronically misses them all, getting into a high-pitched frenzy or a low-level depression, then these multiple crises may be a smoke screen covering something that is more difficult than the crises themselves. What is it that your partner is so scared to deal with or look at?

Is he:

Depressed?
Unable to set limits for himself?
Unhappy with his life?
Under-responsible in the marriage?
Unhappy in the marriage?
Angry at you and showing it indirectly?

Can you find a way to have a conversation with him about discovering or looking at the real issue without putting him on the defensive? Don't confront. Start your queries with phrases such as 'You know, I wonder...' or 'I have something to say, but I'm not sure you'll want to hear it...' (this often arouses so much curiosity, he'll have to find out what it is). Try gently to have the conversation with him. If you can't talk calmly, wait until you can. If you can live *your* life (drop the hot issue) with the way *he* is, learn to do so. If you can't do any of these, get professional help to teach the two of you how to talk about complicated, difficult issues.

Guerrilla Mating Tactic Number 4: Schedule 20 minutes a day to think about the struggle

Try to gain control of the problem by pulling rank on a schedule. Schedule blocks of power-struggle worrying time. During that time you can vent, whine, sob, worry that this will never improve, ask yourself what you are doing with a berk like him. It's not fair. He doesn't deserve to be on top. You should be the drill sergeant, he should be the buck private. When the 20 minutes is over, put it out of your mind, go back to work, get a life.

Guerrilla Mating Tactic Number 5: Try an actual tug of war

One psychotherapist has her couples use a real rope to put this metaphor into action. Set up territory, pull a real rope. See who pulls harder, who drops the rope first, what the exercise feels like. At the moment of your own choosing, one of you can let go of the rope. Who lets go first? What were the surprises in this exercise?

Variation: If you're worried that one of you will get hurt during a real tug of war, you can try this variation related to me by couples' therapist Gayle Golden. Take a set of children's bricks and put them on a table. One of you puts on a blindfold and the other then moves the blindfolded partner's hands to build something with the bricks. You can experience many different feelings when you let your partner lead you and when you take your turn as leader. Talk with each other about what it felt like to be guided and to guide. Which was easier?

Warning: A power struggle is the daily desire to dominate the direction of the relationship because you fear your partner will take up too much of the attention in the relationship. Do not confuse a power struggle with out-and-out brutality or hate or sadomasochistic alliances. Brutality is when one partner perpetrates physical or blatant emotional destruction – the partner explodes in anger, plates are thrown, vicious verbal abuse occurs, you get pushed around by a bully, and/or you feel threatened by the way he talks to you. A sadomasochistic alliance is where two partners set it up so that one partner takes pleasure in inflicting pain, distress and humiliation while the other partner takes pleasure in receiving pain, distress and humiliation. Roles can change, but the game is the same (sort of like Martha and George in Edward Albee's *Who's Afraid of Virginia Woolf?*). If you suspect that you are caught up in something bad, go directly to the end of the book and read the section 'When and Where to Seek Professional Help'.

Guerrilla Mating Tactic Number 6: Never call someone a control freak

Don't start an unhelpful discussion about control freaks. This is a negative term that can only provoke him to behave more unacceptably, rather than less. If you have to name-call or describe his behaviour, keep it less loaded. Call him bossy – it's less provocative than other words for describing his behaviour. Besides, we're all a little bossy.

IN CASE OF EMERGENCY

Nancy and Ivan made an audiotape one night. They told each other they loved each other on the tape. Then, they reminded each other that if something in their marriage went wrong, they shouldn't give up. They have something worth getting back to.

I used to get real bossy. One day when I was being bossy, my husband started to wag his finger at me (like a mother reprimanding a two-year-old) and tap his foot. I started doing that back to him so we were simultaneously wagging fingers and tapping feet. After that, whenever I got bossy, he wagged his finger at me instead of arguing. Soon after, when I felt my bossy urges, I'd wag my finger at him when I talked. Eventually, I stopped talking and just silently wagged my finger. We both knew what I felt, and we would dissolve into laughter. And eventually, as usually happens when you find the funny way out of a psychological jam, I just got over it.

Remember: It takes only one to want all the power, but it takes two to struggle over it.

When he struggles he is feeling out of control, and it will pass. So let him get it out of his system, ask him if he wants to talk about it, and/or wait it out.

Guerrilla Mating Tactic Number 7: Find an effective way to talk about it

Try Telling Him How His Bossiness Affects You. Rather than telling him to stop his behaviour because it isn't fair, tell him how his behaviour affects you. Say: 'When you act this way I feel ...' Then start to talk about how you feel (not how he makes you feel – see Chapter 5)

Try Asking Him If He Knows How His Bossiness Affects You. See if you can arouse his curiosity about his own behaviour. Start your sentences, 'I was curious ... I wondered ...' When you tell him how it makes you feel, ask him if he knew that. (Don't expect immediate results – give him time to mull it over.) It may be something he hadn't really thought about, but if you jump into the power struggle with him, it will be something you will not be able to express.

Note: Karen Kayser's book *When Love Dies* (Haworth, 1995) cites studies that said 53 per cent of all couples who separate cite controlling partners as the main reason. So keep working.

Blowup Number 3: I'm Sick of Being Criticized

Brian is annoyed with Christine. She isn't passionate enough verbally or physically, she doesn't kiss him in the right way, she is too lenient with the kids – he finds one thing after another that upsets him. He tells her, they argue. She makes a few changes. He makes a new list.

The Problem:	One partner's low self-esteem is having a negative impact on the relationship.
The Blow-up:	The struggling partner feels awful and lonely. He wants company. He

	doesn't think he can feel better so
	he wants company in feeling bad.
	He picks on his partner relentlessly
	until she loses control and joins him.
Guerrilla Mating Tactic:	Create a safer, less lonely environment
	where feeling bad about yourself can
	be talked about in a gentle way rather
	than acted upon in a harsh way.

Brian has darling children, a clever, sharp wife, respect from his peers. None of this makes him happy. He feels lousy about himself. When he met Christine, he pinned his hopes on feeling better about himself by being in a relationship, but love let him down. Christine seems to handle separation better than he does; she doesn't seem to feel as needy. This makes Brian wonder what's wrong with him, which makes him feel even worse.

Brian tries to get rid of bad feelings by foisting them on Christine. As long as he can be critical of Christine, he won't have to disclose to her how awful he feels. His intellectualized disagreements provoke Christine, and her anger helps him divert attention from himself. Brian acts critical, but underneath he is a man holding on by his fingernails.

How to Know If the Shoe Fits

You are critical of your partner.

You feel as if your partner undervalues you and could walk out on you.

You feel anxious, empty, and sad and/or angry much of the time.

People have asked you if you are depressed.

You have feelings of hopelessness.

You don't look forward to the day.

There is a major gap between how others see you and how you see yourself.

What to Do When This Describes You

We all have a rough week now and then. When you read this section, please understand that I am talking about rough weeks/rough times, rather than a clinical depression. You may be clinically depressed if you feel hopeless and helpless for more than two weeks at a time. If that describes you, then turn to the end of the book and find out where to get good counselling.

Here are tactics that will assure that a rough week doesn't turn into a rough life:

Guerrilla Mating Tactic Number 1: Teach your partner when you most need contact

The worst thing about feeling bad about yourself is how alone you can feel. It will be enormously helpful if you can teach your partner when you most need emotional contact, when you feel the worst, when it really hurts. Of course, first you have to admit it to yourself. Instead of criticizing, make a disclosure. Ask for physical contact, ask for sex. Without getting upset that your partner can't read your mind and know what you need, say, 'I need a hug,' 'I need a friend,' 'I need you to sit with me for 10 minutes and just hold my hand.' Ask for whatever makes you feel loved and taken care of.

Note: You may want to jump ahead to the next chapter and read about the 'Check-in'. This is an excellent way to let your partner know what you need and to find out what she needs too.

Guerrilla Mating Tactic Number 2: Give the bad feeling a name that makes it easily identifiable and less loaded

Often, we just jump to the word *depression* and use that to describe our mood, but depression is such an 'arrrgh' kind of word – the minute you hear it, it drags you down and makes you sad. It recalls all the other depressions, deaths, hard knocks, missed opportunities. If you can come up with another word or phrase, you can isolate the bad feeling, easily identify it, let your partner know exactly what you feel and when you feel it coming on.

Take two steps forward if, even when you feel bad, you can access your sense of humour through your sadness and give it a silly or affected name:

Godzilla Blues
Señor Mopey
10 pounds of manure in a 5-pound bag
La Grande Tristesse

Start to talk about your feelings using the new name instead of 'aarrgh' depression. When you say, 'I'm depressed', many people's hearts will sink as they anticipate what will come next, or they will run for the hills or, most terrible of all, they will counter with, 'You think *you're* depressed?

Let me tell you about *my* life.' On the other hand, when you have the Godzilla Blues or you ask your wife to call you Señor Mopey, you've already taken one step out of the blues.

Guerrilla Mating Tactic Number 3: Separate who you are from the bad feelings about yourself

Calling your 'depression' by another name as in the examples above can help you separate yourself from feeling bad. *You* are not bad. Feeling bad is what is happening to you when the Godzilla Blues come over you. Then you can take this a step further and look at how the Godzilla Blues – or feeling bad, if you can't really stomach twee phrases – impacts on your relationship and the ways you have successfully handled the Godzilla Blues or feeling bad in the past. Here are some questions you can ask yourself, followed by the answers that Brian gave when he looked at his bad feelings in this fashion. By the way, it was Brian who came up with the term Godzilla Blues, so I'll use that too. *

▶ *What does feeling bad about myself tell me to do or say to my partner?* Brian said that the Godzilla Blues told him to pick on his wife – not to let her feel good when he felt bad. They told him not to let his wife have a moment's peace because he didn't. They told him it was her job to make him feel better – they lied to him.

▶ *What messages does feeling bad give me about myself?* Brian said the Godzilla Blues told him life was hopeless, and he was helpless – they would never let him go.

▶ *When have I been most successful at fighting back over feeling bad?* Brian found that there were days when, as strong as the Godzilla Blues were, he prevailed. These times occurred when he got right out of bed as soon as he woke up, when he exercised, when he spend a day with Christine antiquing or going to a play, thus taking his mind off his feelings. He went back to the charts in Chapter 3 and charted when he felt less depressed. Then he began to look at how to get more of those times.

▶ *When has feeling bad told me to do something and I refused to listen?* Just that week, Brian woke up one day and didn't want to get out of bed. None the less, he rose and jumped in the shower. He began to

---

* These questions are based on Australian psychotherapist Michael White's techniques of narrative therapy. His books are listed in the bibliography.

---

wonder what allowed him to accomplish this – even though he just wanted to crawl under the covers.

▶ *How can I refuse to participate in what feeling bad has planned for me?* Brian began to think about what the Godzilla Blues wanted from him. They wanted him to suffer, to fail, to feel bad, to push his wife away from him. He began to think about ways in which he had said 'no' to feeling bad and how he could continue to say 'no.' He tried all kinds of things from the sublime (having sex with Christine when he felt blue) to the bizarre (sticking pins in a Godzilla doll, purchasing a monster mask in the store, putting it on when he started to feel bad, looking at himself in the mirror, deciding he looked ridiculous, putting the mask away – and the bad feelings with it – going on with his day).

Note: Again, if you think your 'bad feelings' are actually a depression – a situation of a more serious nature – see your family doctor or head for couples' therapy. Today there are medications that can lift a depression and help you lead a happier life. Maybe one of these medications is right for you.

Guerrilla Mating Tactic Number 4: Women – Do something for yourself

Indulge yourself. When you feel the urge to criticize your partner, instead do something wonderful for yourself. Whatever it may be that soothes you – phone a friend and make plans to get together, masturbate to a raunchy romantic novel, eat something delicious and forbidden, get on the StairMaster till the endorphins kick in – do something for yourself. Women get depressed because they aren't getting what they expect from the relationship, so one way to begin tackling this is to expect less. What I mean by this is *not* that you give up on the relationship or agree to accept less from the relationship on a permanent basis. I mean that you try strategies other than investing yourself in a relationship that you experience as disappointing and see what happens.

ON OUR ANNIVERSARY

Chuck and Caroline got married at Gretna Green. So every year on their anniversary they go to Gretna Green and watch other people getting married. Occasionally they've been asked to witness for someone. They say that this trip is like renewing their vows every year, and it has brought them closer.

Try replacing one or two of the things you do for your partner with doing something for yourself. Try some new adventures alone. You may find that you can feel better by giving more to yourself when you feel your partner isn't giving enough to you.

Guerrilla Mating Tactic Number 5: Men – Do something for your partner

Peggy Papp's Gender and Depression Project at the Ackerman Institute has found a man is most apt to win over depression when, instead of doing something for himself, he does something for his partner. Men tend to feel most comfortable denying feelings of depression, which make them feel one-down. Sometimes they hide their feelings in ways that only make sure them feel worse, such as drinking, gambling, womanizing or getting an ulcer. Papp's research team found that for men, long-term discussions about their internal turmoil do not help, but doing for and listening to a partner does.

So force yourself to take over more of the housework, fix that power point you promised you'd fix six months ago, check the smoke alarms to make they are all working, pave the driveway, knit her a sweater. Again, as I quoted earlier and as many therapists say, 'You don't have to like it, you just have to do it.' Getting started is the hardest part.

Guerrilla Mating Tactic Number 6: Be a detective for yourself (keep a journal)

Are there certain situations that trouble you, things that don't feel fair, certain times of the month or year that are worse for you, certain times of the day when you struggle more than others, certain events which have occurred that upset you, old or recent losses that still hurt? Try being a detective who can piece together a picture of what the problem might be. Maybe you will tease out something you can work on now. Writing it down, keeping a journal, is very helpful in getting a bigger picture of what is happening.

Record when you feel good: Don't get overinvolved in feeling bad. After you get a sense of what gets in the way, be sure to start looking at what doesn't! When do you feel better, stronger, more optimistic about life, and what is happening at those times? When you have successfully pulled yourself out a glum mood, ask yourself how you accomplished it. If you need help with gathering more specific information, go back to the charts

---

in Chapter 3, and start using them to chart your good moods and moments.

Beware of hypersensitivity: As you monitor your moods, notice when the fight to hide feeling bad shows up as retaliation for a previous or anticipated fight:

> Maria was watching the last few minutes of a *Chicago Hope* rerun. Jack came over and sat down. Suddenly, Maria started yelling at Jack about why he always criticizes her. Jack hadn't said a word. Perhaps Maria thought Jack was about to pick on her because he'd done that in the past when she'd been watching television. Or she could have been retaliating against remarks he'd made in the past. She saw Jack's sitting next to her as his first step in striking out. Jack sat there baffled – he was just as interested in Aaron's new surgical procedure as Maria was. She saw in Jack's face that he'd had no bad intentions, and she suddenly felt ashamed. So she started yelling even louder.

If you misjudge your partner:

> Say: I'm sorry. I'm having a rough day.
> Don't say: Well, you yelled at me before so I thought were going to yell again.

If you are hypersensitive, disagreements are perceived as personal attacks. When people believe that they are frequently attacked, they stay on the defensive, and they have what could be called 'Sherman Tank' relationships. On the outside they're tough and ready to attack, but on the inside they are extremely vulnerable and scared. If you think you are hypersensitive, easily shamed and hurt, they you need to do extra homework. Go back to Chapter 3 and chart when you feel less sensitive. Try to locate how you are living your life when you feel better and do more of that. You may also want to reread Chapter 4 with the intention of looking at your family root system and your history of hypersensitivity. Most important, read up on disclosures. They will help you to avoid many of these spats.

Guerrilla Mating Tactic Number 7: Ask yourself if this is a fight to test the bonds of love

When we are falling in love, we set up 'if s/he really loves me' tests. Does he love me enough to ignore the FA Cup quarter-finals and talk to me? Does she love me enough to give me oral sex? Does he love me enough to introduce me to his mother? Does he love me enough to give me oral sex? Does he love me enough to attend my school reunion? Does she love me enough to give me more oral sex? Once we enter into the relationship, some of that testing stops – but not all of it. A little part of us wants to know what we can get away with – how far we can push.

Testing comes from several places. One is the childhood place of pushing at the limits that were set for us. You push him to figure out just what the limits are. You start arguments as a taunt, a challenge, a test of love.

Another reason we test each other is to keep tabs on the strength of the bond. Social psychologist David Buss suggests that a woman gets moody to learn her mate's reaction so the woman can gauge the strength of his commitment to her. Family therapist Joel Bergman came up with a similar theory, which he uncovered while watching pigeons in the park. A male pigeon was being pecked by a female. She kept pecking him, following him, and pecking at him more. Bergman thought about the theory of evolution and he thought about a couple he was treating where the woman was 'pecking' at the husband all the time. He realized that the wife was checking the husband to see if he was strong, just as the female pigeon was testing the male. She was testing him for robustness. Suddenly, he had another way to look at their problem in terms of its positive function in the relationship.

If you're feeling bad about yourself, it may move you to test the relationship out more than usual. If you find that you are doing things that aren't all that important to you, but which you know annoy your partner no end – and then, when you are asked to stop, you don't – ask yourself if you may be testing the bonds of love.

What to Do When This Describes Your Partner
When you know your partner feels bad, the following tactics may help:

Guerrilla Mating Tactic Number 1: If your partner is a woman, encourage her to to tell you more

When she feels bad, ask to hear about it. What is going on? How can you listen? Does she want to sit and just talk? Can you hold her hand while she talks? Women can feel awful when they don't feel connected or fulfilled in their relationships. So connect, talk with her, listen to her. Although you may want to advise her or fix her or tell her to get over it, restrain yourself. Don't give any advice unless she asks for it. If you can really listen and hear her feelings, she will feel more connected. When she feels more connected, she'll probably feel better.

Warning: Once my husband scored a hat trick for listening to me for 10 solid minutes, then scored an own goal at the peak of my emotional distress when he picked up the Britannia Compact Disc Offer brochure (five discs for a pound) and started flipping through it. Keep your eyes on her at all times, no matter how hard that is for you. If you are easily distracted, make sure the television is off, both your hands are empty, and there is nothing worth reading in reach.

After you hear about it, learn how to comfort her. Ask her if she wants to be held, touched – take her in your arms and just sit there, holding her, soothing her, *not initiating sex even if you get turned on*.

THE SIMPLE THINGS

Every night after dinner, Carla and Dennis take a walk. This seems such a small thing, but they say it is a big part of why they are so happy. They get exercise and a chance to talk. Carla says these nightly walks mean more than anything Dennis has ever given her.

Guerrilla Mating Tactic Number 2: If your partner is a man, encourage him to help you out

Recent studies suggest depressed men need different treatment from depressed women. Women talk with others, attempting to talk their way through depression. Men pull themselves out of depression by doing. Instead of chronically coddling your depressed mate, tell him you desperately need coddling yourself. Insist he wash your back or take you to the pictures. You may be able to pull him out of his state by letting him know you need him. One woman told her husband she thought she was about to fall apart. She made a list of the things that overburdened her. She asked him to take a few over, and let him decide which ones. She made it clear that if she fell apart, there would be no one to care of him; taking care of her partner was a two-way street.

Also, keep in mind that men work out many of their emotional difficulties through their sexuality, which is the one place men get to be very vulnerable. Having more sex with him lets him feel accepted and wanted and loved. You can say the words over and over again, but when you take his body into yours, it will mean more than your words ever can because men value action over talk. So don't give him what you'd want if you were in his shoes, give him what he wants. See if you can seduce him into feeling better. Forget your foolish pride – grovel naked at his feet, recreate the dance of the seven dishcloths, make like a suburban Mata Hari seeking his secrets.

Guerrilla Mating Tactic Number 3: Sign the two of you up for a movement class

When someone is feeling bad about themselves, there is a tendency to keep away (we're afraid it's contagious) or to coddle them. Try another kind of tactic. Sign the two of you up for ballroom dancing or fencing or acting or tennis or swimming or yoga. You can help your partner's mental state by getting her to move her body in more positive, connected, fulfilling ways. Plus you will be spending time together in a positive way.

Guerrilla Mating Tactic Number 4: Make up 'pep-talk coupons' your partner can redeem when needed

Make up a series of coupons that your partner can hand over when she needs a pep talk. Let her know that when she needs it, you are willing to recount her glories, dance naked, cheerlead her on, perform delectable sexual delights, be her most vocal fan, give her the positive attention she needs.

Note: Sure, this is a plaster, not a cure. But plasters are good for an open wound. Don't discount plasters.

Variation: *Give serious chat coupons.* A serious chat is when you sit for 30 minutes and listen to your partner uninterrupted. All of your energy goes to helping her. You can't talk about yourself – every ounce of your attention needs to go to her. She talks about herself, and unlike a check-in (see Chapter 7), you talk back. You respond, help, empathize, conjure, advise, problem-solve – all on her behalf. Prepare a coupon that reads, 'This coupon entitles the bearer to one serious chat session. Redeemable anywhere, anytime – but only with me!'

Guerrilla Mating Tactic Number 5: Get couples' counselling

If your partner doesn't respond to the tactics you try or your partner seems to be more than feeling bad – to be depressed – and if the resulting conflicts are chronic and eroding the fabric of what is good between you, seek counselling. Recent studies have shown that a combination of medication and psychotherapy has helped people out of long-term states of depression. Since the depression is a relationship issue as well as a personal issue, both of you ought to go. In addition, if you go you can best learn how to give support when needed and how to get support for yourself. Last and most important of all, *depression in a marriage is a couple's problem, not an individual problem*. Turn to the back of the book where you will find a section about 'When and Where to Seek Professional Help.'

Blowup Number 4: He's Out All Night with the Boys

Nancy and Harry stand up in the audience on *Ricki Lake*. Nancy holds a newborn baby in her arms. Nancy describes Harry to the audience. 'He stays out till 3 a.m. with the boys. He refuses to help me at home. He won't discuss how the baby changes things.' When Harry is asked about all this, his response is 'I shouldn't have to give up my friends to be married.'

The Problem:	One person is carrying the adult responsibility for the couple.
The Blowup:	The person who is overresponsible is resentful. The person who is underresponsible wants to hang on to where they are.
Guerrilla Mating Tactic:	Grow up!

Harry is in combat to hold on to a stage of life that is beneath him, a more carefree time. He fights to keep from having to be a full partner and a parent in a relationship between two adults. While this can happen to both men and women, it is more common to see it in men. Women have a social, biological and cultural background that supports them as nurturers. Men don't. Some men make the mistake of thinking marriage is one long party – pass the beer nuts.

What to Do When This Is You
This isn't you, because if it were you wouldn't be reading this book.

What to Do If This Is Your Partner
Well, I'm willing to give you a few tactics, if you can stop pulling your hair out long enough to try them. Some of the tactics from this section I learned from family therapist Peggy Papp. She has worked with hundreds of couples who are in this boat.

Guerrilla Mating Tactic Number 1: Don't nag

Nagging is too hard on you – you don't like how it makes you feel about yourself, and it rarely works. Instead of berating him endlessly (making part of the problem your berating behaviour), ask yourself realistically if he wants to change and if you think he can. Do you have any reason to believe he'd like to be a real partner? Is he more responsible at certain times? Does he ever take appropriate responsibility? Explore his behaviour and think about it.

Guerrilla Mating Tactic Number 2: Ask yourself how long you want to put up with this

Make an assessment. Then set limits for yourself as to how long you can continue if nothing changes. It may relieve some pressure for you if you know it won't go on for ever.

Guerrilla Mating Tactic Number 3: If your partner has a substance abuse problem, join a support group

If your partner has a problem, *you* need support. Go and get it from friends, family and from joining a group of people in the same boat. They have information, feedback, experience, community. In this safe place, you can explore your options and look at how others have managed in the past and are managing now. If your partner isn't a substance abuser, try another kind of support group – a woman's group, for example. Call the local community centre, find a group therapist, scan the newspapers, ask around, or start your own group. You'll find something that will fit for you.

Guerrilla Mating Tactic Number 4: See if he can acknowledge that there is a problem

Without nagging, ask him if his current behaviour is something he wants to keep. Does he see it as a problem for the marriage? If he says he wants to keep it and doesn't see the problem, you may not have much of a chance. If he says yes, it is a problem, he's taken one step. When you can define a problem, you're one step closer to a solution.

Guerrilla Mating Tactic Number 5: Go for couples' counselling

You can attempt getting him into a good couples' therapy even if you don't have high hopes. You will want to know you've tried what you can. It may be that with help he will grow up. Without help, your chances of this relationship working are slim indeed.

Guerrilla Mating Tactic Number 6: Take drastic measures and try a trial separation

Some people don't understand the seriousness of their behaviour until their partners leave them. Then they begin for the first time to see that their behaviour has consequences. If all else fails, you can try a trial separation (not just for two days, after which he'll beg you to come back by promising to change – a promise which will only last two days, I assure you). Make a real plan.

Guerrilla Mating Tactic Number 7: If you don't want to leave, wait a few years and hope he grows up

You can appeal to his conscience. But unless he decides he wants to grow up and take on the responsibilities of marriage, your chances of keeping a marriage with this partner are slim unless you bite your tongue, deny the reality of the situation, take to prayer. Sorry.

Guerrilla Mating Tactic Number 8: If you decide to hang in there, ask yourself what would be the most positive use of your time

If you've been taking the 'Mother Teresa Correspondence Course' and decide to wait and hope he grows up, then get off his case and figure out what would be a good use of your time in the meanwhile. Telling him how bad you feel hasn't worked, so try to handle this by working on yourself rather than working on him. Get some therapy, go back to school, get a promotion, work towards earning more money – you, yourself, grow up.

> Put yourself in a position where you are not dependent on him to grow up but rather where you have options.

That way, if you stay you retain options, and if you go you'll have a life to go to.

Blowup Number 5: Everything She Does Irritates Me

Aisha is a teacher and the headmistress doesn't like her. So she's asked Aisha to stay later, take on more after-school activities, and she watches Aisha like a hawk. Aisha walks out of school, comes home and screams at James.

Betty and Louis had been married for 30 years when he had a heart attack. When Louis recovered, he found that he blew up at Betty at the drop of a hat.

Carl spent three hours trying to renew his driver's licence. When he finally got to the front of the queue, he was told that he had been standing in the wrong queue, and he was sent to the back of another queue. He did what anyone would do in this situation – he came home and screamed at his wife.

The Problem: You have legitimate anger and frustration but no legitimate outlet for it.

The Blowup:	You misdirect it at your spouse and can't be comforted by your spouse.
Guerrilla Mating Tactic:	Learn to express your emotions in the right place, at the right time and towards the right person and learn how to ask for comfort when you need it.

How Anger Gets Displaced

Displacement means you come home from a lousy day at work and kick the dog. It happens to all of us. It's a lot like the hot issue theory in Chapter 2. You have the hot issue and you can't pass it back to the person who sent it to you, so you pass it to your partner. Here is how it happens in the above vignettes:

▶ Aisha can't yell at her boss so she yells at James. Their fight stands in for the fight she will not be having with her boss.
▶ Louis' health scare was terrifying. He gets mad at Betty when he's really angry because he almost died. Of course, what can you do about that? Why not scream at your wife since she's the one you can get to?
▶ The last time Carl yelled at the DLV clerk, he got sent to the end of the queue...

What to Do When This Is You

Guerrilla Mating Tactic Number 1: Seek positive rather than negative attention

Sometimes we want attention very badly but we have a terrible way of getting it. Still, we'll take negative attention over no attention. This kind of fight happens when you need attention you aren't getting, so you start a fight instead of asking for it. If you need attention because you are frustrated, ask for it: Say:

Will you please hug me for one whole minute without asking me
    what's wrong? I'll tell you, but first I need some love.
I will be your slave later if you'll make me a cup of tea now.
I want to make love. I always feel better after we've had sex.
Do you have any ideas that will help me chill out?

Note: Never say, 'I need attention', and end the sentence there. Nobody knows what you mean. When you say, 'I need attention,' you may be offered sex, a cup of tea, advice, respectful silence. People will offer you what they would want when they say, 'I want attention.' Be specific about what kind of attention you want.

Remember: SPECIFIC SPECIFIC SPECIFIC

Guerrilla Mating Tactic Number 2: Learn how to be comforted by your partner

Can you let your partner take care of you and treat you nicely? Many people find this difficult. They are terrific at the skill of giving, but weak on the skill of taking. They think taking doesn't matter as much as giving does, and surely, the response of the world in general is better to givers than it is to takers. However, in a relationship you need to know how to take or you cut yourself and your partner off from a vital aspect of balance in the relationship.

Note: There is a videotape session of family therapist Salvador Minuchin meeting with a couple in their sixties who were fighting frequently. It turned out that the man in the couple was the giver, and he saw it as his responsibility to hold the couple together. Now he was older and not feeling well, but he was afraid to rest and especially afraid to die because, as the giver, he was sure his wife could not take care of herself. So they fought. After working with Dr Minuchin the wife opened a hairdresser's and the husband stayed in bed and did nothing twice a week. The fighting stopped when he learned to ask for comfort and take comfort and his wife learned to give comfort and to comfort herself. Thus, the relationship was rebalanced.

Let your partner soothe you and let her be the strong one for a while. If you don't let her learn how to do it, you short-change her and yourself. Moreover, when you need it most, she will be less experienced at giving comfort.

This advice on learning how to comfortably receive from your partner is good advice for the bedroom, too. There are those who are hell-bent on satisfying their lovers, yet unable to take, to describe what they want, to lie back and greedily enjoy the moment. Your long-term sexual satisfaction depends on your learning to graciously be on the receiving end of the goodies.

Guerrilla Mating Tactic Number 3: Make sure you don't reject your partner's attempts to comfort you

Do you unwittingly reject caring behaviours from others? For example:

Bob threw out his back. Elena began by making him tea and soup as he lay in bed. But Bob said the tea wasn't hot enough, the soup wasn't beefy enough, Elena wasn't fast enough. Soon Elena backed off because Bob made it excruciating for her to take care of him. Bob began doing for himself and bitterly resenting Elena, but with the ongoing belief that he was better off without what he considered to be her inferior caregiving. He felt less anxious when he did for himself, even when if was physically painful to carry on.

CHOPPERS

Dale had to get false teeth, and he felt humiliated. His wife, Kirsty, just kept telling him that his teeth might be gone but his heart and soul were intact. And that was what she loved about him.

Yes, there is a chance that your partner will be less skilled at taking care of you than your mummy was, as well as a chance that you will be harder to comfort today than you were when you were five. Whether you caught the flu, failed your driving test for the fifth time, or lost the lead role in the community centre's production of *The Rocky Horror Show*, accept that your partner will offer imperfect comfort. He or she probably won't find just the right button to push to make you feel better. But don't reject your partner because you feel rejected or mistreated by the world.

Guerrilla Mating Tactic Number 4: Gather information*

It's worth exploring why you turn away any chance of being comforted. So ask yourself the following questions:

▶ How do you let your partner know what you need?
▶ How do you ask for comfort?
▶ Does your partner hear it and can he respond?

* Based on Peggy Papp's model.

- Do you believe that there is enough love around you – is it scarce or abundant?
- Can you join together to comfort each other against the world?
- Do you let frustrations and bad things divide you?
- How could you console each other?

Remember: Yelling never helps you get comfort after you've reached the ripe old age of two.

Guerrilla Mating Tactic Number 5: Explore why you don't express your feelings where they need to be expressed and why you take them out on others.

How did you get into this habit? Sometimes it can be traced back to childhood. Some children, when distressed, were never appropriately comforted.

Note: This is not necessarily about evil mums and dads. This is about large families, difficulty articulating what you want, cranky days, etc. NO PARENT CAN BE PERFECTLY ATTUNED.

At times, your tears may have made your parent frustrated, upset or angry. Your frustration never reached a satisfactory resolution, and you had to find ways to calm and soothe yourself because it was hard to get calmed and soothed by another. You learned that wanting comfort could lead to rejection. Wanting becomes dangerous even though a child both wants and needs his parent desperately. So the question for the child becomes 'How can I have my parent and not be rejected?' The answer is by being undemanding, self-sufficient. The child learns that the way to hold on to love is by showing that he does not need love. So he demands nothing.

Maybe today you can get the comfort you've yearned for all your life – if you ask for it simply, directly, with polite and specific requests.

Guerrilla Mating Tactic Number 6: Think before you speak

Sometimes simple advice is the hardest to take. Thomas Jefferson used to count to 10. With inflation, you have to count to 54. But make a simple, disciplined effort not to attack your partner when the world feels unjust or because you're edgy or frustrated.

Guerrilla Mating Tactic Number 1: Think of your partner as a hedgehog who needs a hug

Your partner may be acting difficult, striking out at you, when what he really wants is to be held. Be courageous. Reach out. Keep alcohol and plasters nearby in case you get a scratch or two.

Guerrilla Mating Tactic Number 2: Recognize that relationships rarely balance out

When you know you didn't do anything and she erupts, carry on under the assumption that your partner is struggling with something. Comfort her, *even when it's on a day you were waiting for her to come home so she could comfort you:*

Carol had to fly to LA on a Monday morning for a Monday night meeting. She got back to her hotel and received a briefing from her office for three hours. She rose at 6.00 a.m. to catch a flight home a little later. The flight was delayed due to a storm. Traffic from the airport was awful. She got home after nine hours of travel in one day and an eight-hour time zone loss. She was starving, crabby and stressed to the max. She walked in the door, and Doug, her husband, was in bed sick. There was not a peanut, a slice of bread, a glass of milk in the house. Taking care of Doug was the last thing she wanted to do, but she did it. And, although she was exhausted, she felt proud that she was able to put her needs aside. She knew she'd avoided a big row.

One couple came into my office, and the man announced up front that the problem in the relationship was that he gave 60 per cent and his wife gave 40 per cent. Funny thing was that she felt that *she* was the one giving 60 per cent. So they fought about percentages for a while, and a few sessions later they realized they were both right – they both gave 60 per cent and got 40 per cent. Decent relationships are always at least 60/40, with both partners giving 60 per cent and only getting 40 per cent. Saying that you have to get back as much as you give will never work. Even though he gives 60 per cent, you will only get 40 per

---

cent. Even though you give 60 per cent, she will get 40 per cent. Twenty per cent is taken out by the relationship tax collector. Based on the fact that you will always be giving 60 per cent and only getting 40 per cent, you're going to have to face the truth:

Everyone is nearly impossible to live with.

Guerrilla Mating Tactic Number 3: Help your partner to take responsibility for his anger

Sometimes your partner is treated unjustly, and he doesn't get mad. He tells you what happened, and *you get mad*. If you get mad at your in-laws all the time or you get mad at your husband's boss or his brother or anywhere that he has trouble expressing anger even when his anger would make sense, think about whether you are expressing feelings for him that he cannot express for himself:

Harold's kids were always hitting him up for money – as if he were a cash machine. His second wife Alice felt furious with the kids for their lack of respect for their father, while Harold never batted an eyelash.

Wilfred's mother called Sunday mornings at 9.00 a.m. even though she knew Wilfred worked late Saturday night and liked to sleep late. Wilfred talked to his mother while his wife, Emily, sat fuming at the intrusion.

Make a conscious effort not to jump in for your partner and bail him out of situations by expressing the anger for him. He may learn to be more expressive and closer to his feelings if you can learn to stop jumping in and taking over. This takes discipline on your part.

Guerrilla Mating Tactic Number 4: Call time out

Take a walk. Groom the dog. Tell your partner that you need to chill out for 20 minutes and leave the room.

Geraldine wrote Frank's name across her stomach in self-tanning lotion. They use this trick from time to time to write all kinds of words and draw pictures on themselves.

Guerrilla Mating Tactic Number 5: Encourage your partner's venting

Invite your partner to rant and rave. Sit quietly. Don't defend yourself. Venting is excellent for the cardiovascular system, so think of it as watching your partner exercise. Coach him if he needs it, offer an electrolyte replacement drink, cheer him on. *But beware of:*

The Night of the Living Vent: If you have a partner who *only and always* vents, who cannot control his venting, who isn't even aware that he is a skip that unloads a psychological manure pile on your pretty little head, you have to handle this differently. There are many things to try. You can use the tactics in Chapter 2 about how to handle a complaining partner. That would mean helping your partner vent, agreeing that he must be nuts to put up with what he puts up with, his situation is crazy – then kiss him and *go meet a friend for dinner.* You can let him know that his behaviour has consequences – affects you. You can, as talked about earlier in this chapter, schedule 20 minutes a day to vent. Tell him he has from 7.00 p.m. to 7.20 to get worked up, then it's Martini time. You can try the alternate-days exercise mentioned earlier in this chapter – one day he gets to vent, the other day he has to put on a happy face. You can try all kinds of things to help him get his venting under control. Don't forget to go back to Chapter 2 and reread how to drop a hot issue so you don't constantly get sucked in and drowned by his problems. If none of this works, then 'Heigh ho, heigh ho, it's off to couples' therapy you go.'

Is This Fight in 4/4 or 2/4?

Anger is a mighty emotion, one deserving respect and attention. And you will probably never stop getting mad at your partner and he will probably never stop getting mad at you. In fact, when you stop getting mad at each other, it's more often a sign that you feel disengaged than it is a sign of love. So don't let anger make you think something is wrong with your relationship. If you learn how to fight fair, your relationship can tolerate anger. Things don't have to be perfect for you or your partner in order to hold on to the love you have for each other.

For your common, garden variety fights, these tactics should help you stop sooner without doing damage to the relationship. There are many more tactics to help you fight less. The next chapters will put them at your fingertips. But let me offer one last tip from professor of linguistics George Lakoff and professor of philosophy Mark Johnson:

> During a fight, it's common to think, 'I want to win,' or 'His behavior is indefensible.' We think of our fights as battles, defenses, counterattacks. But what would disagreements sound like if we stopped comparing fights to wars and started comparing them to dances? You might be saying, 'She can't keep in step,' 'We don't seem to start together or finish together,' 'His time is off.' A gentler metaphor could lead to gentler fights. Think about it. You ought to be able to get angry without getting destructive. *And, by the way, good fighters, just like good dancers, get lots of practice.*

Quick-Fix List: How to Actually Like the Way You Fight

PART I: What to Do

Step 1: Negotiate using the SUPER model
Step 2: Schedule 20 minutes a day to struggle, then set the fight aside
Step 3: Think before you speak
Step 4: Don't reject your partner's attempts to connect with you when you're angry
Step 5: Learn to take turns regarding whose needs get met
Step 6: Call time out
Step 7: Encourage venting so you and your partner can let off steam
Step 8: Find ways to soothe yourself when you are upset
Step 9: Find playful ways of handling the problem
Step 10: Make time for each other so neither of you feels neglected

PART II: What to Think About

Step 1: Ask yourself how you contribute to the problem
Step 2: Ask how you can increase your understanding of the problem
Step 3: Learn to be a good loser

Step 4: Learn when you need contact and how to ask for it
Step 5: Learn how to be comforted by your partner
Step 6: Consider the impact of gender on the problem
Step 7: Think of your partner as a hedgehog who needs a hug
Step 8: Recognize that relationships rarely balance out

Manoeuvres to Dodge an Ambush: Avoid Fights Using a Marriage Counsellor's Tricks of the Trade

Maev and Norman practised fighting until they felt so comfortable that they wanted to invite their entire calling circle over to put on a show and give their friends and family the benefit of their fighting expertise. They found that they could turn an argument into a negotiation, dissolve a power struggle that was in full swing, halt a four-letter word in progress. 'Heh, heh, heh,' they chuckled to each other when they caught themselves getting nasty and switched to fair fighting. 'This is great,' they said when Maev yelled at Norman instead of yelling at her mother and Norman was able to point that out to her in a non-defensive way. 'That is ace,' they said when Norman got too self-absorbed and Maev was able to stop the argument and help him see the impact of his behaviour on her. They had so much to feel proud about. The more they fought, the better they got at it until they were truly fair-fight experts.

Then one night, in the middle of one such fight, Maev looked at Norman quizzically and wondered out loud, 'Norman, darling, could we take civilization a step further? It may sound crazy, but instead of just being good at stopping a fight, is there any way we could … er … avoid having a fight in the first place?' 'What a novel idea,' Norman replied. 'I don't know.'

Well, *I* know. Now that you've learned how to like the way you fight, you may be happy to discover that you can avoid an ambush altogether. When I talk about avoiding an ambush, I'm not talking about being ambushed by your partner, but being ambushed by the fight. There are 12 tried and true methods assembled by renowned psychotherapists. They have been thoroughly tested by the FDA (Fighting Diminishment Agency). Unlike the tactics in the last chapter, most of these require the co-operation of both partners.

Note: When you slip up and you haven't had the presence of mind to avoid the fight, these tactics are useful during or after a fight as well.

Guerrilla Mating Tactic Number 1: Check-in

This is one of the 'tricks of the trade' of marriage counselling. It has proven to be a helpful way for couples to deal with preventing sour feelings from boiling over while keeping the lines of communication unclogged. Let's use Maev and Norman to show you how it works.

In a Check-in, Maev gets to talk to Norman for 15 uninterrupted minutes about what is on her mind. She expresses her frustrations, irritations, anger, sorrow, hopes for the future, pain of the present – she gets it all out of her system. The agreement is that Maev and Norman sit two to four feet from each other and Norman faces Maev and listens to Maev in silence, making no comments. The key to this exercise is that the listening partner, Norman, *cannot respond to what is said*. Norman's function in this exercise is to listen to Maev in a deep, respectful way. When Maev's 15 minutes are up, Norman still cannot refute what Maev has said or respond in any way. Norman must leave the room. Later that day (with a minimum of an hour in between) or the next day, it's Norman's turn to check in with Maev for 15 minutes.

Here is how this exercise has helped other couples:

Brad found that he let minor irritations build up in his relationship with Amanda. He would let things slide and slide until eventually he would begin to feel that he didn't want to be with her anymore. His intentions in letting things slide were good ones. He felt that if he was critical whenever something bugged him, he'd end up a nag. But holding it all in wasn't working either. It only built resentment in Brad, and confusion in Amanda. When he began to do the Check-in exercise, he discovered that he could talk calmly about what bugged him and Amanda could listen calmly to his complaints. Just getting it off his chest, knowing Amanda wasn't going to interrupt or try to defend herself, and then being able to walk away from it, was a big relief. It also helped Amanda because she sensed when Brad's resentment was building and she had been especially unhappy during those times.

Martha got defensive whenever Daryl sounded critical because she was so sensitive to any rejection. Even when Daryl had a legitimate gripe, Martha would pipe in defending herself or shooting cross-complaints before she could ever hear what Daryl had to say. The Check-in exercise taught her to let Daryl finish a sentence. Plus when she listened she discovered that Daryl often had a good point; he wasn't out to hurt her. What Martha needed most and what was most helpful to her relationship was to learn the discipline of listening. This exercise is perfect to build that up in a person.

There is something about being listened to in an uninterrupted way that promotes empathy and understanding. And there is something about listening, knowing you can't defend yourself, that allows new information to get through. However, don't be surprised if it takes you a few tries before you can listen to your partner for 15 minutes without interrupting. My husband, Boots, and I have used this exercise, and it took us several tries before we could muster the discipline to complete it. Either you or your partner can call a Check-in two or three times a week – even when you aren't trying to avoid a fight. Even when you just need to be heard. It is important to use open body language during a Check-in, so don't sit there with arms crossed and a pout on your face.

Note: Sometimes a partner may want to use the Check-in to talk a few minutes and be silent with you for part of the time. This, too, helps couples to calm provocative situations.

Guerrilla Mating Tactic Number 2: Check-out

This tactic was developed by two therapists in the US, Dr Stephen Bergman and Dr Janet Surrey. They have found this tactic extremely valuable in their work, and since they are married to each other, probably at home too.

A Check-out is when you or your partner walks away from the provocative topic. What makes it a Check-out, rather than avoidance of the issue, is this: *You must say when you will return to complete the discussion, when you will bring it up again.*

Say: I need to check out. We can continue this discussion in _____ (a half hour, two hours, this evening), but I can't continue it now.

Time out. Give me 20 minutes to walk around the block, and then we can come back to this.

Either person can call a Check-out at any time. At some point, when the two of you are getting along well, discuss the idea of a Check-out as a possibility to try the next time an argument seems to be escalating. If one of you feels attacked or like attacking, you initiate a Check-out instead.

Guerrilla Mating Tactic Number 3: Checking it out

In the moment your stomach starts to churn and you know where a discussion is headed, make a commitment to check it out before you react: *If you check it out you might discover that you don't have a true fight on your hands.*

You may have had a communication mix-up, a crossed signal, and not a fight at all. For example:

David married Rebecca and she moved into a home he had been living in for seven years. She was a religious Jewish woman who insisted that they make their kitchen kosher. He agreed, saying, 'I turn this kitchen over to you. It belongs to you now.' That week, an ancient man came with a blowtorch and began torching the burners on the stove. His business was that of koshering kitchens, which means purifying them with fire. After he left, David asked Rebecca if he could keep one unit for his box of old tax returns, and she told him, 'Absolutely not.' David said nothing, but went into a slow boil. Eventually he blew up. Rebecca asked to 'check in'. Rebecca explained that when David said 'This kitchen belongs to you,' she took him literally. She had no idea that keeping the tax returns there was so important to him, and, in her head, it made more sense to keep them elsewhere. She had really not understood that he meant that the kitchen belonged *mostly* to her.

When you think your partner is provoking you, ignoring you or treating you without respect, check it out by clarifying your positions.

MOVE OVER, IRVING BERLIN

Deborah and Steven have written a whole album of songs for each other, including 'You've Seen the Last of Not Seeing Me,' and the ever-popular 'How Can I Miss You When You Won't Go Away?' They write them and sing them on long car journeys.

Clarifying positions means that in an honest, straightforward manner and tone of voice you enquire further as to what she meant, and you offer more of what you meant if you think you have been misunderstood. You take what you have already said and you simplify it, explain it, illuminate it, elucidate it, define it. If, on the other hand, you raise your voice, take a sarcastic stance, daddy her like she's a two-year-old, lecture like a school headmaster, you are not clarifying, you are baiting – trying to hook her into a fight. Let me make that clear: When you clarify you offer more of you, when you bait you offer dead worms. Now which one would she rather have?

Clarify Her Position: When I asked you if I could keep my papers in the kitchen, I was totally surprised by your answer. Tell me what you were thinking.

Clarify Your Own Position: When I said you could own the kitchen, I meant it as a figure of speech. I didn't mean that I'd move all my things out.

Tip: Vary the time you discuss the topic. Go back to your charts on the times of day that you feel most well disposed towards each other. Try discussing troublesome matters then. Or any other time you haven't tried. Do something different.

Since many fights are caused by misinterpreted communication, when you try to learn more about your thinking and your partner's thinking, misinterpreted communications become rarer and so do fights.

Guerrilla Mating Tactic Number 4: Stay in the here and now

Keeping it in the here and now means that you focus on the issue at hand and you agree that you cannot switch the issue to a past injustice. However, the here and now is more than not throwing up the past. It means that when tensions build within you, you attempt to be aware of your underlying feelings in the moment. That means going beneath the anger into your self experience – as with disclosures, keeping it in the 'I' of the storm:

It hurts me when...
I'm sad when...
When you said we couldn't go tonight, I got so upset...
When I heard your tone of voice, I felt...

You talk about what just happened and how that makes you feel right now. Staying in the here and now will keep you from getting sidetracked. It takes practice.

Guerrilla Mating Tactic Number 5: Don't take on the attack

When you sense that your partner is getting critical, don't try to defend or explain yourself against her attack. Criticism only works to provoke when the person listening is willing to take it on. Stand, listen, don't try to prove you are innocent – no matter how innocent you may be. Telling her you're innocent won't change her mind. You already know that. Smarten up – let your partner vent and get it all out.

> When she says: ...and last year in June I told you that
> you were supposed to...
> Say: Is there more? Have you said it all?

> When he says: ...and if you want to know the truth about
> your behaviour, you ought to know...
> Say: You've got strong feelings about this.
> Keep talking and get them all out.

Don't fuel a discussion by adding your own set of complaints. If your partner rants while you just listen, there's a good chance she'll actually start to hear her own voice, to recognize what she's saying, and end up stopping herself. It may not happen the first or second time; in fact, the first or second time, the fact that you won't fight may make her even angrier. She may blow up if you won't take her on. But let things get a little worse before they get better. Be patient, keep at it. Eventually she will hear the disparity between herself and you and it won't make her feel good. She'll try a more reasonable path.

Note: If you never engage her in a fight, if you always sit silently, this is another kind of problem. Go back to Chapter 2 and reread the section on the silent treatment.

Guerrilla Mating Tactic Number 6: Prioritize, then specify your wants

You won't get anywhere if you complain about everything at once. So try numbering your most pressing needs from 1 to 10, deciding what you want to work on first. Your chances of success are much better if you can deal with one specific thing at a time. *But it must be very specific.* You cannot say 'I want you to contribute more of your time to the kids' when what you really mean is 'I want you to pick the kids up from school.' It is often very difficult to pinpoint concretely what you want, but you must do so.

Here is a method for that.

If you want more affection, ask yourself: *What would be happening in my relationship if I had more affection?*

Your request may then be:

Kiss me when you walk through the door.
Kiss me more when we make love.
Initiate sex once a week.
Hug me before bed.
Take a bath with me tonight.

If you want more consideration, ask yourself: *What would be happening in my relationship if my partner were more considerate?*

Your request may then be:

Take the kids out a couple of times a week so I can study.
Call me from work during the day to see how I am.
Pick up dinner on the way home.
Let me orgasm first sometimes.
Ask me about my day.

When you know specifically what you want to happen, then you can ask for that. When you use vague terms like 'consideration', 'affection' and 'passion' you leave too much open to interpretation:

Craig was always saying that he wanted more 'passion' from Rosie. It was a gripe that had been going on for years. Rosie tried to be more passionate, but eventually, when the gripe continued, she became resentful. When I saw them, I asked Craig what he meant by 'passion'. His response was 'Passion, you know, passion. Everyone knows what passion means.' I assured him that I only knew what it meant to me, and Rosie only knew what it meant to her. Could he let Rosie know what more 'passion' would look like to him? It turned out that it took him a few weeks before he could put words to it. He had expected Rosie to intuit something which he could not explain himself. Eventually, he was able to specifically describe a sexual favour he wanted and ask for it. Rosie was comfortable with his request – once she knew what it was.

Actually, it may help to remember that if you tend to differ along gender lines, your husband may decide to fix your hair dryer instead of hug you more often if you ask for more tenderness, and your wife may decide to call you by your pet name instead of initiating sex more often.

Always be specific about what you want!

Guerrilla Mating Tactic Number 7: Make a More of/Less of list

This is a four-step variation of prioritizing your wants.

1. Make a More of/Less of list
Make a list for yourself of what you want more of and less of in the relationship. *The first draft of this list is not for your partner to see.* Make sure you don't leave this list on the dining room table 'by mistake'.

More	Less
Heart-to-heart talks	Lectures
Feeling heard	Feeling dismissed
Gentle sex	Morning quickies
Eye contact	Staring off into space
Real listening	Being placated with him saying everything will be all right
Hand holding	Boob groping

Real kissing
Talk about having kids
Help with housework

Rushing during sex
Refusal to discuss it
Stereotyping of roles

2. Refine your More of/Less of list

This list above is a good start, but parts of it are too global. For example, what does a heart-to-heart talk mean? How long does it last? It will be a big problem if you want it to last two hours and he can only probe his emotional depths for 10 minutes at a time. Where are you in the house when you have one? How do you know it's a heart-to-heart talk and not just a talk? What does heart-to-heart mean to him – the same thing it means to you? Probably not. Does he have to participate equally or can he just listen?

You have to find a way to specifically communicate your needs without sounding like a drill sergeant.

Refined More of/Less of List

More: One-half-hour heart-to-heart talks while taking a long walk or sharing a glass of wine together in bed or in the lounge and giving each other our full attention.
Less: Talks while reading the paper at the kitchen table, watching television, or being otherwise distracted.

More: Tackling difficult discussions such as having kids, talking about the obstacles to having children, our options and how we can come to a mutually acceptable agreement. This difficult discussion deserves a half hour at a time to air fully.
Less: Putting off difficult conversations.

More: Pre-foreplay with us occasionally touching, holding hands, paying attention to each other for at least two hours before lovemaking officially begins. Whenever possible, we make sure that the other one knows how desirable they are and what is on our mind.
Less: Turning off the 10 o'clock news and rushing sex so I feel like it's over just when I'm starting to heat up.

3. Beware the all-negative list.

Beware the person *who can only tell you what she doesn't want in a relationship*. When concerned, all of her requests come out in negatives.

Negatively stated:
I want more of him not leaving his wet towels on the floor, more of him not forgetting to call me, more of him not picking on me so much.

Positively stated:
I want a cleaner house, to get more updated on where he is, to have him saying kind things to me.

If this describes you, then the More of/Less of list is a good starting place to point you in a more positive, workable direction. You should try making up such a list for your own thinking, even if you don't use it for anything in your relationship. You might try making up a list like this to address work situations and other relationships as well. You're thinking in a negative fashion, and as long as you do, you won't get what you want out of your relationship.

Note: I entreat you again. If you find yourself naturally thinking and talking in negatives, keep working at it and learn to express positives too. It takes self-training, time and thought. Study after study points out that your thoughts play a big part in shaping your mood. You don't have to be one of the Waltons and live in la-la land, but the person who really loses out when you think all negative thoughts is you!

4. The More of/Less of list and sex
Be careful when you are talking about unfulfilled sexual needs. The More of/Less of list does not work so well here. Nothing is a bigger frustration and turnoff than when someone says, 'I want more anti-clockwise motions with your first finger and less clockwise motions with your thumb' or 'I want more rhythmic movements with your tongue and less uneven movements.' Your partner can feel inadequate and confused and angry when there is too much direction in sex. Try pleasing yourself and letting him watch to get the hang of it, instead of constantly moving his hand and rerouting him. Of course some instruction is definitely desirable – he can't read your mind. Just don't make each lovemaking session a pass/fail quiz.

THERE IS A SEASON

One old Javanese custom has couples copulating in the rice paddies to celebrate a fruitful crop. You may not pass a rice paddy in the next few weeks, but you could plant a carrot in a yoghurt pot.

Guerrilla Mating Tactic Number 8: Be a little sneaky once in a while

From time to time, be slightly sneaky. There is nothing so rewarding as getting your partner to change his behaviour by slipping one past him.

Ask for Help: Instead of approaching the problem as a couple's issue which needs solving, reframe the problem as one for which you need assistance, such as:

I need help with...
I have a problem...
Something feels wrong to me with...
I can't decide about...
I can't figure out...
I could use more information about...

Offer Help: Ask your partner how you can help him along with questions such as:

How can I give you more support regarding your picking up your socks?
How can I make it easier for you to pick up your socks?
How can I make it easier for you to listen to my feelings about your socks?

This is what Diana actually tried with Zack – regarding his socks. Zack actually had an answer. He hated where the laundry basket was and he wanted something more accessible. He took off his socks after he got in bed at night, and he didn't want to then have to walk to the basket. Diana put the basket next to his side of the bed – and that was the last time she found a sock on the floor (almost).

Note: A glint in your eye that makes you seem humorous rather than maniacal may allow you to pull this one off. However, keep in mind that if your inflection is slightly off, you may sound patronizing and you will have a whole other fight on your hands.

Guerrilla Mating Tactic Number 9: Create a character and/or alter egos for troublesome emotions

My husband Boots and I had a high-conflict period of time in our relationship during which he had a particularly short fuse. We were trying to figure out what to do about his anger and we weren't having much luck. Around the same time he came into possession of an infamous audiotape of the late renowned drummer Buddy Rich talking to the musicians who worked for him. Buddy was explosive and had a foul mouth. His outbursts were the stuff of legend. He screamed and shouted and swore, and he didn't care who heard him.

Without planning it, when my husband got mad, I started calling him Buddy – humorously saying things like, 'Uh oh, Buddy's back.' We thought of the tapes and laughed. Soon my husband began to tell me when Buddy was coming and to identify his anger as a visit from Buddy. This allowed both of us a sigh of relief. We didn't have to blame my husband, it was Buddy's fault – we could have a good laugh at Buddy's expense. My husband didn't have to feel bad about himself for getting angry. From the grave, drummer Buddy Rich helped us avoid many fights.

Lena used the same idea and called the situation a visit from 'Uriah Heep' when her husband Sam got a little too careful with the pennies, and Marcus called his wife 'Lady Dramatica' when she flung her arms in the air melodramatically.

Guerrilla Mating Tactic Number 10: Find the comedy, not the drama

Although she knew her second husband, Joseph, was a much better guy than her first husband, Quentin, Irene still found that in her new marriage she had feelings she'd had when she was still married to Quentin – feelings of not being a priority, of not being valued as a person. In her heart she knew that Joseph loved her, but the feelings kept coming up, rising in her throat like bad pepperoni.

One day, she told Joseph a story that she thought captured the feeling. Her first husband, Quentin, had a daughter from a previous marriage who was being confirmed in church. Even though Quentin's daughter had invited Irene to attend, Quentin's ex-wife called and told him Irene should not be allowed to come to the church because she would only destroy the day for the entire family.

Irene was nearby at the time and overheard the conversation. It was devastating for her because Quentin's response to his ex-wife was 'Well, Irene wants to come and I can't stop her.' For Irene, this was very different from saying 'Irene is my wife and she'll be there.' His comment hurt Irene in a profound manner, and the hurt never went away.

As Irene told the story to Joseph, he took her hand, winked at her, and said, 'You never have to worry, Irene. I love you more than I love Quentin's wife.' They both laughed, and Irene was able to put a name to her feeling and to change her perspective on it. Now, whenever Joseph did something where Irene felt as if she was not a priority or whenever she felt insecure she would say, 'You love Quentin's wife more than you love me.' Joseph then knew exactly how she felt, he didn't feel blamed, and they both knew what Irene wanted.

Many painful moments in your life are also comic moments in retrospect. Find the comedy in your sorrow and use it to alleviate tensions. Use a story from the past, a buzzword that gives you perspective on today:

Marianne decided to lose two stone. She went on a strict diet, and after many starts and stops, she managed to lose a stone. She was ecstatic. Shortly thereafter, Kevin came home from work on a Friday with a box of chocolates and a bottle of wine. Marianne felt sabotaged and a terrible fight followed. Finally Kevin was able to talk about the fact that her weight loss threatened him – he felt less in control, less loved, and he was getting sick of hearing her talk about her diet. He was angry and he couldn't say so, so he brought home the chocolates. Now, when he feels resentful or angry, he calls it a 'Chocolates Day'. Marianne knows exactly what he means and they can talk it through.

Early on in their relationship, James was desperate to paint the apartment he had moved into, which Don had lived in for years without painting. Don was reluctant to move all the furniture and submit to the intrusion. They argued about this for weeks, an ongoing stream of really nasty fights. Years later, they still use this story when they find themselves in a power struggle. When James really wants something and Don is really reluctant, James will say, 'C'mon, it's easier than painting the apartment.' They use an old fight to keep them grounded and in good humour in a current fight.

Tracy was Will's second wife. Early on in their marriage she found a note he'd written some time before they'd met about how much he loved his first wife's large breasts. Tracy, who was flat-chested, fell into a funk. Nothing Will said seemed to help. One day, close to Hallowe'en, she was passing a fancy dress shop where she saw on

---

display a plastic flesh-coloured set of strap-on boobs that would make
Pamela Anderson weep with envy. She purchased them and, on her
husband's birthday, she put them on over her own breasts and
marched into the room. Neither she nor her husband could stop
laughing about it for weeks.

Guerrilla Mating Tactic Number 11: Learn to deal with issues directly

Linda and Tony avoided many fights when Linda learned how to stop making
confusing, provocative, indirect statements that only made Tony angry.

Don't say:	Who's going to return the video to the rental place?
When you really mean:	I'm tired of bringing them back.
Don't say:	What film do you want to see?
When you really mean:	I really want to see the new Bill Pullman pic.
Don't say:	...whatever you feel like, dearest.
When you really mean:	If we eat Chinese once more I'll croak.
Don't say:	Where should we go on holiday?
When you really mean:	I want to go to Corfu.

I hadn't realized this when I started to write this book, but I do this all the
time. Last week, I was sitting in the living room and I said to my husband,
'We should put on the air conditioner.' He said, 'Okay,' and he sat there.
A few minutes later he pointed out to me that I frequently say 'We should'
when I really mean, 'Will you...?' Now, as I am suddenly aware of it, he's
right. We should do something about that.

Guerrilla Mating Tactic Number 12: Create a joint narrative

Every third husband or so (just kidding) you will find a partner who
actually wants to work on improving the relationship in an organized
manner as much as you do. When that happens, bow to the great anger
gods and try a technique used by my sister, Dr Michelle Wolf, who is a
professor of communications at San Francisco State University. She uses
an exercise meant to help students initiate dialogue, an exercise which
can be adapted to help couples initiate dialogue with the purpose of
understanding each other's differences and point of view.

A couple is watching *This Life* or they have rented *Casablanca* or any programme where they are observing the relationship of another couple. They have a pad and pencil (or a good memory), and during the programme they write down their opinions about how the couple they are watching are getting along – opinions such as:

- When were the couple the closest to each other emotionally?
- When were they mad at each other and harbouring resentment?
- When was their love for each other clearest?
- Who was more in love with the other?

HELLO, SAILOR

Hamish checks in and goes to the hotel bar where his wife, Ruth, is already seated and waiting. Hamish and Ruth pretend they don't know each other and are meeting for the first time. They make quite a scene. Sometimes they've done this when Hamish's been at the bar with a few acquaintances who have never met Ruth. She shows up, they pretend they are strangers, and Ruth chats Hamish up. He then invites her to his hotel room as his astonished peers wonder what Hamish has that they haven't.

Kendra and Charles decided to try this 'assignment' because they never felt they knew what the other was thinking when it came to their relationship. They constantly misinterpreted each other, and they were looking for a way to understand each other's point of view more clearly without going over and over old business between them. They taped a sitcom on television that they usually watched together anyway, but this time they answered the above questions as they watched. Kendra was shocked that Charles thought the husband was not mad at the wife, whereas she felt the husband was picking on his wife for the entire programme. She was able to rewind the tape and look at exactly the place where she thought the husband was mad and discuss it with Charles. Charles was surprised that Kendra thought that the wife loved the husband more because he thought the husband was at least as much in love with the wife. He was able to rewind the tape and show her the places where he thought the husband showed his love. They went back over the programme and their opinions, which shook up their thinking by making them aware of how differently they perceived the same exact action. It helped them to realize that the same kinds of differences occurred within their relationship. Charles would do something he thought was affectionate, such as giving her a little cuff on the chin as he gave his male friends affectionately, and Kendra would see this as Charles bullying her. Kendra would think she had let Charles know that this annoyed her, but Charles actually had no idea she was annoyed. They were able to use a third couple to discuss their own feelings and behaviours and, with one degree of separation, discussions felt less loaded for them. One thing they realized was how differently they thought about the same action, therefore how different they must be from each other, therefore hoping the other would read one's mind and know what he or she was thinking wasn't working between them.

Taking a step back from your own relationship and conferring about the relationship of others is a tool for understanding your own differences. Always use a videotape you can watch over and over so you can check out what your partner is talking about.

Warning: Never use home videos of your own family. If you ignore this advice because you want to end up on *You've Been Framed*, start taping your chihuahua's tricks instead.

You Fight Because Your Relationship Is Growing Up

Well, there you have it: 12 ways to avoid an ambush. If learning, trying and getting this stuff to work for you takes time, don't get discouraged. It takes a long time for two people to grow into each other. Think of it this way: Cupid is a baby, and that's no coincidence. The honeymoon is the infancy of your relationship. That's why it's happy and carefree. When the honeymoon is over your relationship enters puberty and, like any adolescent, *its voice is changing!* There's a struggle as your relationship grows into itself. Just as every teenager would give anything to avoid massive acne breakouts (face *and* back), that first bra, uninvited erections and clothes that don't quite fit, you will want to avoid that parallel time in your relationship when your relationship doesn't quite fit.

Both growing up and growing into our relationship make us feel out of control.

Emotions run haywire, moods swing like Tarzan on speed. None the less, if you live you grow, and if you grow you've got to get more creative about your relationship. It's unavoidable. You will have to try different tactics until you find the ones that work for you. In addition, something may work great for the two of you for a while and then stop working completely. You need to be flexible, inventive, undaunted to keep coming up with ways to soothe each other. Again, think of it this way – if you have a colicky baby, you don't give the baby back. You become more creative. Apply the same commitment to your relationship and see what happens. Of course, you could always run for the nearest exit. But first, look at all your divorced friends – how happy are they?

Quick-Fix List: How to Avoid an Ambush

1 **Check in**
Speak uninterrupted for 15 minutes each.
2 **Check out**
Take time out, but you must say when you'll bring it up again.
3 **Check it out**
Make sure you have a real disagreement on your hands.
4 **Stay in the here and now**
Be aware of your underlying feelings.
5 **Don't take on the attack**
Don't fuel it with your own set of complaints – it takes two to tango.
6 **Prioritize and specify your wants**
Determine what you need most so your requests aren't overwhelming and global.
7 **Make a More of/Less of list**
Learn what you really need to make you happy.
8 **Get slightly sneaky**
Ask for help or offer help.
9 **Create a character or alter ego**
Find a metaphor, a character from the news, the movies or a book who can represent your anger.
10 **Find the comedy instead of the drama**
What's funny about this?
11 **Deal directly with problems**
Don't be indirect about what bothers you.
12 **Try a joint narrative**
Talk about other people's relationships as a way to discuss issues in a less provocative manner.

IV

PEACE TREATIES

IV

Conclusions

SURVIVAL SKILLS THAT WILL SAVE YOUR RELATIONSHIP DURING A MARRIAGE-THREATENING FIGHT

Silent weeping, bouts of screaming, Jekylls and Hydes, puddles of tears, slammed doors, high blood pressure, snide remarks, contemptuous laughter, picking at her like she's a scab, taunting him like he's a bull – we each have our own unique talent for creating fights. For some people, fights just represent a chronic pattern of superficial bickering. Neither partner seems devastated, but you do start getting fewer dinner invitations because no one can stand to be around you. However, we've all had the other kind of fight – the one that is so damaging that the relationship nears maximum fracture. Here's how couples have described them:

> The worst fight we ever had happened when we were driving in the car. Words flew and it culminated when Kevin hit the windscreen of the car with his fist so hard, he actually broke it.
>
> We were off on holiday in a caravan with our kids. We started fighting in the Midlands. When we got to Scotland I threw my wedding ring out of the window onto the motorway. My wife ended up stopping the caravan and ordering me out. The kids were crying. I stomped off.
>
> My wife is Korean. I got so angry one night I called the airline and made a reservation for her to go home to her mother. The next day I picked up the ticket at the airline office and brought it home and handed it to her. She didn't speak to me for a month.

These are the fights you know your neighbour heard, the fights you never forget, and each has the following three qualities:

1 *Lasting scars.* With most fights, you won't remember in a week when you had them or what they were about. The hurt brought on by marriage-threatening fights, however, is remembered for years. The memory remains a source of pain.
2 *One or both of you seriously contemplate divorce.* The residue of the fight can last for weeks, even months. You consider that the relationship may not be worth it.
3 *Uncharacteristic behaviour.* You and your partner act uncharacteristically cruel and contemptuous. You lose control, your fights escalate and assaults fly back and forth. You hate each other and you don't care who knows it.

People's fighting styles can be as various as their fingerprints. No two people fight exactly alike, no two people brew anger in exactly the same way, no two people hurt each other in exactly the same way, no two people make up in exactly the same way. But sometimes the seeds of marriage-threatening fights fester for days and days when you are mad and *you don't want to make up:*

> Gail gets up early and goes downstairs. She knows Bob worked late the night before. She yells up to her kids to wake up. She empties the dishwasher noisily, she slams the pantry door.
>
> Today, Gail *wants* her anger, wants to play out all permutations of the feeling. There is someplace in her that needs the intensity of anger – needs to have that kind of impact on Bob, that kind of power over him, needs to probe her own anger. There are times when she's sure the only way she can get through to Bob is to yell. Her anger may be the truest feeling she owns, or it may just be the best way she can function at that moment. She stokes her emotional inferno by repeating angry messages to herself over and over again: 'If he thinks I'm going to put up with this ... He's had a second chance – no more chances. I've had it.'

For you, as for Gail, when you need to be angry nothing will keep you from it. Then, in some real way, your anger isn't even about him, it's about you. He just happens to be there. You have to respect that kind of anger because it comes from a profound place inside of you. There are periods in our lives when we need more anger than we need at other times; we need the anger to change, the anger to grieve, the anger to heal. Then, the worst thing you can do is to try to shake the anger off or pretend it isn't there. You can't wipe that anger away. It's a Lady Macbeth thing – the 'spots' are on the inside.

SOMETHING YOU CAN'T BUY

Fran and Harry had been married for years, and both were very successful. When it came to material things there really wasn't all that much they could give each other that was exciting anymore. But Fran came up with a gift that brought Harry to tears. She took him on a blindfold trip, back to the neighbourhood he grew up in. She had made arrangements with the people now living in the house he grew up in to give them a tour of the house. She found Harry's old barber and they visited him as well. It is a day Harry will never forget.

The tactics you've read about in the previous chapters will help you *start* to use your anger for positive change instead of for unfocused explosions, but this can be a slow process. Be ready to go slowly and to give yourself time to take in all these new ideas. Meanwhile, use this chapter in case of emergency or if you know that you have a problem with anger. The goal of this chapter is to teach you how to survive a marriage-threatening fight. You will learn techniques that keep fights from escalating out of control. You can take what you need.

Four Things to Do When You Can't Get Past Your Anger

Here are my first four pieces of advice, my attempts to move the chairs around on the *Titanic* so you will be more comfortable. These are the kinds of things a person usually thinks about afterwards, when it's too late. But on the chance that you are highly suggestible, keep these in mind:

1 *Stop stoking the anger coals*. The muttering to yourself, the angry thoughts you repeat inside your head – such things serve to keep you angry. A person can work herself up or calm herself down. Try to calm yourself down by replacing the muttered phrases and angry thoughts with more reasonable thoughts:

When you think: He isn't getting a second chance. He'll pay for this.
Replace it with: This too shall pass. This too shall pass.

When you think: He'll never change. I want out.

Replace it with: He's already made changes for the relationship. He may make this change and he may not. Either way, battling over it won't help, and trying to figure it out might.

Note: I'm not asking you to give up being angry, just to give up further inflaming yourself.

2 *Get enough rest and a proper diet and try to protect yourself against extra stressors.* Many terrible fights happen when you are already overburdened with stressful situations that life throws at you:

You have crabby, cranky nights when you didn't get enough sleep the night before. Your defences are down and you blow.

You have visits to relatives over Christmas where you are all supposed to feel jolly but you find yourself fuming inside.

Do the best you can to protect yourself from more stress when you are already anger-sensitive. Get extra rest and exercise, and watch Marx Brothers movies.

3 *Imagine how you will feel about yourself after your outburst.* Recall marriage-threatening fights of the past – did they help your marriage? Imagine the one on your mind now, and then imagine how you will feel after you've had the fight. Will you really feel better or will you hate the way you acted? Will the fight be a fight for change or just a way to get more deeply entrenched on the battleground?

4 *Show self-control even when it's the last thing you want to do.* Being angry is fine, but you know when you are about to cross the line into a marriage-threatening fight. Don't do it.

Yes, as you learn more productive anger skills you will take two steps forward, and occasionally you will take 10 steps back. And when you take 10 steps back and you blow up and you don't want to make up, it's worthwhile not to turn your anger into a marriage-threatening fight.

15 Tactics to Avoid a Marriage-Threatening Fight

Guerrilla Mating Tactic Number 1: Look for the hurt underneath the anger: Discuss feelings versus issues

When you or your partner raises a truly heated issue, know that you are treading on a matter that hurts you a great deal. Nastiness will be greatly reduced if you can respond to the hurt in yourself and your partner rather than the issue itself. So if you are mad about something, you need to add the step of figuring out what hurt you have that corresponds. You must do this before you say something you'll be sorry for.

Anger	Corresponding Hurt
He's late	He'll leave me
He flirted with another	I'm not attractive to him
She won't pick her clothes up	She doesn't respect me
Our sex life is flagging	I'm sexually inadequate

Acknowledging what hurts you can stop you from attacking, and it will curb your partner's counterattacks. Even though this is hard to do, when you feel like you'll blow up, ask yourself instead what the *pain*, rather than the anger, is about. Know that when you get the feeling that you want to attack your partner, it is usually a way of trying to protect your own vulnerability. Remember the Sherman Tank allusion in Chapter 6? Your marriage-threatening fights will be greatly reduced and the health of your relationship will be greatly elevated when you can respond to the pain you feel and the pain your partner feels, rather than responding to the attack.

Guerrilla Mating Tactic Number 2: Validate your partner's experience

An important thing to keep any fight from getting out of control is to validate your partner's experience. This means you make a statement that directly addresses your partner's experience, rather than your partner's complaint. In the following interactions, the validating statement is italicized.

Bruce: How could you do that to me? Calling my mother behind my back and telling her we're fighting. I don't want my mother in on our problems.

(Say this)

Demi: I see what you're saying. I had to talk to someone. Your mother and I get along. You and I weren't speaking.

(Not this)

Demi: Get off my case. Well, I had to talk to someone. You and I aren't speaking.

Marla: When you feed Tiffany, I expect you give her a real meal with vegetables and milk – not a pepperoni pizza because that's what you want.

(Say this)

Donald: You have a point. She likes pepperoni pizza.

(Not this)

Donald: You're overreacting. She likes pepperoni pizza.

Nothing makes someone fly off the handle more than feeling as if he isn't getting through to you. Validation of your partner's experience lets your partner know that, even if you don't agree, you take his feelings seriously and you hear his point of view. You are listening, you are paying attention, you want to solve the problem. That does not mean you don't express your feelings or feel just as angry. Validating your partner's experience means adopting phrases such as:

I see what you're saying, and...
I understand you feel strongly about this, and...
You have a point, and...
You're furious and...

(Notice that all of these use the word *and* rather than the word *but*. We'll talk more about that later.)

When you fight, the point is not to agree with each other, but to let each other feel heard.

Guerrilla Mating Tactic Number 3: Watch your facial expressions

One morning after breakfast Nina is trying to talk to Julian about ways to save on the electricity bill. The principal way would be if he turned off the lights when he left a room. Julian cannot take his eyes off his cereal bowl. When he finally looks at her, he rolls his eyes. Nina explodes.

Fights escalate when you:

Sneer
Contort your facial muscles
Purposefully divert your eyes
Use your body to show disdain
Roll your eyes
Stare off into the sky
Turn your back on your speaking partner
Swing your foot feverishly and impatiently
Play with things on the table during the fight

Make an effort to keep your facial expressions open. Do the same with your body language. You may not realize that your body language is provocative. In a calm moment, you might even ask your partner about it. Disagreeable facial expressions are guaranteed to up the ante in any quarrel. Face your partner, face the music, and don't act like a put-upon 12-year-old.

Guerrilla Mating Tactic Number 4: Avoid the kitchen sink fight

> You never take out the garbage, and you never talk to my
> mother when she calls, and you never pay the phone bill
> on time, and you never pick up Audrey from school.

This is a major fighting cock-up. It's easy in the midst of a fight to want to add in other past unresolved fights and issues. The fight takes on the quality of the kitchen sink – everything is thrown in it. Stay focused on the fight you are having and do not bring in other fights and other information. You can only tackle one thing at a time. Your partner can't possibly address several accusations at one time. This behaviour escalates the struggle, and you make it impossible for the fight to be resolved. Remember, fight fair now and there will be ample time to have all of those other fights in the future.

Guerrilla Mating Tactic Number 5: Don't get hung up on the accuracy of your partner's statement

Liza: Last Tuesday you said we would.

Bob: Last Tuesday, I worked until 10. When I came home you were sleeping. I never said we would last Tuesday.

Liza: Yes, you did. I was up when you got home.

Bob: No, you weren't.

Proving the accuracy of your statement and disproving the accuracy of your partner's can take over a fight when the accuracy is the least important part.

Arguing over accuracy is a perfect way to avoid resolving a real issue.

The point in a fight is not who said what when and how many times but to hear the heart of her hurt, her emotional rather than her literal truth.

The Literal Truth	*The Emotional Truth*
You said that	I'm hurting
No, I never said that	I won't help you
Yes, you said it	Can't you hear me?
I did not	I won't hear you

As long as you get stuck in his literal truth, you will not be able to have the relationship that you want. You need to focus on the process of your fights (the interaction between you) rather than the content of your fights. When you get mired in disproving his literal truth you are saying that, for the time being, you have little interest in your inner life or his inner life or ending the fight – you are more interested in proof. And the hard fact is: *Proof won't help your relationship.*

For most fights it won't matter who did what or who is telling the truth, it is how the two of you interact that matters. This is one of the hardest things for couples to get past in a fight. I have seen countless couples get captured by trying to prove which one is telling the truth. It never works.

What to Do When You Have Got Over the Need to Prove Who Is Right While Your Partner Has Hired Johnnie Cochran and Three Forensic Psychologists to Prove Her Point: Wait.

Believe it or not, when you aren't trying to shove your competing set of facts down your partner's throat, the joy of the 'proof' game wears thin quickly. In fact, she can't play it alone – it's not fun anymore with no jury, no verdict, no judge. Initially, she might get angrier because you changed the game, but soon after, she'll probably start to hear what she sounds like, and she won't like what she hears. When she tries to offer up proof, go back to validating your partner's experience.

Guerrilla Mating Tactic Number 6: Avoid Sarcasm

Jack: I'm not going to put up with the way you treat me.
Maria: Oh darling, when you talk like that it turns me on.

Maria: How dare you introduce me as 'the little woman'?
Jack: You're right. You're not the little woman I married. You've gained two stone since then.

Wisecracks, denigrating humour, getting a laugh at your partner's expense, taking a most sensitive issue and mocking him about it – all are to be avoided. Sarcasm directed at a partner is experienced by her as humiliation. Sometimes it is hard to distinguish sarcasm from humour. Your sense of humour comes from goodwill, your desire to help the two of you out of a terrible spot by sharing something funny. Sarcasm happens when you want to make a point at your partner's expense. Sarcasm is cutting – it is done with the intention to hurt or wound your partner. Sarcasm actually does feel like a wound – a dagger in the heart. Weeks later, even years later, such cruel outbursts still sting. So don't do it. If my telling you isn't enough, let me ignore my own advice and hit below the belt:

People get sarcastic during a fight when they feel weak, ineffectual and awful about themselves.

When it comes to gender differences, men are *very sensitive* to feeling mocked. Women have learned to rely on a wide range of verbal styles for conveying emotions – mockery can be one of these. Keep in mind that nothing gets a guy going like feeling that you've mocked him.

Guerrilla Mating Tactic Number 7: Don't bring up old failures

Never bring up the erection he didn't get, the pay rise she was passed over for, the exam he didn't pass. As with sarcasm, this is an attempt to humiliate or shame your partner, to grab the power in the fight when you feel as if your power is tottering. It is a primitive left jab to the jugular. All you do is act in a way that is beneath you and that damages your self-esteem, and you push the relationship towards a state of incontrovertible disaffection.

Guerrilla Mating Tactic Number 8: No name-calling

The hurts caused by name-calling linger well beyond the fight, and they can cause a deep pain that is hard to turn around. So stuff a sock in your mouth before you call someone a moronic, fat, bitchy loser.

Note: Sarcasm, bringing up old failures and name-calling are unacceptable. There are absolutely no excuses for such behaviours. If you get cruel in this way, it would be a worthy goal to devote your life to trying to stop. STOP! Do whatever you need to do to gain self-control. You simply can't say that you lose control and can't help yourself and expect that to be okay. You aren't a child. It's not okay. Get control or get therapy!

Guerrilla Mating Tactic Number 9: Don't get global

> *Andy:* I forgot the bread.
> *Ellen:* You're oblivious – you never remember anything.

> *Ellen:* Where's my chequebook?
> *Andy:* You can never find anything because you are so irresponsible.

These are 'all or nothing' statements in which you attribute what your partner did to who they are. You can only hope to feel more agitated and more anxious and make your partner feel the same way with these kinds of accusations.

Variation: You Always ... You never...

   Linda: You always promise to call and you never do.
   Tony: I got held up in traffic.
   Linda: You always have an excuse.
   Tony: That's what happened.
   Linda: You're never late for your own mother, only mine.

All you can expect when you use 'always' and 'never' is for your partner to respond to the criticism rather than to the issue itself. Always and never statements are *never* true. *Always* think twice before you use them because the only place for your partner to go is on the defensive.

Guerrilla Mating Tactic Number 10: Don't qualify an apology

Last week I was watching one of those 'confessional' programmes on the telly. Three adult daughters were on with the mother who had put them in foster care when they were teenagers. The daughters were still furious with their mother, and at the same time they deeply loved their mother. They wanted an apology from her for sending them away. The mother was unable to say she was sorry without qualifying it: 'You have to und-erstand the stress I was under,' 'You don't know what things were like for me,' 'I tried to find other ways,' 'I thought I was doing the right thing under the circumstances.' All these daughters wanted was a real apology – no excuses, no explanations, just a validation of their experience. A simple 'I'm sorry' could have been the first step in turning the relationship around, but the mother was unable to give that.

GOT ANY JACKS?

My husband, Boots, and I both have demanding schedules, but sometimes at night, before we go to bed, we play Fish. It's a mindless childhood card game. We wind down by getting silly together.

When you are fighting and you know you've made a contribution to the battle, don't make excuses. Say you're sorry – period. That's the real fighting spirit because that takes courage.

Guerrilla Mating Tactic Number 11: Give each other equal time

Jim: Your behaviour at my office party was indefensible. You actually snubbed Dr Klugman, and he is someone whom it would benefit me greatly to spend more, not less, time with.

Rena: I ... I ... I...

Jim: Moreover, when I introduced you to Mrs Klugman and she invited you to join the hospital auxiliary, you didn't even have the decency to say yes blah blah blah blah blah blah blah blah blah blah blah blah blah blah blah

Rena: I ... I ... I...

Jim: Furthermore, blah blah blah blah blah blah blah blah blah blah blah blah blah blah blah blah blah blah blah blah blah blah blah blah blah blah blah blah blah blah blah

No fight can be handled fairly unless both partners get equal time to air their complaints and feelings. If you yell for 20 minutes and then cut your partner off, his deep resentment will pay you back in the long run. So use a stopwatch if you must, but make sure both partners have equal time to air their side.

Guerrilla Mating Tactic Number 12: Be civil in voice tone and volume

If she yells and you yell and you are both comfy with that, consider sound-proofing your flat or documenting your fighting cycles in such a way that you can forewarm your neighbours. But recognize that, for many people, yelling makes issues and anger escalate. Also, if one partner yells and the other doesn't, the one who doesn't feels bullied. Not to mention the fact that the partner who is screaming starts to feel like a meany. Fighting escalates when there is asymmetry in vocal tones and volumes, when people's vocal tones don't match each other. And fights escalate when you yell. So the question to be answered is: *How can you maintain the intensity of your message without pumping up the volume?*

Guerrilla Mating Tactic Number 13: Never say, 'You're just like your mother'

> *Nina:* I needed that new dress.
> *Chris:* What do you mean you needed that dress? You need food, you need shelter. Nobody needs a dress.
> *Nina:* I want to look great at that party. I need to look nice. It's important to me to fit in.
> *Chris:* All you care about is appearances. You're just like your mother.

In-laws bear the brunt of many of a couple's frustrations. Criticizing your in-laws is a way to bash your partner, one generation removed. But in addition to criticizing your partner when you use her parents to do so, you also evoke all the ambivalent feelings about her parents that your wife struggles with on her own. Many of us have ambivalent feelings about our parents, feelings that frequently run deep and strong and are troubling to us – especially as we watch ourselves turn into them, more or less, in ways that do not always please us. So one way to escalate any fight and cause long-term hurt feelings is to break into the phrase 'You're just like your mother.' This is guaranteed to raise the stakes and to drive your partner nuts.

Guerrilla Mating Tactic Number 14: Never say, 'Yes, but'

> *Kim:* You're late.
> *May:* I said I'd be home at seven.
> *Kim:* Yes, but you said you'd call.
> *May:* I said I'd call if I was going to be later than seven.
> *Kim:* Yes, but I told you how important this night was. It's my mother's birthday. The reservations are for seven.
> *May:* So, we'll be a few minutes late.
> *Kim:* Yes, but why didn't you call? I could have let people know.
> *May:* We'll be there in 10 minutes.
> *Kim:* Yes, but you said you'd call and you didn't.

'Yes, but' makes it seem as if you are waiting for her to finish her sentence because you've already planned your rebuttal. It is experienced by the other person as if you don't hear a thing she is saying. It is a whinging, combative phrase. It is a dismissal of your partner's feelings and words, so it cuts off any empathy between the two of you.

If you're willing to break the 'yes, but' habit, it's easy to find a replacement for it. Instead of saying 'yes, but,' you'll get a lot further practising saying 'yes, and.' 'Yes, and' validates what your partner has said and adds additional information to it. 'Yes, and' is not experienced as an attack. Getting over the 'yes, but' habit takes practice. It's like when you learn a new word and suddenly you see that word in every other paragraph. Once you become aware of your 'yes, but' habit, you will hear it everywhere.

Here is what the 'Yes, and' conversation might sound like.

Kim: You're late.

May: I said I'd be home at seven.

Kim: Yes, and you said you'd call.

May: Oh. I thought I was supposed to call if I was going to be later than seven.

Kim: I thought you were going to call no matter what.

May: You did?

Kim: Yes, and this night is so important to me. It's my mother's birthday. The reservations are for seven.

May: So, we'll be a few minutes late.

Kim: Yes, and I hate to be late. They are waiting for us.

May: Do you want me to ring the restaurant, and tell them we'll be there in 10 minutes?

Kim: Yes.

May: Okay. You bring the car round, and I'll ring. I'm sorry. I think we crossed signals.

Guerrilla Mating Tactic Number 15: Never say, 'I hate you, I want a divorce'

May: I can't believe you're pulling this on me now. You're crazy.

Kim: What do you mean I'm crazy? You're vicious. You knew exactly what you were doing.

May: Goddamn it, it slipped my mind. What is the big deal? We're taking 10 minutes, we'll be 10 minutes late.

Kim: No. I'll be 10 minutes late. You stay here. I don't want you with me because I can't stand to look at your face.

May: I hate you and I want a divorce.

It almost seems as if it would go without saying that you shouldn't get vicious and cruel in a fight, you shouldn't say things that you'll be sorry for later. Sometimes, terrible things fly out of our mouths and we think we can be sorry later. We think our partner will just forget what we said in the heat of the moment, and, in the heat of the moment, 'I hate you' feels real. We are unaware of the long-term impact such words have on our partner and how easy it is to truly hurt someone in a way we will truly regret. Words such as 'I hate you, I want a divorce' linger in the mind. We don't get over them easily, even if we know they are not deeply felt. The most important thing I can say is *never underestimate your power to do real damage*.

What to Do When What You Say Only Makes It Worse

When your partner gets out of control, and you know there isn't much you can say, let your partner vent and then you can say:

> You sound so angry that I don't know how to respond, but I want us to be able to talk this through.

> You seem so hurt that I realize that whatever I say may hurt you more, and that would be bad for us.

This moves the issue of the fight from the specifics to something about the experience of the fight. It validates that you are a couple in this together.

I Feel Like I'm the One Doing All the Work

You've now read three chapters about fighting, and all of these tactics can be put immediately into use. Perhaps at this point you are saying to yourself, 'Why should I do all this work? He doesn't seem to respond anyway. I'm trying to learn new ways to improve the relationship and he's trying to figure out how he can avoid discussing anything with me ... ever.' Well, even if that's true, if you sink to his tactics the two of you are guaranteed never to make progress. Sometimes it's absolutely true that two partners in a couple make progress at different rates. You may have moved ahead of him for a while, but what you want is *not* to dump him but to help him catch up. Have faith that your partner will catch on. If he watches you doing better, he may be tempted to join you. He can't keep his current fighting style if you won't play the game anymore.

Understand Gender Differences in Anger

A puzzle and a paradox – when women get angry, men withdraw, and when men withdraw women get angry. Women also tend to prefer no yelling while men spend years practising yelling. Watch any hockey match – you'll see the players push and shove and go wild. But – and here's the rub – yelling doesn't stop men from continuing in good camaraderie. They fight, say horrible things, sometimes even smack each other – and they keep playing the game.

However, men know they shouldn't fight with women in this way. Fighting with women confuses them because they aren't supposed to get worked up, but they are used to getting worked up as they do when playing sport. Studies, particularly psychologist John Gottman's study, have shown that men are physiologically aroused by fighting more quickly than women are. Their hearts beat faster, their pulses increase. It takes longer for their heart to calm down. They stay madder longer than women. They tend to hold grudges. This is part of the reason why, during a fight, men leave the room, pace, don't make direct eye contact, walk in and out, fight from behind a door. The direct contact is too stimulating for them. Also, direct contact makes them too mad, and they know that they don't seem to control their anger as well. Men are trained from infancy to be rougher, tougher and more aggressive, and many of them stay that way. So don't be upset if your husband paces or leaves the room and comes back when you fight. He is trying to control his anger. One woman I know has a husband who stands outside the door of the room when they fight in his effort not to blow up. Don't assume that your husband is avoiding the discussion. Instead recognize that your husband's behaviour may be an attempt to control himself.

Tip: You never hear a woman say she is getting hot under the collar. Men say this, and it's true. Their body speeds up, they flush, they literally do get hot. So, if your man is mad, hand him a glass of water and tell him to drink it down. Men need more liquid when they get mad.

Men, you ought to recognize that when a woman starts screaming, it is usually her last-ditch attempt to engage you. Chances are good that she's brought up this issue a number of times and you've avoided it. Eventually, she will feel that yelling is her only vehicle for capturing your attention. Don't make her resort to that. Find some way to listen to her before she gets so worked up.

Conclusion

When you do fly off the handle, think about how what you say may haunt your relationship for years to come. Even if, in the moment, you think you won't hang around long enough to know about that, you could be wrong. You could work it out. And even if you're right and you won't be there to have to deal with it, you will still have to deal with yourself. That may be the one way in which life can feel very long.

Quick-Fix List: What to Do for a Marriage-Threatening Fight

1 Look for the hurt underneath the anger: Discuss feelings instead of issues.
2 Validate your partner's experience.
3 Watch your facial expressions.
4 Avoid the 'kitchen sink' fight.
5 Don't get hung up on the accuracy of your partner's statement.
6 Don't get sarcastic.
7 Don't bring up old failures.
8 No name-calling.
9 Don't get global.
10 Say you're sorry.
11 Give each other equal time.
12 Be symmetrical in voice tone and volume.
13 Never say 'You're just like your mother.'
14 Never say 'Yes, but...'
15 Never say 'I hate you, I want a divorce.'

nine

BEST WAYS TO CALL A TRUCE

At the end of the First World War, 32 nations large and small that had either been at war with or severed relations with Germany gathered to create the Treaty of Versailles, a peace-keeping treaty which was supposed to settle the future of 422 million people affected by the war. This peace treaty was so badly mishandled that it is considered to be a leading cause of the Second World War. First of all, the Allied leaders argued viciously among themselves and were unable to agree with each other on the terms of the treaty. Each country was out for itself and wanted something that it did not get. The premier of Italy stomped out of the negotiation sessions altogether and did not come back for months.

Promises were broken, demands escalated, what countries asked for in order to 'make up' was exorbitant. Eventually, the Allies came up with a set of humiliating 'peace' terms which they delivered to a stunned and angry German delegation, who were told that no discussion of its terms was permitted. Among the other points, the Allies demanded five billion dollars in gold from Germany. However, as negotiations continued, the Allied blockade, which prevented food and supplies from being delivered to Germany, continued as it had during the war, so while Germany was getting together the five billion dollars, its inhabitants were literally starving to death.

In the end, though the treaty was signed, though you could point to something that said that there was peace, many countries – especially Germany and Italy – left the treaty divided, infuriated, and dangerously rankled. It was only a matter of time...

The mistake made in the Treaty of Versailles was to think that the way to right the wrongs lay solely in punishing the guilty. It's true that the Germans were wrong and deserved to pay, but that wasn't an excuse to starve the German people. What was learned by the end of the Second World War is that the real purpose of a peace treaty is to make a stable peace, and you cannot make a stable peace using only the tools of humiliation and punishment. At the end of the Second World War war criminals were tried in the courts, reparations were made, but simultaneously the focus was on how to stabilize the world so this would not happen again.

The lesson to be learned is that making peace will never work if it centres solely on punishing your partner, even if your partner was wrong. Making peace is about reparations and restabilization, soothing the relationship in a way that can last, rather than clamping down on your partner such that it is only a matter of time until the Third World War.

Just as good fighting can bring a couple closer, good making up can bring a couple even closer than that. Couples ought to have a formal ritual truce period so that you can show respect for your own and your partner's anger. In an interview about anger, Margaret Mead says that most cultures have ritualistic ways of dealing with anger and other unpleasant feelings. In Zambia, when there is anger, Zambians believe that one of their ancestors' teeth has got into a person. The tooth won't come out until the entire village tells the truth. They gather to do so and cleanse the village. We too need rituals to cleanse our relationship and reconnect with each other after a fight. The formal ritual of making up is important. You both take time to acknowledge you've fought, to apologize, to connect around the healing process.

Simple makeups are lovely. Any way, anytime, anywhere you say you're sorry is cause to celebrate. But besides simply approaching your partner with an apology, there are all kinds of creative ways to say you're sorry. Following are a few tactics, but you must, you simply *must* also invent your own:

Guerrilla Mating Tactic Number 1: Play the blues

Put Albert or B.B. or Big Mama Thornton on the stereo full blast. The blues help us bear anguish and make it creative. If you got the blues, then you've got a pulse.

Variation: Sing a bluesy apology to your partner to the tune of 'Heartbreak Hotel' or 'Stormy Monday'. Example:

Heartbreak Hotel Makeup Song

Since we had that big fight,
my life has been a mess,
I want to kiss and make up
So please pull up your dress

Guerrilla Mating Tactic Number 2: Elaborate your evil ways

Don Jackson, who until his death was the director of the Mental Research Institute, came up with a way for couples to clear the air when built-up frustrations threatened the goodwill in the relationship. The couple sits face-to-face for 10 minutes and reveals to each other their evil ways. Each partner makes up a list of how she or he contributed negatively to the problems and fights in the relationship:

I nagged you about raking the lawn.
I was critical of you when you did rake the lawn.
I flirted with the waiter in the restaurant.
I own these evil ways.

Your partner reciprocates:

I didn't call you when I knew I'd be late and when I did come home I was
    drunk.
I erased an important message for you from the answering machine.
I was nasty to your mother.
I own these evil ways.

These aren't cure-alls, they are illuminations. After you've made them you can prioritize what is most important to change and work on that. Plus *it feels so great* to know that your partner acknowledges and remembers what he did that really made you nuts.

Guerrilla Mating Tactic Number 3: Find an old birthday or anniversary card

– the one you got from her where she speaks of her undying love and affection for you. Attach a note reminding her of her undying love and affection for you, and let her know things can be that great again. Send her own card back to her.

Robert saved the first card Melanie ever gave him. He crosses out her message, writes a new note, and recycles the card when times are tough. This ongoing affectionate joke between them has been a great makeup ritual.

Guerrilla Mating Tactic Number 4: E-mail your apology

Catherine was thrilled to turn on her computer and get an e-mail apology from Frank. There were 20 pages, all the same, and they all looked like this:

I'm sorry. I love you. I'm sorry. I love you. I'm sorry.
I'm sorry. I love you. I'm sorry. I love you. I'm sorry.
I'm sorry. I love you. I'm sorry. I love you. I'm sorry.
I'm sorry. I love you. I'm sorry. I love you. I'm sorry.
I'm sorry. I love you. I'm sorry. I love you. I'm sorry.
I'm sorry. I love you. I'm sorry. I love you. I'm sorry.
I'm sorry. I love you. I'm sorry. I love you. I'm sorry.
I'm sorry. I love you. I'm sorry. I love you. I'm sorry.

I've found e-mail to be a wonderful way to pass notes to my husband. We develop ongoing jokes that we pass back and forth, write lusty notes, create characters. He's a musician, so he might get an e-mail with a review from a famous jazz scholar (of course, I really wrote it) after he does an important concert. I might get a congratulary note from 'the President' after a television appearance. E-mail can make you a very creative partner.

Guerrilla Mating Tactic Number 5: Build an anger altar

After the Vietnam War, Latino veterans mourned by building an anger altar where they could express their angriest feelings. You can do something similar at home for being angry and for making up. You don't need a whole altar. The top of a chest of drawers is fine. You can leave a token of your anger on it (a sliver of a plate you threw at the wall), or you can cry there. You can kneel or stand at this altar and let out your anger and grief. More important, you can meet at this altar when you want to connect and/or make up. You can leave apology notes on this altar when you know you were in the wrong. You don't have to be religious. The altar is a place for you to leave your bad feelings so you don't carry them with you all through the house. The altar is a place to make up.

Guerrilla Mating Tactic Number 6: Dance like a monkey and say, 'Me sorry'

Remember the therapist in Chapter 7 who had his couples beginning sentences with 'Me' instead of 'I'? It's hard to stay mad when you feel ridiculous.

PET NAMES

Many couples have pet names for each other, even pet names for each other's genitals. Those who revealed these include a psychologist, a writer, a City banker, a homemaker, and a musician.

> Pot
> Goofy
> Amazonia
> Chicken bottom
> Fluffy (referring to a bad perm)
> Accordion Toes
> Shuggy Shughead
> Miss Chesty Cough
> Boobs Collucci
> Jelly head

When asked how these names came about, very few were willing to part with that information. However, they did say that the names went through many permutations.

Guerrilla Mating Tactic Number 7: Buy him something special and give it to him with an apology note

From a pair of socks to a yacht. Let your bank balance be your guide.

Guerrilla Mating Tactic Number 8: Complete five positive interactions for each nasty thing you've done

Psychologist John Gottman interviewed two thousand couples to see what they did that kept them together. He discovered that it doesn't really matter how much a couple fights; what matters is that they ultimately perform five positive interactions for every negative interaction. The ratio of bad to good is what matters most. What he discovered through taping couples was that they didn't deliberately say to themselves, 'Oh, I was an idiot. I must now do five good turns.' This was just how it happened to work out in couples who stayed together, in a consistent five-to-one pattern. Like so:

1 BAD INTERACTION
Blame him

5 POSITIVE INTERACTIONS
Buy him flowers
Say I love you
Make him cocoa
Find his lost chequebook
Clean his glasses

2 BAD INTERACTIONS
Blame him
Argue in a mean fashion

10 POSITIVE INTERACTIONS
Pop him popcorn
Give him oral sex while he eats popcorn
Massage his feet
Buy him a card
Cook his favourite meal
Fix his drill
Wax his car
Compliment him
Clean his wardrobe
Tell him he's gorgeous

You can see that if you don't learn to fight fair, you will have to quit your day job just to make up for it.

Guerrilla Mating Tactic Number 9: Do a household task she hates to do

When you say, 'Let me make it up to you,' find something she hates to do, and do it for her. Clean out the refrigerator, cook for the kids, sew a button on her shirt, give the dog a bath, water the plants (score extra if it's something you hate to do, too).

YOUR PET'S PET NAMES

Really proper people who hesitate to give each other pet names may want to start slowly by giving their pets pet names before they graduate to giving their partner pet names.

Guerrilla Mating Tactic Number 10: Start an apology conga line with a Carmen Miranda hat and fruit

You may do this in any location from the supermarket to your living room floor. You may ask others to join in. Borrow maracas or carry two pears.

Guerrilla Mating Tactic Number 11: Use hand puppets, stuffed animals, or your pet to say what it is hard for you to say yourself

Jim can have difficulty articulating his feelings sometimes, but he does a great John Wayne voice. Mary started to talk through her two stuffed animals to express difficult apologies and emotions. When I mentioned these stories to other couples, they regaled me with stories of their own.

Deborah and Steven use fictional characters from novels they've read. Olivia and Nell talk in the third person through their basset hound.

Guerrilla Mating Tactic Number 12: Go sit between his legs when he's watching television or kiss him when he wakes up and climb into his arms

Physically showing affection says you want to make up.

Guerrilla Mating Tactic Number 13: Take an emotionally cleansing bath together

A bath cleanses the body, but it can also cleanse the soul. Make it spiritual and sexy with candles, lotions, water pillows, music. Wash the bad away.

Guerrilla Mating Tactic Number 14: Take her most obnoxious relative to lunch

If you were really impossible, double penance is required. Take her whingy cousin Martha or her opinionated father Fred to lunch. She will know that you know the egregious nature of your mistakes.

Guerrilla Mating Tactic Number 15: Dance

After Boots and I invited our two newly married friends out for dinner and dancing to celebrate their marriage, we realized that we didn't know any dance steps. Boots went out and bought two videotapes called *How to Do the Fox Trot* and *How to Do the Merengue*. We began to practise. One day, after an argument, Boots signalled that he wanted to make up by putting the tape in the video recorder and asking me to dance in the middle of the living room floor. It is our number-one makeup routine. The music immediately reconnects us with our good feelings for each other.

BEYOND PET NAMES

Peter and Roberta have a secret language of almost 100 words they've made up to describe things. They try to slip the nonsensical words through when they are in public as a kind of private joke between them.

Guerrilla Mating Tactic Number 16: Make love

Not only is sex a sweet makeup, it can be especially earthy and erotic after a fight. In fact some couples fight to improve their sexual encounters. So sweep the dishes off the kitchen table, use the snooker table, drop to the lino, hop in the backseat of the car, and say you're sorry where the sun don't shine.

Guerrilla Mating Tactic Number 17: Make a peace treaty

Boots and I were fighting over money. I didn't want to share the expense of our costly New York City parking space. Boots needed to have a car for his job, but we used the car together on weekends. Our fights about money (what is joint money, what is personal money, how should the money be spent, who decides about money) were distressing. We didn't seem to be able to come up with a set of rules for our relationship that we could both live with.

Well, no matter what I knew about therapy, I couldn't be my own couples' therapist. So, at one point early in our marriage, Boots and I sought outside help from psychologist Mark Finn. When we saw Finn we were both still trying to prove that our own complaints were the justifiable

---

ones while the other's complaints were off-target. What Mark Finn did was to make a written peace treaty that honoured our different points of view. I liked his treaty so much that I wanted to pass it on to you. Here is what it said:

We Agree That:
Everybody's anger is justified and understandable.
Being mean to the other person never helps.
Attacking the other person never helps.
Blaming the other person never helps.
Validating the other and apologizing is never a defeat.
Peacemaking is never wimpish.
Being close is scary – it's the spiritual crisis of our time.
You always give more than you get.

When we thought about this treaty, we were able to think about our problem in a different way. We had dated for seven years before we got married. It was scary to have taken this step, and we weren't sure about how to join our lives or our money. When we realized that this was what we were fighting about, we were able to find compromises.

However, Mark Finn's peace treaty didn't stop there. Part of the treaty included questions we could ask ourselves when we felt pitted against each other in the future. These questions were phrased like this:

Ask Yourself:
How can I assert myself without being mean?
How can I assert myself so I can be heard?
How can I assert myself without injustice collecting?
Why am I impossible to live with?

We taped this piece of paper to the refrigerator. It helped us to remember that we each contribute both to what works and to what doesn't work in our relationship, and that we have a great future to look forward to.

Guerrilla Mating Tactic Number 18: Practise forgiveness

When you cannot forgive, the future seems troubled and dim. Peace is won not just by a cease-fire. You must also let go of the past, level the playing field, and think about your future together. This is a conscious act. Apologize. Accept your partner's apology. If it is hard for you to do so, search your heart and soul or pray or talk to a shaman or to a five-year-old who knows all about forgiveness. Do what you must. Come up with a way. Forgive. Practise.

TEAMWORK

Some couples have paired, complementary nicknames such as 'Big Bubba' and 'L'il Bubba' or 'Tank' and 'Tiny' or 'Mickey' and 'Minnie'.

Guerrilla Mating Tactic Number 19: Become an expert in how you end fights

Think back on your previous fights. Instead of recalling what you fought about or who won the fight, try to remember when, where and how you managed to end the fight. What exactly were the conditions that were present when you stopped fighting – that allowed you to stop? Once you know what it takes to end a fight, *do it*. Throw in the towel. (In fact, you may want a 'makeup towel' – an actual towel that one of you can throw to signify the end of a quarrel.) Hug him even when your arms are stiff as boards, kiss her even when your lips feel like dead weight, stop talking even if you're not finished with your side of the story. Use your expertise in how you've ended fights in the past to invent ways to make up in the future. In the words of couples therapist Michele Weiner-Davis, *you don't have to feel like doing it, you don' t have to like doing it – you just have to do it.*

Guerrilla Mating Tactic Number 20: If all else fails, QUACK

I travel frequently to promote my books. I went on a long book tour with my second book, *Guerrilla Dating Tactics*, which put me in 16 cities in 17 days without a trip home. My husband and I talked a great deal before I went about the importance of separating well, of supporting each other during this separation instead of getting angry with each other. We said a tearful good-bye at the airport, and we'd never felt closer. We were very proud of how we'd handled the separation. When I came home, however, things did not go well initially. There was a lot of yelling. We fought for days. We had talked about how to separate well, but we had forgotten to talk about how to get back together, how to reconnect well.

When we have this kind of problem to solve, we are particularly fond of finding stories that fit it – stories that don't make us look bad. It was not comfortable for either of us to think of ourselves as people who yell that much. Sometime later he found the perfect story for our trouble with separation and yelling, a story which we have held on to ever since:

The Love Ducks

> My husband reminisced one evening about his childhood friend, Hugh Churchill, who, at one point, kept two baby ducks in his backyard. The ducks were very, very young. All day, they sat cuddled with each other, one head lying on the other head, bodies touching. They were quiet and totally content in this position. But if you moved them – even as little as six inches apart – they began turning frantically in circles and quacking loudly in great distress. They could not find each other even when they were only a tiny distance away from each other. When you moved them back together, they immediately resumed the position and stopped quacking. My husband said he thought that he and I were like the love ducks – we were lost without each other.

It was then that we realized that sometimes yelling is not yelling, it's quacking. Sometimes we can be only six inches apart, but we feel so alone – so we keep quacking loudly until we find each other. These days, we try to quack when we feel like yelling, we try to quack when we need attention – if one yells, the other tries to quack back instead of yelling back. We have managed to avoid an awful lot of fights by dissolving into laughter.

When I returned from my next trip my husband hung streamers covered with pictures of love ducks in the doorway. We left them there for days to remind us to quack instead of yell.

Quick-Fix List: Best Ways to Call a Truce

STEP NUMBER 1: CLEAR THE AIR
1 Admit when you've contributed in negative ways to your relationship
2 Practise forgiveness
3 E-mail your apology
4 Become an expert in making up

STEP NUMBER 2: PAY YOUR PENANCE

1 Do a household task she hates to do
2 Complete five positive interactions for each negative interaction
3 Take her difficult relative to lunch

STEP NUMBER 3: DEVELOP APOLOGY RITUALS

1 Play the blues
2 Send an apology note reminding her of a special past moment
3 Consider what the ape doctor suggested – say 'Me sorry'
4 Try using hand puppets or stuffed animals to articulate your feelings

STEP NUMBER 4: RECONNECT

1 Make love
2 Climb into his arms or put your hand in her hand
3 Dance
4 Take an emotionally cleansing bath together

STEP NUMBER 5: REMEMBER MARK FINN'S ADVICE

Everybody's anger is justified and understandable
Being mean to the other person never helps
Attacking the other person never helps
Blaming the other person never helps
Validating the other and apologizing is never a defeat
Peacemaking is never wimpish
Being close is scary – it's the spiritual crisis of our time
You always give more than you get
Ask yourself:

How can I assert myself without being mean?
How can I assert myself so I can be heard?
How can I assert myself without injustice collecting?
Why am I impossible to live with?

Emergency Plan: If all else fails, QUACK

V

Be the Lovers You Were Meant to Be

ten

For Men and Women: Decipher the Sex and Housework Code

On a recent afternoon talk show a couple in the audience stood up to speak about their sex life. It seemed that when they were first married they'd been thrown out of several restaurants, an underground car park and a ladies' room (this was a heterosexual couple) because they could not resist fondling each other in public. Now, a few short years later, the husband was upset that they had no sex life at all. The wife protested that it wasn't true. When the talk show host asked him how often they did have sex, he replied, 'Every three months'. The wife blushed. The audience groaned. The couple sat down. If we had a pound for every couple who swore that this would never happen to them and then had it happen to them, we could lick the deficit. As an after-thought, the talk show host asked the couple why their sex life had dwindled so miserably. The wife replied that after she'd come home from work, fed the kids and cleaned up, she was too tired.

Each evening after work Grace picked up the kids, came home, tended to what needed to be done around the house, made dinner, put the kids to bed and fell into a stupor of exhaustion around 10 p.m. – just about the time that Gary felt a tingle of sexual stirring. He had tried pouring Grace a drink to put her in the mood, buying her flowers to capture her attention, renting an X-rated video (produced by women because those were the ones Grace found sexy). But nothing he seemed to do made Grace's libido lambada. Grace used to ask Gary to help her hoover, do the dishes, etc., but arguing with him about it turned into one more task of the evening, so she stopped and just carried on doing it herself. When she tried to raise the subject with Gary he was unresponsive. To him, the subject of housework felt trivial

> compared to the subject of their flagging sex life. Besides, the dirt doesn't bother him, so he considers it to be Grace's problem.

Face it. No guy sits and contemplates whether his sex life would improve if he cleaned the toilet more often, but Arlie Hochschild, author of *The Second Shift*, says that there is a greater relationship between these two things than we imagine – or at least, than men imagine. Psychologist John Gottman agrees. In his studies with over two thousand couples, he found that *women consider housework as a major issue affecting their interest in and availability for sex.*

So join me in a two-part chapter which discusses sex and housework. (I decided to put the housework section first because I knew that after you'd read the sex section, you'd be so turned on that you might not get to the housework at all.)

We'd be having a lot more sex and a lot fewer talk-show addicts if we could grasp the concept that sex and housework need to be discussed together. The way male and female psychotherapists write about sex and the way they write about housework says it all. I looked up the separate subjects of sex and of housework in over 20 self-help and psychology books by men and women. Many of the women had sections on house- work as well as sections on sex, or at least they talked about housework. However, in the books by men, housework was rarely found in the index, rarely mentioned, but sections on all aspects of sex took up pages – sexual frequency, sexual preferences, sexual problems, sexual positions. One renowned male therapist dealt with housework by saying he wished all couples could get a maid. Other male therapists don't mention it at all – as if housework wasn't a part of the struggles that couples are having today. Finally, after quite a search, I found a book by two male co-authors that had housework listed in the index. Excitedly,
I looked it up to see how they were addressing it as an issue, and I discovered that they weren't addressing it, they were mentioning it as part of a list of things couples fight about, *with no explanation, nothing but the word itself.*

Which brings us to:

Basic Truths About Men and Housework

Men and Dishes: Men soak. Pans remain in the sink for weeks on end collecting rare microscopic growths. If you ask a man why this pan has been in the sink for three weeks, he will look you in the eye with great sincerity and say, 'It's soaking.'

Men and Sight: Just as certain people have no night vision or bad peripheral vision, men have no bin vision. Even when they sit and use envelopes for basketballs and the basketballs all land on the floor because there is no room in the waste-paper bin for them, men do not see that the bin is full. This vision deficit extends to the refrigerator. A man will open the refrigerator door and yell, 'Darling, where is the mayonnaise?' when it is right in front of his face. However, a man *is* able to spot the can of lager tucked under two pounds of grapes in a brown bag.

Men and Smell: At a certain point in life men lose their sense of smell. I walk over to my husband's desk on a regular basis and find empty or half-eaten tins of tuna, slivers of salami, etc. The entire area stinks – I can smell it from the bedroom, while he cannot, even when I point it out. I soothe myself by saying, 'Better a salami than a gas leak.'

Note: This phenomenon of men losing their sense of smell only occurs *indoors*, in their own home. If you drive down the street with a man and pass a dustbin lorry, he will be the first to hold his nose.

Men and Credit: When a man does lift a finger to contribute to the maintenance of the home, he requires credit, which extends to 3.2 times the amount of time it took him to do the household task. That means if he spent five minutes dusting, you must thank him 16 times. Plus, if he empties the rubbish he will want peace and quiet for the next 6.4 hours – the recovery period is 3.2 hours per minute spent cleaning.

Men and Retirement Plans: Should you corner your man with a record of how much you do around the house, he will start yelling about how little you appreciate what he has done for your future. He will then cite retirement plans and pensions and suggest that in some ways these are more exhausting to keep up than four rooms, 1½ baths.

Later in this chapter I'll discuss ideas for a steamier sex life, but now I'd like to draw a connection between Gary's complaint and Grace's complaint; sexual frequency and housework.

Honey, I'll Feed the Kids Tonight

Is the following familiar?

It's Gary's night to cook for the kids because Grace is taking an evening class. Grace has just received the results of her exams. 'I got a C,' she mutters to herself, 'after 15 hours of study... pretty depressing.' She is in the mode of reconsidering her idea to advance her education when she walks in the door and sees an empty pizza box on the kitchen table next to a half-empty bowl of jelly. Gary has fed the kids pizza and jelly for supper. Gary has left the empty box on the table – and the entire clean-up to Grace.

Among women's complaints are men who 'help' with the housework and the kids. 'Helping' implies that it's her domain and that you are doing something out of the goodness of your heart. Women want a partner, not a helper. Psychologist Lois Braverman talks about men who agree to cook two nights a week and then feed the kids chips on their two nights, figuring that on the wife's cooking nights the kids will get the vegetables they need. This is more than a lack of respect for the wife; it's subparenting. Then there are the men who agree to do the laundry and then only do it once a month, or men who agree to tasks and then turn them into a power struggle. 'I will do it, but I will do it my way and on my timetable.' Then there are men who grumble constantly about the contributions they do make.

As far as I'm concerned, any psychotherapist who treats a couple with lack of sexual frequency or lack of sexual desire complaints and fails to take a detailed housework history along with a detailed sexual history isn't doing her job.

Note: This is not men-bashing. If the roles were reversed, I too might fight quite heartily to maintain the status quo.

Note: Lastly, if you are a man who already does housework, please let me say that, of course, I am not referring in this section to *all* men: I am only referring to my husband.

What to Do When ... You Want Change

Men, I don't ask you to take my word about this. Instead, start by taking your own sexual/housework history to see if there is a connection between the two.

FOR MEN ONLY: A SEXUAL/HOUSEWORK HISTORY

When we first met, we had sex _____ times a week.

The last time I scrubbed the toilet was _____.

When we began living together we had sex _____ times a week.

I have purchased _____ bottles of washing-up liquid in the past two years.

I would like to have sex _____ times a week.

Rotten food is regularly removed from the refrigerator by _____.

After we lived together for a year we had sex _____ times a week.

The last time I removed and washed the microwave tray was _____.

In the past three months we have had sex _____ times a week.

I clean the grill _____ times a week.

Sex is initiated by me _____ times a week – by my wife _____ a week.

Tile fungus generally builds up for _____ weeks before I notice it.

Men, the biggest turn-on might not be a lacy negligee you bought her but you changing the sheets, making the bed, fluffing the pillows and inviting her to join you under the duvet which you recently washed. A tray you've placed next to the bed containing a spray of flowers, a bottle of mineral water for dehydration, a snack just in case you're there longer than you thought – all these things can only add to her pleasure.

Clinical Impressions Regarding the Sex/Housework Connection

The anecdotal results of this questionnaire have suggested the following clinical impressions:

Men who do housework live longer: They have less conflict at home, and less household stress, feel better about their marriage/partners/ significant others.

Men who have lost their senses regain them: Men who do housework regain lost senses of vision and smell in remarkably short periods of time. They enjoy the aroma of foods and the redolence of sex more when they learn to smell the bad with the good.

Men who do housework feel more loved: Why not? They have happier wives.

Men who do housework have happier children: Since there is less resentment between husband and wife, the greatest beneficiaries after the husband and wife are the kids, who don't have to learn about teamwork from their school coach – they see it at home.

Men who do housework have partners who initiate sex: Relationships feel fair – or they don't. When women feel that their relationships are fair, they are more able to get in touch with their own rhythms of sexual desire and more inclined to act on them.

Men who do housework get promotions, win lotteries, can drink three pints a night without gaining weight, and get free season passes to all important sporting events: Okay ... I'm exaggerating a little.

Three Tactics to Turn This Around

Guerrilla Mating Tactic Number 1:
Document what needs to get done and set up a schedule

Sometimes it is hard to get each other to understand what you are already doing. This leads to the kind of chronic bickering where she says that he has no idea how overwhelmed she is and he says she has no idea of what he does around the house. This is a stupid fight, because it is the most easily solved of all household disagreements.

TABLOID NEWS

One night, before Boots and I got married, I woke up at around 3 a.m. with a terrible headache and shooting pains. We went to casualty and it turned out I had meningitis. Boots never left my bedside for five days. Each day he came in and read to me out loud from the *News of the World*. He read to me how they found the captain of the Titanic in a dinghy with his cigar still lit, he read me about Elvis sightings. He was

---

> so there for me that I learned a valuable lesson. Less than a month after I got out of the hospital, we got married.

All you have to do is make up a list of all household tasks and the frequency with which they are done. It's best if you can do this together. Stick a list on the refrigerator and the two of you can fill it out over a week or two as you do the tasks.

Then sit down with that list and take a look. Talk it through. Figure out how long the tasks take. Frequently there are contributions men make, such as maintenance of the car, recycling newspapers, etc., that go unnoticed. Note the things you both hate doing and the things you like doing. Maybe you will want to switch some of those things with each other for a spell. Maybe you will even want to switch roles completely for a week and see what that is like. It may give you knowledge you can't get in any other way, plus it may get you on a talk show.

> I actually tried switching roles for a week with Boots. He was always the one to drop me off at the door and take the car to the lock-up four streets away (even after midnight in the rain). When we switched roles, I hated doing it and had never realized what a pain in the neck it was to do it. I was glad to go back to dusting. In fact, in our documenting I discovered all sorts of things that he did that I had never considered 'housework' – taking the car for its MOT, reading the manual to learn how to programme the video. In fact, a peculiar thing just happened as I was writing this chapter. I got the flu. He went to the chemist's for me, got food in, and then went to the optician's to get the glasses fixed that I'd inadvertently stepped on. In my head I was thinking that he'd better get home soon so he could start cleaning up. I then realized that I frequently did not consider his contributions at all. When I looked for what was right about his purview of housework, there was some truth in his complaint that his tasks went unnoticed. But –

Research shows women do five times as much housework as men.

So read on.

Guerrilla Mating Tactic Number 2: Negotiate to split things up

Using SUPER negotiation skills from Chapter 6, negotiate as to how tasks will be split up. Family therapist Marianne Ault-Riche says it is better not to speak to men in terms of percentages, and my experience has proven that she is right. Whenever I say to my husband that I want things 50/50 he blows up. Then he walks around the house muttering for a few days about retirement plans. And what I realized is that it isn't percentages that set men off, it's the 'F word' (fifty) that makes them nuts because they feel their contributions are never noticed. The 50/50 is about what women notice. Men never feel as if they get the 50 per cent of anything they ever want. And, as I said earlier, they're right!

Shoot for 60/40. Things end up 60/40 at best – you give 60 per cent and you get 40 per cent. So stop using the 'F word' and if you must use a percentage, learn to live with 60/40.

Focus on your mission task by task. Get him to do the dishes one time, to hoover one time. If you get him to do a task once, there is an imprint of it in his brain, whether he wants it there or not. Getting him to do it again will be a little easier. I have known couples where, focusing on one task at a time, things ended up going from 90/10 to 60/40 in five years. That may not be fast enough, but it sure beats keeping it 90/10 and fighting about it for 50 years.

Don't scowl if he doesn't know where the hoover – or even the sink – is. Be cheery in spite of yourself.

Make men who do housework the social norm. Cultivate friendships with other couples based not on mutual interests, but solely on whether the men in those couples do housework.

For the truly desperate: *Convince your children to do housework and then mention how much faster it will go if Daddy helps them.* Do not pay your children. If you're going to pay them, you may as well get a maid. You see, men hate *being told* to do housework more than they hate house-work itself. Being told to do it makes them feel one-down. So get someone who is already three-down to ask for help. Then the man can't ever feel one-down.

Remember: One small jay cloth for men, one great step for womankind.

Guerrilla Mating Tactic Number 3: Create a Sex/Housework Saturday

Ursula had a creative idea. On Saturdays, she and her husband do housework and make love. When she told a friend the friend asked which they did first, sex or housework. Ursula laughed and said she wasn't crazy. The housework got done first. Then they showered together. Then they had sex. Ursula said this arrangement resulted in her husband moving the microwave and cleaning behind it for the first time in eight years. Moreover, her husband took over a few duties on days besides Saturday that he had never been willing to do before. The only problem was that he got an erection every time he did them.

Final Thoughts for Women

Do not expect your husband to welcome housework with open arms. It is much more fun to do less housework than it is to do more. However, according to Ms Ault-Riche's research, the more money you earn and the more evenly expenses are split, the better chance you have of more equitable house-keeping arrangements. And new research by Rosalind Barnett of Radcliffe College in the US supports this research. So, if you aren't getting any co-operation at home, *see if you can get a big pay rise at work*. Some (not all) women say this has worked for them.

Also, try to refrain from using those two little words – 'or else'. They are a challenge – fighting words. When you utter them you may as well picture yourself in a Roman amphitheatre, deciding whether your weapon will be clubs or bare hands, gazing towards the spectators with your final conscious thought, 'Look at that fat man with the wine dripping down the front of his toga.'

Last, when your man is angry with you, and you don't want to hear it, I can guarantee you that it won't be sex that he will be withholding...

Final Thoughts for Men

1 When a woman feels powerful – that she is heard and that life is fair – outside of the bedroom, it frees her to feel sexually powerful in the bedroom. If a woman does not feel powerful outside the bedroom, if the bedroom ends up as the only place she can exert power, then she'll

use her power there. But her power will be the power to deny you access to her sweet body: *You can' t separate sex from the rest of the relationship*. These are the real facts of life.

2 Even if you do all of the housework, your sex life on a week-to-week basis may never be what it was before the honeymoon was over. That was a time to treasure, a time to remember – with a consenting partner, a time to take Polaroids. None the less, when your behaviour around managing the household drudgery makes a woman feel powerless, even though she's promised herself never to do this, she may use her power in other places. Several studies have suggested that women bristle at the idea of having less sex because they don't get help with the housework, but that they know it happens: *If you make room to share the drudgery, you make more room to share the passion*.

SMOOTH OPERATOR

When Al travels for work, his and Evelyn's phone bills soar because they use separations to refine their phone sex skills. They used to talk sexy on the phone when they first met, and then gave it up. Now, six years later, Al swears that some of the best sex he's had *with* Evelyn has happened when he was in a hotel room *without* Evelyn.

---

3 While the sex you had when you first met was grand, this doesn't mean that the best of your sex life is behind you. In the next section, we'll talk about how to have more sex and how to expand upon your sexual repertoire to make the best sex something to look forward to rather than something in your past.

4 Lastly, sure, when you met you probably didn't have to do much of anything, and your sex life was great. Then, the two of you were in hormonal overdrive – isn't that part of what the honeymoon is for? What I am saying is:

There is no housework on the honeymoon. No housework is the definition of the honeymoon!

More Adventurous Sex, More Romantic Sex, More Satisfying Sex

The steps you've already taken ought to make a difference not only in frequency of sex, but more important, in the quality of sex. However, there are many additional things to know and do about your sexuality as a couple that will increase the interest and enjoyment of any sexual encounter for both of you. Here are 11 tips to get you into orbit.

Guerrilla Mating Tactic Number 1: Foreplay begins before you walk in the door

I appeared on an *Oprah* show where they sent out undercover cameras following a man who wanted to get a date. He borrowed Oprah's cocker spaniel as a conversation piece to attract women's attention. When a woman would stop to pet the dog, he would say, 'Like my dog? Want a date?' He was unsuccessful most of the time.

For men, foreplay may begin 10 minutes before intercourse. For women, it helps enormously if foreplay begins before you walk in the door that night. That does not mean that you need to fondle her breasts before you take off your coat. What it means is that you can't expect to not speak to her during the day, watch television all night, turn off the television, and then and only then turn your attention to her.

This is not a criticism of men. Men compartmentalize. They are able to watch a football match, jump up and down over a final goal, turn off the television and then get a hard-on. For men who want to make love to women, it is helpful to know that women don't work this way. We have overall experiences, though this doesn't mean we never want a quickie. It's like the old joke about men going to a mall to buy something and women going to a mall to experience the mall. For women, her partner's behaviour from the moment he walks in the door (and even earlier than that – like if you called her at work to say hi) constitutes foreplay.

On a night you want sex, think about the steps between 'Hi honey, I'm home' and turning off the 10 o'clock news to have sex. When you turn off the television, climb into bed and reach for her with no warning, she can feel more like a receptacle than the woman you love.

Here are moves you can try out that make her feel like the woman you love and with whom you want to create more sensuality. These pave the way to a logical transition of the day into a sexually charged night:

- During dinner, play footsy under the table.
- Take her wrist and kiss the inside near her pulse.
- Pull a romantic old snap out of the photo album of when you first met and leave that on the bed with a note.
- When she's drying the dishes come up behind her and kiss the back of her neck, putting your arms around her.
- Without saying a word to her, run a warm bubbly bath with a favourite-smelling potion and light candles.
- Leave the handcuffs on the bed with a satin ribbon and a note.
- Massage her with exotic oils (buy two or three and let her choose the scent she likes, or shop together for them).
- Take a shower, shave and put on cologne.
- Invite her to cuddle, telling her you want to be near her.
- Have a T-shirt made up for yourself with her photo on it and come home wearing it.
- Offer to take over child care for a weekend day and buy her a day pass to a spa.
- Give her a pedicure, complete with soaping her feet, massaging them and putting nail varnish on her toenails (you can find a book to tell you how to do it, or ask her).
- Wash her hair, brush her hair and/or condition it.
- Hold her hand.
- Hug her unexpectedly and look in her eyes.
- Surprise her with something she never expected.
- Kneel at her feet and profess your love.
- Serenade her with your trousers down.

The key is, before bedtime, don't forget to touch her, hug her, keep in contact with her during the evening.

Note: William called Ivy at work to tell her he couldn't wait to see her that night and he was making dinner. When she came home, he was serving hors d'oeuvres – in just an apron.

Please note that putting this emphasis on foreplay when you walk through the door is not a way of saying that men control a sexual encounter. Women who report the most satisfying sex are those who take responsibility for their own arousal. After all, our anatomy favours a man's orgasm over a woman's orgasm. So we women have to make sure we aren't left out in the cold.

As for men's foreplay, just because they wake up aroused and ready, just because they climb into bed at night aroused and ready, just because they turn on *Baywatch* aroused and ready, doesn't mean that men don't appreciate mental and physical foreplay. Men, glorious men, love fore-play too – especially foreplay that goes straight to their groin, hinting of pleasures to come. So, make your foreplay verbal, visual, kinaesthetic, more erotic than romantic:

- Bite him lightly on the back of the neck when he isn't expecting it.
- Drop the shoulder strap of your black, see-through bra or wear anything that drapes off the shoulder.
- Run your hands over your body as he watches.
- Tell him that instead of putting perfume behind your ears, you touched your vagina and put that scent behind your ears.
- Surprise him with a sexy video.
- Have a professional photographer take sexy shots of you in various stages of nudity and present them to your partner.
- Leave an explicit, erotic note in his briefcase telling him what he can expect when he comes home that night (do not tack on the end of the note a reminder to pick up bread on the way home from work).
- At a moment he doesn't expect it, take his hand and put it underneath your shirt.
- Make Marilyn Monroe lips, licking and pouting – being always careful not to cross the line into Miss Piggy lips.
- Shop for a few 'speciality' items from a lingerie catalogue or take one of your own old bras and cut out the fabric that covers the nipples.
- Take a pair of scissors and, while standing in front of him, cut off your underpants, snipping them off at the sides.

Whatever you do, don't assume that because men are more easily aroused, you don't have to work at your sex life.

Guerrilla Mating Tactic Number 2: Create desire

Men, don't figure that you can have a formula, such as bringing home flowers, and you will get sex. Be more creative. Don't always bring the same flowers. It sounds terrible to say it, but when you always bring the same thing, it can get boring and feel too predictable – although we'll never really tell you this. Try different types of flowers, exotic blooms, flowering plants, a little pot of herbs such as spearmint or rosemary, a delicious vanilla hand cream, a scented massage oil, a sultry lavender soap – things you like the smell of, the taste of, things you want buried in her hair, her arms. Women, bring him his favourite bottle of bourbon, rub him with almond oil, tell him stories about your own or other couples' wildest sexual encounters, unplug the phone *and* the answering machine.

JOYFUL SEXUALITY

One night George and Penny were drinking wine in bed and began pouring it on each other and licking it off. They didn't stop there. Penny started taking the cheese dip they'd been nibbling on and spreading that over George and licking that off. Soon they were breaking crackers over each other and licking those off. They made love in a messy bed to peals of laughter and erotic delight.

Men, don't forget to write a note to accompany the gift you're giving her. Women like to see your love written down, they want to save it in their pile of saved notes. Here are ideas to create desire in a note or what to hand her:

- Ask her to tell you something you shouldn't repeat.
- Call her by the pet name you have for her.
- Find a card that will have special meaning for her and in it describe her favourite sexual pleasure in detail.
- Write a line from a romantic movie she loves (*Casablanca, While You Were Sleeping, Gone with the Wind*).
- Quote a romantic poem (if you don't know one, go to a bookstore, browse the poetry section and find one).
- Buy her a book of romantic poems and inscribe it.
- Remind her of the most romantic time you had with her and tell her you still can't get it out of your head.
- Tell her that all day you couldn't stop fantasizing that you were licking her between her thighs.

Note: For Delia's birthday, Bruce went to an international bookstore and bought 12 books of romantic poems, each in a different language.

Women respond positively to the written word. That's why we buy romance novels.

Use that, capitalize on it.

Creative variations on the written word: be Henry Miller. Men like the written word, too, and since women also respond, why not pen your own erotica for each other? Think about what your partner might like to see written down. Some women prefer to have a sexy scene set. They like the sights, the smells, the feelings. Other women like the kind of erotica more preferred by men, erotica that is visual, earthy, right to the point. Find out whether your partner prefers romantic erotica or sex erotica. You don't have to make your note long, and it's not a competition. But pen a scene of your own and read it to him out loud. One of the nicest things about penning your own erotica is there don't have to be those perfect bodies that we see in videos, the ones we'll never have. You can say,

> And then Joe lifted his strong round frame, brushing his potbelly over Melinda's...

Remember that men tend to like their erotica to be explicit. If you aren't sure how to do that, take a closer look at that dirty book he has hidden in his night table drawer.

Give redeemable coupons for erotic pleasures. Is there something your partner has told you that she or he can't get enough of? Well, make up a few coupons s/he can redeem when s/he wants.
    Examples:

> This coupon entitles the bearer to 30 minutes uninterrupted oral sex. This coupon is not transferable.
>
> This coupon entitles the bearer to a hot oil massage lasting no less than one hour. RESTRICTIONS: This coupon cannot be used until after the kids are asleep.

In talking about desire, it is generally true that men have a higher sex drive than women. You may as well get used to it.

For men: Have you ever played 'The Alphabet Game'? What you do is give your partner oral sex, making sequential capital letters on her clitoris ... slowly and decisively ...A ... B ... C ... D...

Guerrilla Mating Tactic Number 3: Take a tip from the animal kingdom

First, kill all your competitors ... just kidding. In the bird kingdom females choose a male by watching who builds the best nest, who finds the best branches, the finest twigs, the most shapely bough. This is encoded in our genes. You can capitalize on biology by taking a few tips from the birds. Turn your bedroom into a love nest:

▶ Take the photos of Mom, Dad, Rover and the little darlings out of the bedroom, and put out photos of the two of you at the point where you were totally smitten with each other.
▶ Keep a drawer with lotions, vibrators, gels, magazines, erotica – *whatever the two of you find sexy.*
▶ Keep a tray where you can put chocolate-covered strawberries and water, wine ... maybe even a little Lucozade if you plan on losing a few electrolytes.

Tip: Feed her the strawberries, pour her the drink and hold the glass to her lips. Anthropological studies show that when she takes the food from your hand, she's yours.

▶ Put a lock on the bedroom door so you don't have to worry about the kids bursting in, and teach them about private time; yours and theirs.
▶ Put a tape recorder in the bedroom along with his favourite mood-heightening tapes (surprise him with a special tape he loves).
Rates high: Luther Vandross, Jeffrey Osborne, Johnny Hartman, Anita Baker, Sarah Vaughan, Antonio Carlos Jobim, Boyz 2 Men, TLC and The Ron Carter Quintet.
Rates low: Tiny Tim, Twisted Sister, Metallica, The Three Chipmunks.
Variation: You can drive him wild if you decide to tape the two of you making love (or of you masturbating) and play that back for him another time.
▶ Sprinkle the bed with rose petals. Robin tells of an occasion where he brought a dozen roses to his lover's place, filled the bathtub with warm, soapy water, pulled off all the petals and put them in the water as she watched. Nan and Johnathan tell of the time Johnathan put rose petals all over their bed and they made love on top of them.
▶ Make a bed hamper. Ask your partner what her favourite things to have in bed are and then take a picnic hamper and fill it with things

that the two of you like in bed, such as oils, food items, candles, sexy books, sex enhancers, different type of vibrators, fake fur glove, several types of lubricant, towels, hairbrush, lingerie, mineral water, wine. Make it look pretty, inviting, surprising.

The key aspect for women is that we need to feel as if we aren't an afterthought, as if you thought of us during the day, as if you thought about what might make us feel special. The key aspect for men is that they need to feel that you aren't just doing something to make them happy, but that you are deriving pleasure and feeling turned on too. So make sure that you choose things that do that for you – don't pretend – keep looking for your own sexual pleasures as you look for what pleasures him.

Guerrilla Mating Tactic Number 4: Talk in bed

As you plop your heads on the pillow, you may not realize that bed can be the only place a busy couple ever gets time alone. But here, as in other places, men and women have different ways of reconnecting after a long, hard day. Women want sex (oh ... do we ever), but they want as much talk as sex. In fact, talking makes them feel close to men, and then they want even more sex. Men's emotional life opens through sex. This is part of why men like to have sex when they are angry or feeling fragile – having sex gives them a voice to express difficult feelings. It isn't true for all of us, but generally:

> For women, talk is the way into sex.
> For men, sex is the way into talk.

So women, don't make the mistake of thinking that because men prefer sex *before* talk, men only want sex. And men, don't make the mistake of thinking that because women want talk before sex, they don't want to have sex with you. For women, talk is as much about sex as sex is about sex.

Guerrilla Mating Tactic Number 5: Talk more about sex

In addition to talking about feelings, you can move your relationship into a more satisfying sexual arena if you both talk openly and *a lot more* about sex: It's time to start talking about sex in the same way you talk about other relationship matters – through disclosure, negotiation, positive feedback, More of/Less of lists, seeking co-operation on a wish, increasing creative solutions to sexual problems, offering generosity and most of all remembering that in sex, as in other parts of the relationship, both partners will have times of feeling that they give more than they get (at least as you're working this stuff through).

As liberated as we are, talking about sex may be the last taboo. It takes practice, trust, time to get the words out. Here are six reasons to work at talking about sex today:

1 Your sexuality has probably changed a great deal since you met. You like different things done in different ways, and your partner can't read your mind about this.
2 You may not even have a clear picture of what you do like. You may only know what you don't like. If so, you've got to think about what you want sexually. If you aren't making a commitment to be thinking about it outside of the bedroom, you'll only think about what you don't want in bed, and that leaves little chance of improving things.
3 When you met, everything you did turned each other on. Today you may want to refine this to certain things that turn you on more than others.
4 If you can talk about sex without getting defensive, you've really broken through to the front line of love.
5 All sexual encounters won't be the same. Some will be more satisfying and sexy than others. If you can't talk about the times when the sex wasn't what you hoped for, you'll never know that the reason was that his back went out or she was preoccupied with something else. You risk taking something personally that was never personal.
6 Women in long-term relationships tend to become aroused more slowly than their male partners. Women need to state specifically what they need for arousal, how long they need, when he should know to move forward. If we leave men guessing in bed, we can never have the sexual relationship we want.

These are the reasons to talk. Here are seven things men and women may want to talk about:

1 What you want in bed to feel good:
   I want to be held more.
   I want you to slow down.
   I want more oral sex.
   I want to stimulate myself.
   I want to use a vibrator. Please hold me while I do.
   I want you to initiate sometimes.
   I want to have a quickie once in a while.
2 What could help you feel better about asking for what you want:
   I want to talk about what I like in bed.
   I want to practise being more direct about my sexual needs.
   I want to know you won't reject me even if you don't want to do it the way I want to do it.
   I want to know that sometimes you will be willing to have sex even when you aren't totally up for it, just to make me happy, and I don't want to feel guilty about asking for that.
3 Better ways to hear what your partner wants:
   Please tell me in detail what you like most.
   Let me try things and tell me while I'm trying what feels best.
   Show me with your own hand.
   What do I do that you'd like more of?
   What was our best sexual encounter for you and what made it best?
4 How to help your partner ask for what she wants:
   Tell me how I can make it easier for you to ask.
   Tell me how I can make it easier for you to show me.
   When you want to use a vibrator, tell me where you want me to be – should I touch you? Get behind you and hold you? Move me how you want me to hold you.
   Tell me what I do that makes it hard for you to speak openly.

5 Willingness to hear about your sexual technique without getting defensive:

I want to learn the best ways to please you with my hands, my mouth, my penis. Let's talk about that.

Tell me what I do that takes away from you being hot.

Some things I do seem to give you more pleasure than others. Do you want me to stop doing some things?

Which ones?

Am I doing _____ long enough? Should I touch harder? Softer? It excites me when I know I'm exciting you.

6 Willingness to talk about your partner's sexual technique without being critical:

I love it when you touch my balls lightly. My balls are sensitive.

Touch them like this ... lightly ... even lighter ... yes, that's perfect.

I like it best when you take as much of my cock as you can into your mouth, but I never feel comfortable because I worry that I may push too deep. I want you to show me how much you can take and still feel comfortable.

Before I'm really hot, my breasts are too sensitive to be touched. I'll move your hand to them when I'm ready.

7 Ways to praise what is going right sexually:

When you nuzzle my vagina before oral sex, it makes me feel like you want to be there. I love that.

I love the way you hold my balls when I start to orgasm. It's so intense ... I love it.

Tip: Women can be uncomfortable using a vibrator to reach orgasm with a partner. You can help by reassuring her that it's okay. One man named his wife's vibrator 'ET' because it looked like the alien in the Steven Spielberg movie. By giving the vibrator a funny, non-threatening name, he signalled his acceptance of the device to her.

The more easily and openly you can discuss sex, or better yet narrate as you are having sex, the better your sex will be. This takes time and work; it will not happen naturally. Because honeymoon sex happened naturally you may feel that devoting time now is a sign that the thrill is gone. Sex, just like love, blossoms in a relationship because people work at it. They learn each other's bodies, they explore each other's fantasies, they tell their secrets. It's a parallel process to how love deepens when the honeymoon is over. In short, if you become educated about the difference between 'first honeymoon sex' (which anyone can do) and 'multiple honeymoon sex' (the domain of those brave enough to take the risk and make the commitment), you will discover that your sex life can provide you with a glow that can light up the sky (if not a few neighbouring solar systems). Getting to multiple honeymoon sex will test your ability to tolerate discomfort (you'll have to talk about things that are hard to talk about), it will test your ability to listen, it will test your ability to be open – in other words, learning to converse about sex will make you a better person all round and bring you closer to the full range of your potential as a sexual partner.

If it's too uncomfortable, then try to talk about that. Try writing down what you want. Try discussing it with your partner's back turned towards you to make it easier for you to speak. Show him with props (vegetables, feather dusters, biscuit dough) what you want.

Guerrilla Mating Tactic Number 6: Expand beyond penis-centred sex

The difference between men's and women's styles can be reduced to the difference between men's and women's sex organs. Women's sexuality is deep, internal, mysterious. Men's sexuality is concrete, instrumental, here in your hand. Men often complain that women don't want as much sex as they do, and sometimes they go to sex therapists wanting this problem fixed. Their idea of how to fix it is centred on how to get their women to want more frequent sex – but what if the way to fix it was by making men only want sex once a week? That could fix it, too. I'm not advocating that, but I am saying that the idea of a couple's entire sex life revolving around the satisfaction of the penis is limiting. One way to get more sex and take some of the pressure off yourself for having to have the perfect erection is to put your penis on the back burner – er ... let me rephrase that ... to broaden your expression of your sexuality.

Sexuality is a complex system, and to keep it thrilling you have to move in a long-term relationship beyond sex to the realm of eroticism. Sex is for procreation. Eroticism is pleasure for its own sake, fulfilment in the act of giving and accepting. Sometimes men who have more frequent desire to have sex get in the habit of trying to outperform themselves or get in the habit of thinking that each stirring should be satisfied:

Lionel could have three orgasms in one sexual encounter. Because he had done this when he was in his teens, he felt he had to keep trying to go that long when he was in his thirties. Sex became an Olympic event.

When Barry and Sue were dating, Sue was willing to have sex any time Barry got an erection. Two years into the marriage, Barry still expected Sue to drop what she was doing to have sex with him. But Sue no longer felt that she could be that available to Barry.

To broaden your sexuality so that it includes more than penis-centred sex, you can try many things. Besides simply masturbating more to manage your sex drive, you may even, once in a while, masturbate before sex so that in some sexual encounters your focus will be less centred on getting off and more centred on connecting emotionally with your partner. Other ways of increasing your repertoire include experimenting with ways to increase your partner's desire that don't include your penis. This again could mean massage, romance, ways of developing more sexual self-control on your part. In addition, you may want to see what happens if you start avoiding things that excessively stimulate your desire, such as certain movies and magazines. Some men purposefully stimulate themselves frequently – which is fine, unless it leaves you chronically frustrated because of your partner's differing desire. Also, men and women need to understand differences in desire and not perceive lower desire as a lack of love. Last, take up an activity outside of the bedroom where you can divert some of your sexual energy.

LET'S EAT IN

Susie and Jim have created a sexual take-away menu. The choices include:
- oral sex
- sexual fantasies
- romantic dinner
- sex in an unconventional place
- sexual position

They leave it on the bed with their choices ticked when one of them is in the mood.

Think about trying sexual encounters that are less frequent and 'storing up your goods'. Think about sexual encounters with lips, hands, entire evenings in which the penis isn't part of the big story. Find out where your other erogenous zones are. Check out that spot behind her knees and inside her wrist. Practise self-control. Don't have a single idea of what sex should be like. Think of sex as many different ways of interacting intimately.

Note: At the same time this is going on, the partner with lower desire must realize that, for a long-term relationship to last, there must be times when she has sex because her partner wants sex – even if she's not in the mood. Consideration goes both ways.

One of the benefits of expanding beyond penis-centred sex is that as we age the penis may need more time for arousal, more direct stimulation for arousal; having many other ways of making love increases sexuality and the potential for sexual encounters. Good sex comes from expanding your ideas about sexuality rather than narrowing them.

Guerrilla Sex Tactic Number 7: Get an erotic education

Almost any man can put a penis in a vagina and reach orgasm. And this is a fine thing to do. But why not bone up on (sorry, I can't help it) all the other ways to do the fine thing to do? Since people have been having sex for centuries, there may be quite a bit you don't know. Go to the sex section in the book shop as well as the sex and marriage section. Wear a red wig, sunglasses and Groucho Marx nose if you're the shy type. Buy books on ancient Asian sex and Indian sex practices, enhancing sex and marriage books, books that offer sound advice – and pictures. Read the table of contents and learn to tell the gems from the rip-offs. Learn more about your body and your partner's body. Find where others have elicited great pleasure. Bring these books into the bedroom. Better yet, bring your partner to the book shop to choose with you. Tell your partner that you want to learn more about what pleases her and turns her on now (this may be different from what pleased her and turned her on when you met). Talk with each other, experiment, make lovemaking your greatest creative act. You may even want to consider taking a trek to the local sex shop, set on the outskirts of town. The only thing you need to plan in advance is what you'll say to your cousin Ruth when you run into her there.

Erotic Toy Catalogues. These are places that discreetly offer catalogues (for a small fee), and they won't sell your names. You may write or order by phone.

Sexy Videos. The Lovers' Guide series and others produce sensitive, erotic videos where partners actually seem to love each other and where women's needs are just as important as the men's.

Guerrilla Mating Tactic Number 8: Take your eroticism to a deep, intimate place

Once you learn ways you can feel loved and safe with each other, take your eroticism to a deeper level. Try different locales, times of the day, lengths of lovemaking sessions. Use mirrors, watch each other. Build stamina, trust, and then go for the gusto:

Try having an orgasm while you are looking in your partner's eyes.

Now *that's* intimate.

Guerrilla Mating Tactic Number 9: Give sexual homework

Both of you should write your best sexual fantasies down as homework assignments, independently of each other. What would an ideal sexual encounter be? What would you wear? Where would you be? Who would make the first move and what would that be? What would you be listening to for background noise? Write down your fantasies and agree to share them. See where that takes you. Write down role-plays you'd like to try out too. Assign books, films ... anything that can give each other a picture of what you each really want from sex. Then take turns. One night it's her fantasy, one night it's yours. See what you learn about each other from these fantasies and what you learn about yourself. Never be critical of a partner's fantasy. It takes courage for a reluctant partner to share such stuff.

Note: Men, who feel daily that they must be strong and in charge, often have sexual fantasies of being weak and bossed around. Their behaviour in the bedroom can be in direct opposition to their behaviour in the boardroom.

FROM HERE TO ETERNITY

On a romantic Mexican holiday, Joe and Evelyn decided to live out their fantasy of making love on the beach. They waited until after five in the morning before they walked along the shore a mile or so, dropped to the sand, and began to passionately devour each other. They never noticed when the sun came up, but suddenly they heard a noise that brought them back to earth. They turned round and discovered that, unbeknownst to them, they were only 50 feet from a small seaside town. Several residents of the town had lined up to watch Joe and Evelyn. One or two had even set up deck chairs.

Guerrilla Mating Tactic Number 10: Honour your partner's sexuality

Men and women's sexuality is different and needs to be honoured and celebrated in different ways. It is quite silly to assume that men value women less because men get hot like a flamethrower. For men, sexual urges are E-mailed to their penis – in a nanosecond. Urges are strong, with desire for immediate copulation, immediate gratification. That's the way men are built, and isn't it great to have the ability to procreate in the Ice Age with your back end freezing, and later in other tight spaces, backseats, against corridor walls, on rickety chaise lounges with a broken fence while the neighbours barbecue next door. Men are fearless about risky edifices, inclement weather and wacky encounters. Yes, as I said, it's the way they're built.

And it is equally silly to jump to the conclusion that women are sexually withholding because they get hot like a slow cooker with a slow, tender, roiling triumph of unexpected oils and flavours. Yes, sometimes women are just like men – we have all known our share of getting sand in our deepest orifices on the beach, getting caught by the university porter while we struggled through how to do it without getting the stick shift of a '78 Mini embedded in our back, or casually heading towards the airplane loo one moment after he has casually headed for the same place. Overall, however, women's sexual urges are a delicate combination of biology, temperament, surroundings, sense of where the relationship is as a whole and so on. Our gift is that we can absorb everything that is going on and relay the messages to our vaginas – deep, internal, mysterious. We are hottest when we have the time, energy and romance that makes that slow cooker bubble.

Male or female, you are not being asked always to have sex the way your partner wants to have sex. You are simply being asked to respect and honour these differences in each other. When he feels angry or fragile, he may want sex. When she feels angry or fragile, sex may be the last thing on her mind.

So start asking how you can hear the other's sexuality in a way that does not leave you feeling diminished. What I mean is that if he comes at you sexually at a time when you can't even imagine wanting sex, you might be wise not to think about what you would do if you were in his shoes, but rather to think about what it's like for a flamethrower. Don't judge him. At the same time, if you approach her with vigour and she wants to put on the music, asks you to take a shower and slow it all down, you might be wise not to assume she's trying to make your life difficult. Don't judge her. Don't use individual sexual styles as weapons to hurt each other. And never ever say, 'HOW CAN YOU THINK OF SEX AT A TIME LIKE THIS?' But do talk about it. There's probably a good reason.

Guerrilla Mating Tactic Number 11: Build mutual fascination

The biggest stone in the way of long-term sexuality is its predictability. Many of the mysteries feel gone (although having orgasms looking into each other's eyes rarely becomes boring). So make a decision to nurture mutual fascination and unpredictability between you. The only way to do this is to develop yourself as an individual and as part of a couple so you can bring new things to the relationship. So:

- *Have periodic separations.* Spend a weekend at the home of friends, take a class, do something that keeps you apart long enough for the absence to make the heart grow fonder and short enough to keep you from responding anxiously to too much separation.
- *Find something new together.* Discover a project that gives you both pleasure and that you begin equally together. It can be cross-country skiing, hiking, bird watching, antiquing, line dancing. Get sweaty together.
- *Do the best you can with packaging your body.* Sounds simple, but exercise your body to keep limber and healthy. Try a little lingerie

even if you aren't wild about the shape you're in – after all, he knows the shape you're in, so why not accentuate your assets with something sexy? And don't wear that T-shirt you spilled strawberry jam on to bed!

▶ *Keep sweet at both ends.* Get regular dental cleanings. Wash your genitals before sex. Nothing is a bigger deterrent than unpleasant odours from both those places (unless you are Napoleon, who asked Josephine not to bathe for two weeks before he saw her). Spontaneous sex is great, but sometimes no surprise is the best surprise. PS Clean your fingernails, too.

▶ *Be unpredictable.* The bad news is that the better couples get along, the more brotherly/sisterly they can get when it comes to sex. You have to work to keep the edge. Plan trips away, skip work, go in late to work, go to a motel with a double showerhead, buy a massage showerhead, work at thinking how to bring novelty to your sex life.

Note: Guys, one thing you might try, if you are constantly chasing her for sex, is to think about trying something new. She expects to be chased, so stop chasing her. You may get more sex merely by stopping your trying to get it. Make yourself less available, sleep late, go to bed after she does. Turn the struggle around and soon she could be chasing you. It will take a few weeks. If weeks go by and she hasn't even seemed to notice that you aren't chasing, go back to chasing.

Last Words

Get over the idea that since sex on the honeymoon was great, something must be wrong now because sex is not as exciting. Good sex is acquired, learned, worked for. One well-known sex therapist says couples don't have really good sex until they hit 50. This is how many years it takes to appreciate and hone your sexuality. Don't shortchange yourself. Put the same energy into your sex life that you put into other aspects of your relationship.

Working on your relationship as a whole will help your sex life, and the tactics in this chapter should give you the extra ideas and help. There are many books on sex that offer 300 pages of ideas and positions. So try those. Keep talking. Keep breathing heavy. Don't forget feathers, ice, edible sex gels, lubricants and your beat-up copy of the *Kama Sutra*. Remember, the better your relationship works as a whole, the more work you will have to do to stay or to get sexually outrageous. And, in case you need something to aspire to because you aren't sure what sexually outrageous really is:

> Lisa and Jeff were living in New York City at the time that Dino De Laurentiis was making the movie King Kong. The body parts of Kong were separated and stored nightly in lower Manhattan. They were kept outdoors under tarpaulin to protect them from bad weather. On impulse, Lisa and Jeff took a late-night subway ride to where Kong was kept. They climbed under the tarp and Jeff boosted Lisa up into the gorilla's eight-foot hand. With much effort, he scrambled up after her. There, they made the most passionate love of their lives.

You may never wake up pulling small tufts of fur out of your hair, but apply yourself to this chapter's ideas to come up with a few fast-breathing, slow-moving surprises of your own.

Quick-Fix List: Sex and Housework

HOUSEWORK: A SIX-TACTIC PLAN FOR MAKING HIM (AND HER) INDOORS HAPPY

1 Document what needs to get done and set up a schedule.
2 Negotiate to split things up.
3 Pull your weight without complaint.
4 Create a Sex/Housework Saturday.
5 Keep up with your tasks in a reasonable manner.
6 *Remember:* When you make room to share the drudgery, you make room to share the passion...

SEX: AN ELEVEN-TACTIC PLAN FOR MAKING EACH OTHER HAPPY

1 Remember that foreplay begins before you walk in the door.
2 Create desire with creative gifts.
3 Take a tip from the animal kingdom: Make a sexy nest.
4 Talk in bed: Use some of that time to talk about feelings.
5 Talk more about sex.
6 Expand beyond penis-centred sex: Think of all the ways you can make love.
7 Get an erotic education.
8 Try having an orgasm while you are looking in your partner's eyes...
9 Give sexual homework.
10 Honour your partner's sexuality.
11 Build mutual fascination.

eleven

NINE WAYS TO GET (MOST OF) WHAT YOU WANT AND AVOID (MOST OF) YOUR FRUSTRATION

> Grace and Gary, after much arguing, discussing and soul-searching,
> set up a regimen for getting the housework done. The last person
> out of the bed would make it, the first person up would make coffee,
> Grace took care of the bathroom and kitchen, Gary took care of the
> hoovering, etc. It ended up not totally equitable but vastly improved.
> The problem is that Grace is never happy with how Gary makes the
> bed. He doesn't seem to care where the pillows are thrown – plus his
> hoovering leaves much to be desired. And, when he does the laundry,
> he rolls the socks before he puts them away, which pulls them out of
> shape. Gary doesn't care deeply about the elastic around the socks,
> and this upsets Grace. Poor Grace is too busy checking up on Gary
> to enjoy the lessening of her household responsibilities. Instead of
> getting a pedicure or discovering a cure for heart disease, Grace
> spends her time stewing over the way Gary folds the socks.

One of the sad truths of life is that you can convince your partner to
do something you've always wanted him to do, only to discover that
it doesn't make you feel any better about the relationship. It all boils
down to the theme of control: *When you convince your partner to take on
something new, whether it be housework, doing the taxes, teaching your
daughter how to drive, you must then give up controlling the task
yourself.*

Grace did a good job of convincing Gary that she expected more from
him as a partner. She thought when she accomplished that she'd be
happy. She didn't know that her job in fact had two parts:

Part I: Convincing your partner to change
Part II: Giving up the control you had over things when you did them

You'll have a hard time enjoying success unless you accomplish both parts of this task. Grace has not yet been successful because although she wants Gary to pulls his weight, she wants Gary to pull *his* weight *her* way. This is a tug of war, and they may as well use one of her stretched-out socks for a rope.

Gender Bender

Women almost always make the space at home, choose the decor, the wallpaper. Women have a feeling about a home, what it should look like – how home should feel when they are in it. The stereotype of a bachelor pad is a place with plenty of beer, a card table, and little else. After months, the sheets go on strike and walk off the bed in disgust. Certainly, many men are great cooks and great housekeepers, but men tend not to care about the details the way that women do. One highly respected sports editor acknowledged that comic Paula Poundstone is right when she says that left to their own devices most men would live 'like bears with furniture'.

Note: Walk into almost any couple's bedroom. How often do you get the feeling that he picked out the duvet?

Home Is a Woman's Space

Recently, I decided to buy new dishes. I chose yellow. I told my husband before I bought them. He said, 'Are they masculine?' Then he told me he felt that there wasn't enough 'masculinity' in the house. For most men, it's a woman's space they're coming into. Often a man has to fight for a place to put his tools, the old chair he loves so much, that silly poster he still keeps. Women send the men off to the garage or the garden shed and tell them *that* is their space. The woman tends to feel that the home is her domain, her responsibility, her pride. And she wants it to look a certain way – *a way which may not have much of the man in it.*

The more strongly she feels about how the home should look and what it means if it doesn't look that way, the more out of control she can feel when she sees how her partner, left to his own devices, takes care of it. I remember staying one weekend with my aunt and uncle who, after 35 years, have one of the best marriages I've seen. My uncle made the bed, and within 10 minutes my aunt remade it. I find myself frequently caught between what she did, my urge to complain to my husband to do a better job, and my resentment that I'm spending my time doing this instead of getting a pedicure or discovering a cure for heart disease.

TO ABSENT FRIENDS

Tony and Elaine had lots of out-of-town guests because their tiny flat was right by the ocean. They found they were fighting all summer because of all the disruption in their lives. When it came time to get a new settee, they decided *not to buy* a sofa bed. Now their relatives stay in a hotel, and Tony and Elaine rest easy.

How to Reclaim Your Power in the Household

If there is one thing I've learned from my own life, it is that nothing is too small to have a power struggle over. And, whenever there is a significant change in the power structure, whether it is for better or for worse, there are struggles that go with it. During times of stress, power struggles escalate – people feel out of control as something new is happening, and the balance shifts. Once Gary had the power to refuse to do his share around the house – now he has the power to not put on a top sheet, the power to stack the dishwasher in a different way. And in considering all his power, Grace has forgotten her own power. Grace has the power to learn all the ways the dishwasher can work besides her way. Grace has the power to go upstairs and play with the kids and let Gary muddle through his tasks on his timetable even if it takes him two hours to do what Grace formerly got done in 10 minutes. She has the power to let Gary be Gary and do things Gary's way even if that seems inefficient to her. Here are tactics for Grace to reclaim her power and for you to reclaim your power in this matter:

Guerrilla Mating Tactic Number 1: Let him grumble

So what if Gary grumbles over the housework? Grace has done plenty of grumbling over housework. Does she expect him not to grumble? Just as Gary has the power to complain about what he's doing, Grace has the power to say, 'You're right. It's no fun at all. Thanks.' Grace needs to let Gary complain. The more comfortable she gets with letting him complain, the less she will feel provoked when he does it. She may even decide to complain for him before he gets the chance. When she sees him open the dishwasher, she can say, 'Thanks. It's such endless drudgery, isn't it?'

Guerrilla Mating Tactic Number 2: Give ample positive feedback

Praise his efforts, praise his accomplishments, praise his trying. Let him know you notice he is working at it. Let him know when he does a good job. The more positive reinforcement and validation you give, the more motivated he will be to keep trying. Award him a silver star for his contribution.

Note: I'll never forget a story I heard many years ago, long before I became an author or psychotherapist. Ed, a man who worked in a shop I used to go to, left his wife of 23 years. I asked someone in the shop what had happened. They told me that the kitchen taps needed replacing so Ed installed new ones. It took him hours, he cut his finger, and finally he got it right. Proudly, he called his wife in to look and she said, 'You left the box on the counter and a mess in the sink.' That day he packed and left.

Guerrilla Mating Tactic Number 3: Accept that things will be less than perfect

Become more comfortable with things being less than perfect. You can't have it both ways. Although it is reasonable to set some standard, you cannot insist that the bed be made your way. If you hover over your partner insisting that he is not doing a good enough job, if you keep a checklist of his housekeeping shortcomings, you are not likely to get far. He will never, ever care as much as you care about housekeeping, and he will never, ever put as much into it as you do.

Note: So keep this in mind when you make purchases. If your bed has a complicated duvet where the pattern needs to be just right, if you buy a brown rug that needs to be hoovered almost daily, then your home is not husband-friendly.

You could also do some tasks together, so you can give the task the finishing touches you want.

This little piece of advice, 'Accept that things will be less than perfect,' applies to more than the hoovering – it applies, excuse my grandiosity, to your entire life. In fact, you can fill in the blanks:

Accept that your _____ will be less than perfect.

first marriage	pregnancy
second marriage	career
third marriage	in-laws
judgement about relationships	state of mind
children	bottle of vintage wine
sex life	Christmas and all other
health	major holidays
body – even if you work out daily	visits home from the kids
teeth	_____
partner	_____
family reunion	_____

I know I've left many important imperfect things out of this list, so I've included extra spaces for you to fill in as you live your life. Any time you hit a major disappointment or big slump, turn to this page and fill it in.

POSITIVE SELF-IMAGE

Selma was a physically plain woman and her husband, Sammy, was gorgeous. Every morning Selma would get out of bed in her pyjamas, stand in front of the full-length mirror in her bedroom, put her hands on her hips, look into the mirror and say, 'Sammy, you're the luckiest man in the world, and I'm the most beautiful woman in the world.'

Guerrilla Mating Tactic Number 4: Make requests instead of complaints

If you want him to do tasks differently, then frame your request as a request instead of as a complaint. Instead of saying 'You never put the glasses in the dishwasher right,' say, 'Please put the glasses on the top row.' Give positive feedback when he does it. Repeat if necessary. Then go back and read the 'Let him grumble' section.

Tip: Your choice of words is key. Never say, 'Would you mind...?' or 'Can I ask you to...?' Most of us have a sarcastic streak. If you use these phrases, he will tell you he does mind.

Guerrilla Mating Tactic Number 5: Accept that men and women have different standards for the home

There are times when I am deep into writing a book when only the minimum gets done around my house. I slack off, so my husband does too. Invariably, during one of those weeks we'll need a plumber or some friend will drop by. My husband doesn't blink an eye when someone enters our home, which has magazines and clothes scattered all over the living room floor. He doesn't pick anything up – such a thought never ever crosses his mind. Meanwhile, I feel shame. My heart pounds. I run around trying to hide things. I apologize to a plumber whom I have never seen before: *I am fused with my home. When it's a mess, I am the mess. To my husband,* the mess *is the mess.*

He follows the philosophy of my renegade late Great Aunt Irene, who lived much like the Collyer brothers (two men who saved every newspaper they ever read until they were piled floor to ceiling) and said, 'If you want to drop by and see me, you are welcome at any time, but if you want to drop by and see my house, make an appointment.'

You will never get him to know the shame you feel. If you take on the battle of trying to get him to feel as you feel, care as you care, clean as you clean, you divert your energy to a fruitless quest. Whether it's his nature or his nurture doesn't matter. The important question to ask yourself is: *What would you be doing with that energy if it wasn't all going to him?*

Guerrilla Mating Tactic Number 6: Have patience

After my husband and I agreed mutually (although he swears I give orders and we never agreed mutually on this) that the last one out of bed makes it, I had to remind him – and then he just threw the duvet on and did a messy job. I clamped my tongue between my teeth. Days later I made the request that he put the pillows neatly on the bed. He grumbled. I smiled a friendly, empathic smile, not to be confused with my sarcastic, hostile smile. He put the pillows neatly on the bed.

I am not talking here about men who purposely try to sabotage their tasks, although there may always be a little 'testing' from him. I am talking about real embedded differences in the way men and women see this. You must have patience.

If you are valiantly changing the status quo, expect to know the moment in the life of the mountaineer facing Everest. It won't be easy, but you'll do just fine.

Guerrilla Mating Tactic Number 7: Don't give up.

I do not advocate being in constant conflict about this, but I also do not advocate giving up. Be realistic. Expect conflict and resistance – especially if your previous housekeeping arrangement was very different from what you want now:

> When Donna and Nick moved in together, they never had a discussion about how the housework would be managed. Neither one can say why when it would seem so logical for them to have done so, but the honeymoon makes you think that housework will never be an issue. For the first year or so, Donna took over as she had done in the past – it took a long time before she was able to clarify for herself and communicate to Nick that she wanted a new deal. It took a long time after that for them to be able to have a civil conversation about it.

As long as you keep yelling about housework, nothing has to change. The yelling can stand in for change. When you think about fighting, think about fighting 'for' something, rather than just fighting. Keep your goal in mind. Keep at it. Things do get better.

Guerrilla Mating Tactic Number 8: Be ready to change course midstream – don't overreact

Update on My Duvet: After one month of 'working with my husband' about the duvet, after repeated requests for him to put his heart and soul into making the bed, he turned to me calmly on 15 May, 1995, and soberly announced, 'I'm not Bed Man.' 'What?' I asked. He repeated his words, and he said he would not make the bed even if he was the last one out. After having spent three years working on a book about relationships, however, I knew something that I did not know four years previously: *There was a way out of this one*. I chose not to blow up or overreact. Instead I turned to him cheerily and said, 'Okay, what will you do instead?' He thought deeply for a minute and replied in a profound manner, 'I'll be Dish Man.'

And he is. I haven't washed more than 10 dishes since that day. If you find that your arrangements aren't working out, ask your partner *what he'd like to do instead* of what he is doing (or not doing).

Guerrilla Mating Tactic Number 9: Create comic rituals

You will not survive this without your sense of humour. So hold on tight to your skewed vision of the world. All couples need to enter a playful state around chronically difficult material. Next time you feel irritated, go for the laugh instead of the tears.

The Ritual Passing of the Olympic Mop Ceremony: Gather family members to see this event, which takes place once every four years. Put grape leaves in your hair, run once around the kitchen holding the eternal cigarette lighter and the mop. Ask your husband to go where no man has gone, and pass the mop to him.

Naked Dusting à la Marvin Gaye: Last weekend Boots and I were housecleaning (it's taken me six years to accomplish this, so hang in there) and something didn't feel right. We were both crabby. Suddenly, he turned on the stereo and the sounds of 'I Heard It Through the Grapevine' filled the flat. We continued to clean, meeting every 10 minutes in the living room for 30 seconds of bump dancing, and, in higher-tension moments, 30 seconds of slam dancing. Always play loud music when you clean the house. It will get you through. PS: Being naked is not required, but it helps.

As I told this story to others, I heard about a wondrous variety that had never even crossed my mind. These items included:

> Tile Regrouting à la Nathan Lane (*Guys and Dolls*)
> Semi-nude dishwashing *avec* Garth Brooks
> The Annie Lennox annual packing away of summer clothes
> The Hootie and the Blowfish scouring of barbecue tools

The Pant Hat Promenade: As you are cleaning, it is inevitable that you will discover a partner's underwear and socks in small feral piles. Place said pants over your head and promenade through the house. You may substitute a clean pair if you cannot bear to wear the dirty pair.

Offer Unforgettable Sexual Delights: You have the ultimate gift in your hands: sexual satisfaction. He will be more inclined to try to give you what you want around the kitchen, living room and lavatory if you give more to him in the bedroom. Men connect through sex. They feel most vulnerable, closest to their emotional lives in the bedroom. So help him feel close to you, to connect, to want to be there for you by being generous with your sexuality. Then hand him the Jif and put him to work.

What If You Don't Feel Any Better

Sometimes, your partner will take over more chores, make an effort and, although not enthusiastically, he will begin to contribute to the daily upkeep of the home in a more equal manner – *but you don't feel any better.* You are still angry, still frustrated and nothing he does feels right. If this happens, consider the possibility that something else is going on here – that what you thought was wrong may be wrong but something else is wrong, too. When this happens, go back to Chapters 4 and 5 and reread. They may point you in the direction of issues that may be at the root of this problem. The chances are that something unrelated to laundry and dishwashing is going on for you. You owe it to yourself and to your relationship to try to figure out what it is.

Conclusion

Men want a home too – that safe place to come to, that feeling of warmth. Home conjures up many of the same good feelings for him as it does for you, as long as he can feel part of it.

Quick-Fix List:
How to Get What You Want and Avoid Frustration

CAN YOU...?

Accept that things will be less than perfect

Let him grumble

Give ample positive feedback

Make requests instead of complaints

Accept that men and women have different standards for the home

Have patience

Be ready to change course midstream and not overreact

Create comic rituals

Keep at it and not give up

twelve

COUPLES: WHY THE BEST IS YET TO COME

Rachel and Charles used to play seven-card stud before bed in order to wind down – usually with one-eyed jacks and suicide kings wild. Then Rachel developed a list of winning hands and wild cards, particular to her unique mind. In February, she wanted the king and queen of hearts to be wild. Then one night she got upset because she thought that a six-card straight (which she was holding) should beat a full house (which Charles was holding), except if the six-card straight has a wild card in it. 'You can't reinvent the rules of poker just to suit your mood,' Charles said sternly as he told Rachel to find another poker partner if she was going to be so fussy.

Mark rings Patty at the office. Patty kicks off a shoe and launches into a discussion of the reason she was sure he'd rung – today is her birthday. 'Well,' Mark pipes in after two minutes, 'I just wanted to say happy birthday – gotta run.' He hangs up, leaving a semi-stunned Patty trying to figure out why his phone call felt more like a slap in the face than a thoughtful gesture. How can he ring to say hello and then not even want to have a proper conversation?

Danielle has waited patiently for Guy to come home from work so she can tell him that she's just found out that tomorrow she has her annual review – she's nervous. Guy sits with her on the couch and starts to channel-surf with the remote control as she speaks. 'Guy, I really need your attention,' Danielle says. 'You have my attention,' Guy replies as the cable box clicks 42 … 43 … 44 … 45 … 46 … 47 … 48 … 49…

Tara and Martin were both feeling pretty sexy after watching the Playboy Channel for an hour. Martin jumped into bed. But where was Tara? She was lighting candles. Then she reappeared with a bottle of massage oil, and told Martin that she wanted a full body massage before sex. Martin, with an image of a particular bunny belly-dancing across his scrotum, was uncertain as to whether he could complete such a massage without exploding. Why does Tara have to create all these exotic conditions as a preamble to sex?

We are all TDT or ODT. To find out which you are and what that means, take this short quiz:

When I come home from a long day at work, I
A Reach for my partner
B Reach for an electronic device

When we fight, I
A Think about how it makes me feel
B Think about what I should do

My favourite adult indoor game is:
A Barbie meets Ken, then deeply tanned cabana boy
B Barbie offers Ken oral sex

My favourite child outdoor game is:
A Hopscotch
B King of the castle

When I played this game as a child, after I had my turn I
A Gave someone else a turn
B Took another turn

If it is suggested that another might want a turn, I
A Step aside
B Debate the philosophy of turn-taking

If I do give another a turn at king of the castle, I
A Empathize with the difficulties of ruling
B Offer harsh tips on how to rule

If you answered mostly a's, you are an ODT, or an Oestrogen-Driven Thinker: *There is a certain amount of empathy in all your interactions.* If you answered mostly b's, you are a TDT, a Testosterone-Driven Thinker: *There is a certain amount of one-upmanship in all your interactions.*

Just in case you landed on earth with the crew of *3rd Rock from the Sun*, we earthlings are divided into two sexes which are socialized differently. Women (the ones with milk) tend to be socialized to be ODT, placing a high value on talking about feelings, sharing secrets, making decisions by consensus. Men (the ones with ... oh, never mind) tend to be socialized to be TDT, placing a high value on winning, staying on top and keeping a strong front. These two styles can complement each other, if you keep in mind that it can mean different things to a man and a woman to be:

Available to each other
Interested in each other
Open to each other
Understanding of their effect on each other
Connected with each other
Safe with each other

When a woman longs to feel safe, she asks a man to sit with her for a long time and hear her deepest feelings. When a man longs to feel safe, he rewires the smoke detector. When a woman wants to show interest, she'll ask him about his day. When a man wants to show interest, he'll initiate sex. When a woman feels anxious, she'll talk. When a man feels anxious, he'll channel-surf. Whether it's in the DNA or whether it's all learned behaviours, no place more than in our journey to be lovers for life do we walk the thin blue line of gender.

Take a Look at How We Got Here

When I was growing up I loved watching old war movies. I guess that's why I end up using the motif of the soldier in all his paradoxical ideology. There was something simultaneously terrifying, heroic and romantic about the scraggly band of marines facing hostile beaches, the enemy dug into the sand. The sergeant, a grim-faced man, would turn to his few remaining men and say, 'We gotta take that hill.' One man would reply, 'But Sarge, I'm only a cook. Besides, there are 100 of them and only seven of us.' Suddenly the seven men would realize the enormity of their task and the sacred need to succeed and win the war. And they would do it. Maybe when it was over, I'd flip the channel and catch the end of *The Titanic*. Every man over the age of 13 was asked to go down with the ship – bravely, without fussing – singing.

It's growing up with exactly that kind of expectation of what it means to be a man that causes men to numb out and lose contact with their feelings. Knowing that your life is what you may be asked to sacrifice, who wouldn't want feelings like a tap – feelings that can be switched off at will?

Put a group of women at the battle scene, and we'd be fighting a lot fewer wars – and that would be a good thing. Women are as brave as men, yet we would figure out another way. (My husband says women are kidding themselves if we think that women would fight fewer wars, pointing to Margaret Thatcher and Golda Meir.) We don't need to be heroes in that way. But we have a culture that thrives on that kind of hero, and that kind of hero is a man.

That kind of thinking about love and pride and heroes follows men and women into relationships. Women think about what they must do to hold on to love, while men tend to think about what they must do to hold on to pride, to heroism.

Note: What do you think about the story of the *Titanic* today? Do you still think the saying 'women and children first' (not even 'children and women' first) makes sense? Should it be primary caretakers and children first? And, on the night you two are going to the Christmas Ball and the tyre goes flat, and it's freezing, and you're in a gown and he's in a tux, who gets out to change the tyre in the freezing, drizzling cold? Do you really think he feels the cold less than you do?

Be Respectful of Gender Differences

This is a short chapter, as all I really want to say is that the point of relationships is not to get men to be more like women or vice versa, not to blame men and women for acting like ... er ... men and women, but to think about ways to be a couple fully aware and fully engaged around differences: *Use your differences to bring you closer to each other* rather than trying to get closer by dissolving differences. Figure out how to move towards your differences rather than away from them.

Maybe you will channel-surf along with him, maybe he will sit and witness your feelings in the way you'd like or maybe you will take turns.

Each couple will find a different way to join with each other and respect what makes them different, but here are some ways to begin to move in that direction:

Accept Basic Differences

At the risk of a terrible pun, maybe you can see his rewiring the smoke detector as an attempt to connect rather than an attempt to disconnect. Maybe he can see your desire to talk as an *invitation* rather than a *demand*.

Look at Intentions

She can look at his intention in rewiring the smoke detector when she really needed to talk, instead of being captured by what she thinks he isn't doing. He can look at her intention when she asks him about his day instead of focusing on that question as yet another demand.

THE GREATEST GIFT

On one cross-country trip, my husband, Boots, met my Great Aunt Irene, who lived in Arizona. She adored my husband because she said he reminded her of her own father, who had been dead for 42 years. A few years later my aunt was dying, and I made plans to visit her. She asked if my husband would come because it would be like seeing her father again. She said she wanted to lay her head on his shoulder like she used to do with her father when she was a little girl. My husband said he would come, even though he'd only met her that once. He climbed into her hospital bed with her and let her rest her head on his shoulder.

Check TDT and ODT Levels
When You Feel Provoked or Alienated

When you feel your spine stiffening up, do a quick gender check and you may avoid a problem. This is my story:

> One morning my husband told me that if I waited 20 minutes he and I could travel to work together and be together for another half hour that day. Even though I was in a bit of a rush, I decided to wait. His interest in 'togetherness' was too appealing to pass up. Imagine how I felt when I got into the driver's seat and he immediately pulled out the newspaper. I said, 'You said we could go to work together.' From behind the *Guardian* he patted my leg and replied, 'We are together.'

If I hadn't done a gender check, this might have made me sit pouting through the entire journey, in addition to feeling angry, hurt and confused. Because I did my gender check, I only sat through the entire journey pouting.

Think of Your Relationship as a New Infant

You can view your relationship as an infant that hasn't been around as long as the two of you have, so it requires much care and attention. Maybe you can think in terms of how to care for the relationship. What does a relationship need to thrive?

Ask Each Other for Help in Understanding Gender

She can ask him how she can express a desire to talk in a way that doesn't feel like a demand. He can ask what he might do that would help her see his doing as connection rather than distance. What could he do that might help her feel like they are more connected? Maybe there needs to be a way of expressing when you feel connected or disconnected. Maybe you need to come up with a phrase or signal that expresses that so your partner knows.

Do you have such a phrase or signal between the two of you already? Can you come up with one helpful thing that can be done or said when one partner feels disconnected?

Don't Try to 'Solve' Differences

Elie Wiesel said, 'A mystery that has no words ought to be transmitted as a mystery.' Maybe we could celebrate the strength of a mystery, the strengths of each gender. Here are just a few gender strengths to celebrate:

WOMEN	MEN
Taking in everything at once	Focusing on one thing at a time
Tenacity in holding on to relationship	Tenacity in protecting the family
Ability to discuss things	Ability to fix things
Ability to emote deep feelings	Ability to bench-press heavy objects
Nurturing	Removing dead animals

It would seem that any relationship could benefit from this enormous repertoire – but let me add a note of caution:

Acknowledging gender does not mean using gender to let your partner – or yourself – off the hook.

Although there are gender differences, they should not be used to accept the unacceptable such as in 'Oh, he doesn't communicate because he's a guy' or 'Oh, she's got PMS – that's why she's angry.' Gender differences are something that we can twitch over, something we can create cartoon strips about, something we can rue, but they are never something we can use to write off vital issues of our responsibility to each other. They are never something we can use to dehumanize each other (he's a caveman, she's a bitch). They are never something we can use to pigeonhole each other.

Thoughts for Men and Women

The more we can move in and out of the gender roles in our culture, the more interesting our relationships will be. The siren, the anchor, the sister, the nurturer, the daddy – loving relationships allow us to try on many hats that help, enhance, tickle, soothe each other's lives and our own. And it's not likely that we'll ever really get away from gender stereotyping. Just look at a cinema marquee. Clint Eastwood, Jim Carrey, Holly Hunter. And, here's something I've wondered about: if you think of a film script, a set of circumstances, you know what Clint Eastwood would do, you know what Jim Carrey would do. However, you probably don't know what the late Jessica Tandy or the much-alive Holly Hunter would do. Female film roles tend not to have sequels. I guess *Driving Ms Daisy* and *The Electric Piano* never made it off the drawing board.

Television makes up for this dearth with an abundance of predictable, stereotypical, beloved women's roles. Look at *Terry and June* or *Till Death Us Do Part*.

What Does It Mean to Be a Woman or a Man?

We're in a time of transition – a time of re-evaluating what it means to be a woman, what it means to be a man. The roles of men and women have never offered greater possibilities than they do at this very moment. We can laugh at Alf and Else but we don't have to be them. Men and women have never worked harder than they do now at stepping out of stereotypical roles. But transition rarely happens without a struggle as we redefine what we've taken for granted.

As you two define or redefine your relationship, there will be a struggle. The reason to keep going is that having a large repertoire of roles and behaviours will take you towards a stronger bond, greater rewards in every part of your relationship. You will reach a point where your relationship goes beyond co-operation and becomes live energy between two people.

The next chapter will define what you need to do to get there and stay there. Meanwhile, remember this is new territory. Go slowly. Try to protect each other. Look at the possibilities, rather than the limitations, of making this trip as a unit.

VI

GUERRILLA MATING TACTICS: MAKE YOUR RELATIONSHIP A MASTERPIECE

thirteen

The Front Line of Love: Victory for Both Sides

Have courage – get in formation – take heart – eat a good meal and make all the phone calls you need to make because this chapter will require your full attention. It's time to use Guerrilla Mating Tactics to push yourself forward to the front line of love. The front line of love is where you relinquish your armamentarium, drop your defences, face your partner, end the struggle *against* each other, join forces *with* each other and revel in a mutual victory. Yes, the manoeuvres you've mastered, the obstacle courses you've run, the gender jungle you trekked through were all leading you here – to a victory for *both* sides.

This victory for both sides means you will be taking a leap that's higher than any Baryshnikovian spiral into space, further than Evel Knievel's hurdle over a stack of 36 lorries, wider than Kierkegaard's leap of faith, loftier than Maria Callas's high C:

> Take the leap to looking at yourself and your partner as part of something that is bigger than either of you individually.

To do so, you will need new eyes for seeing a problem, new ears for hearing a problem, new skills for tackling a problem and new words for describing a problem: *Problems once defined as your partner's are now seen in a way that includes a vision of your impact on them.*

You proceed carefully:

▶ You aren't falling in and taking over a problem and redefining it as yours.
▶ You aren't falling in to 'help' him with 'his' problem.

The front line of love requires a perceptual shift, not an offer of aid.

It works like this:

Stage I: The Honeymoon: *We Are One*. Here, a couple shares one mind. When you say 'we' it is with the belief that differences between you are insignificant and won't matter to either of you.

Stage II: The Honeymoon Is Over: *We Are Two*. The couple separates into a 'you' and an 'I' pitted against each other. They think in terms of what is good for them as individuals. Is this the right relationship for me? Is he the right person for me?

Stage III: The Front Line of Love: *We Are Three*. Here, the 'you' and 'I' are transcended for the 'we'. It is not the Stage I 'we' where they feel lost in each other. In Stage III, the 'you' exists, the 'I' exists, and the 'we' is a third entity which exists. Here, you balance your actions based on what is good for you while you simultaneously holding an awareness of what is good for the 'we' the relationship – this is the front line of love.

On the front line, you change your posture within the relationship from the 'I' to the 'we' – from the individual position to the couple's position, from 'his' problems to 'our' problems. By no longer opposing each other, by facing each other on the front line and joining forces, the two of you gain a victory for both sides.

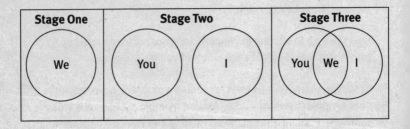

Caution: Tread carefully, because doing this doesn't mean that your relationship is all smooth sailing. We are human, we are full of surprises (thank goodness), and one surprise that shouldn't be surprising is:

Men and women assimilate the idea of 'we' differently.

A woman is more attuned to a shift in feelings, more sensitive to changes in her inner world. She wants to *feel* differently about the relationship. She makes an internal shift from the 'I' to the 'we'. She talks differently about the relationship, now saying, 'How can we solve this problem, how can we have a better conversation about it?'

Men assimilate the idea of 'we' with an external shift. Men tend to *do* something. Men think, 'What can I *do* now to feel more like a couple? What can I do to co-operate? How can I show by doing that I'm in a new place? What can I do right now, this minute, when I've got to do something?'

So, if a woman is responding to change in talking and feeling about what it means to be 'we' while a man is responding to change in what he does to be 'we' you can see that women may not feel that men are working at it, and men may feel that women aren't working at all. All this at a time when we are both working at it.

Keep working at it. Here are just some of the benefits you will reap after your thinking shifts from what is good for you as an individual to what is good for you as a couple.

The Top 10 Benefits of 'We'

10 Heals old hurts: A lot of the anxiety in a relationship comes from fear of separation and abandonment. When you talk in terms of 'we' both you and your partner feel more secure, less likely to be abandoned, less like abandoning. Childhood ghosts of being left begin to dissolve.

9 Builds confidence and vitality: When you know the two of you are struggling for the good of the relationship, you feel more motivated to stay with issues. You feel much more confident in the face of a problem. Because you feel more confident, you feel more energized. Conflicts in the relationship no longer deplete you, but instead they promote creativity and spirit.

8 Strengthens the relationship: There are many couples who view marriage as an 'institution' worth saving and work at marriage on that basis. In truth, it ought to be the 'relationship' that feels worth saving. When you think in terms of 'we' your investment is in each other rather than in the institution of marriage. Thus the connection with your partner feels more loving and more real.

7 Elevates empathy: You can truly see your partner's point of view. When she disagrees with you about an important matter, you look at what makes sense about what she has said, rather than what is wrong with what she has said. Because there is more empathy it is easier to have an open expression of difficult issues without being afraid that the talk will disintegrate into a blame-filled fight.

VISITS TO AND FROM RELATIVES

Meera and Adam found that visits to their out-of-town relatives were the source of their biggest fights. The relatives argued over who would get the most time with them, and they felt overwhelmed. So they made a pact with each other to decide in advance exactly how many hours they would spend with the family. They also decided to stay in a motel rather than staying at their relatives' homes so they could have private time to unwind. Since they both knew exactly how long they were staying, tensions eased. They were even able to enjoy their families more.

---

6 **Empowers the couple:** You become a strong couple, able to tackle more, to handle closeness and conflict, to handle the good times and the bad times equally well. It's easy to stick by each other during good times. It's great to know that you are a strong couple during tough times too.

5 **Stretches you as an individual:** Your behaviour feels more honestly connected to your feelings, so the range of your capacity to enjoy yourself and your partner increases. You don't repress your reactions to unpleasant situations, you work them out.

4 **Increases altruism:** Since you feel more empowered as a person, you have more goodwill, more capacity for kindness. You see the benefits of thinking in terms of the good of the relationship. That does not mean you ignore your needs. Rather, you are able to enjoy a more complex inner life, attain a higher level of self-fulfilment, where you feel most yourself and most fulfilled when the needs of the couple are met.

3 **Ends the impasse of a tired issue:** Couples tend to have the same whingy fights over the same whingy issues over and over again. These fights lessen when you understand what it means to be 'we' because you are then able to negotiate solutions. From time to time, you may want to have that same old fight just to prove you can still be as out of control as the next fellow, but overall you'll be doing less fighting and more problem-solving.

---

2 **Promotes relationship growth:** A relationship grows just as an individual grows. It becomes more complex, able to tolerate and understand more, able to function better in the world. Your relationship will grow as it teaches you how to savour and enhance the many ways in which you can relate to another person.

1 **Leads to endless, richer honeymoons:** You gain a new and deeper respect for your partner based on who she really is and not on your fantasy of her. Thus, feelings of romance and love deepen and are enduring. A new appreciation of the person you fell for is born. You fall in love with her over and over again. You have honeymoon after honeymoon after honeymoon.

Note: Countless studies have shown that couples who refer to themselves as 'we' – we had a problem, we wanted this for ourselves, we tried that – these couples do better, stay together, make love last. Speaking, thinking and acting as a 'we' is not just a nice idea, it's essential to intimacy – the key to a deeper and more satisfying relationship. You enter new territory, stretch out to explore new feelings, discover new aspects of yourself if you want to keep your relationship fresh and moving.

On the front line of love, we face the essential questions of lasting love as our point of view shifts and we develop a whole new set of questions to consider:

▶ If you thought in terms of 'we' in addition to the 'I' what would you do differently?
▶ How might it change how you feel about decisions you make?
▶ How can you engage in a way such that women do not feel unheard and men do not feel shamed?

You start to see love as something that evolves. You will understand people who have been married for a long time and tell you that their love has grown. You will know what they mean as you move towards a higher, more adaptive way of loving where:

▶ You move towards your partner without the fear of being either rejected by or swallowed up by your partner.
▶ You initiate contact without the resentment that you have to be the one to initiate to get it.
▶ You improve communication without feeling rancour.

- You deal with your expectations of the relationship instead of projecting them onto your partner.
- You show more caring by modifying your blaming behaviours.
- You show an ongoing capacity to respond to and to have impact, a give and take.

On the front line of love you find meaning for yourself as part of a team.

Here are four examples of the front line in action, since actions speak louder than words:

Frontline Situation Number 1

Rick's mother rings too often. What did they have for dinner? Did she forget to tell Mandy that Rick likes Romano cheese and not Parmesan? When will she have another grandchild? Eventually Mandy automatically hands the phone to Rick. Now it is Rick who is always answering the phone. No phone call lasts less than 15 minutes. The calls come at dinner, early Sunday morning – intrusive times, intrusive calls. Mandy fumes. Why can't Rick handle his mother?

The Situation: A third person intrudes on your life.

The Foxhole: Mandy blames Rick for not telling his mother to ring them less. Of course, Mandy isn't sure how to handle Rick's mother either, but she isn't *her* mother. She says,

> You have to tell your mother not to call so much.
> It's your mother, it's your problem.
> Who is more important to you, your mother or me?
> We don't have a normal life.
> Widdle Wickie want to talk to Mummy?

The Front Line: Mandy joins Rick to solve this problem. Rather than the problem being identified as Rick's refusal to stand up to his mother (Rick's problem), a problem where Rick needs to stand up to his mother (Mandy's solution), the problem would be reframed as a problem between the couple, Rick and Mandy. Mandy would stick with the problem and say:

How can we talk to each other about this without fighting?
How can we talk to your mother about this?
Should we talk to your mother?
What do we say to her, if we decide to talk with her about this?
Which of us should handle this?

Can you see how different the problem looks, feels, sounds, seems? Can you see how the problem can join two people instead of dividing them? The real problem was that Rick and Mandy hadn't found a way to talk openly to each other about an intrusive relative. They pitted themselves against each other instead of working together to solve a problem. When they are no longer pitted against each other, they can co-create multiple solutions for the problem. For example, they can screen calls, or turn the thing off completely if necessary – eventually Rick's mother may get the message and know what times of day they answer the phone and when they do not. Or, Mandy can coach Rick through a heart-to-heart talk with his mum, and even though he may feel it won't make his mum completely happy, he'll still have more courage about doing it. Or, Rick and Mandy can decide Mandy should take his mum out to lunch and talk with her about it. Or, Rick and Mandy can decide to talk to his mum together. Or, they can convince his dad to take his mum on a world cruise so they can have time off. Or, Rick and Mandy can enlist Rick's siblings to take turns taking calls. Or, they can encourage Rick's mum to visit the garden centre on Sundays so she'll be busy Sunday mornings. What matters is that Rick and Mandy stick together as they find out what works. And the big surprise for them is that, if they stick together, it won't matter as much if nothing works! When the phone rings early on a Sunday morning, they'll be able to offer each other a sad-sack smile and say, 'Whose turn is it?'

Frontline Situation Number 2

> James purchased a used car from his friend Bill that turned out to be a lemon. First the carburettor went, then the steering, then the brakes. Aisha blames James for getting them into a mess. If he'd only listened to her and not bought from a friend, none of this would be happening. The car sits in a heap on the drive and does not run. And James and Aisha don't seem to be getting anywhere either.

The Situation: You aren't happy with a decision your partner has made.

The Foxhole: Aisha blames James for the lemon. James feels awful. Of course it's true that James picked the car. Aisha felt that James knew more about this so it made sense to let him do it, but now she's saying:

> Call your friend right now.
> Why didn't you listen to me when I told you this was a mistake?
> You aren't holding up your half of the relationship if you can't make a lousy phone call.

The Front Line: Aisha would see her contribution to the problem and her impact on the outcome. She delegated all the power to James and then she didn't like how he used it. She didn't want to be bothered with looking for a car, for thinking about how to choose one. On the front line of love, instead of blaming James, she would join him in how to handle this lemon on their drive. After all, they are both stuck and it could have happened to anyone. Aisha and James would both move from an individual stance to a couple's stance about the car. Aisha might say:

- This is a mess. Now what do we do?
- It looks like we need to contact Bill and tell him what is happening. It's awkward, so let's talk about how to do it and who should do it.
- What are our options? What should we say to Bill? What if Bill doesn't want to do anything?

Aisha and James might go to see Bill together or invite Bill over and figure out what to do. Or, since James handled buying the car, they may decide that Aisha should handle the aftermath. Meanwhile, Aisha and James need to figure out how to get through a legitimate crisis without feeling demoralized. There will be other crises, and when a couple respectfully faces each other on the front line, they can join together, avoiding some crises and bouncing back from the rest.

Frontline Situation Number 3

> Ron gets a call at his office to tell him that Little Betty's not handling playgroup well at all. She wets. She won't play with other kids. She can't throw the ball. Ron is in shock and he calls Tanya, his wife. 'Little Betty is having trouble at playgroup, did you know that?' he bellows. 'Why aren't you making sure she adjusts to it?' 'Why don't you come home in time to play with her?' Tanya snaps back.

The Situation: Someone the two of you love has problems.

The Foxhole: Ron and Tanya are so wrapped up in their struggle to prove who failed Little Betty that they don't have anything left over to help Little Betty tackle the problem. Ron blames Tanya for not watching over Little Betty carefully enough (as if that is Tanya's job) and Tanya blames Ron for working so late. For Little Betty's part, her playgroup antics may be her effort to keep her parents involved with her so they will fight less with each other. Now that plan has backfired. She has no chance of getting into a private nursery, let alone the public school her parents have chosen for her and her parents have one more reason to have a go at each other.

> ### SICKNESS
>
> Sharon gets bad stomach aches and it helps her to take a hot bath to ease the pain. Her husband, Clyde, sits on the edge of the tub the whole time, even if it's after midnight. She says she feels so loved, so safe with him there.

Ron and Tanya feel such failures that blaming each other seems like the only way out. But in blaming Ron, Tanya is saying she feels powerless to help Little Betty, and Ron is saying he feels the same way. So blaming is not a way out, it's a way to feel even worse. They say:

> You're her mother. You should help her.
> You're her father. You're better equipped to teach her how to throw a ball.
> You weren't a good mother.
> You weren't even there. You're not a good father.

The Front Line: Ron and Tanya would team up to explore solutions – how to deal with Little Betty and her playgroup problems would become their joint issue:

▶ We're upset that Little Betty isn't behaving. It makes us feel bad about ourselves – as if we've failed Little Betty.
▶ Little Betty needs more attention. How can we set up a schedule for spending time with her and practising correct behaviour with her?
▶ What is a schedule that we can stick to, that works for both of us?
▶ We have to talk to Little Betty about this, so what is our best approach?
▶ What should we do if Little Betty gives us backchat? How do we handle that?
▶ Maybe Little Betty is just going through a phase.

Ron and Tanya want to help Little Betty, but as long as they blame each other, they express their belief that they can't. When they join forces, they may decide to change their priorities. Ron may get home earlier and coach Little Betty. Ron and Tanya may set up a schedule for spending more time with Little Betty. They may even sit down with their daughter and ask *her* how she sees the problem and what she thinks might help.

Frontline Situation Number 4

Selena was working in a retail store and it was Christmastime, so her boss was making Selena's days longer and longer. She kept insisting that Selena do more overtime. George, Selena's husband, was alone six nights a week. He eats alone after he's put their three girls to sleep. Goodness knows, George and Selena need the money. He's been made redundant. But George is upset. He can't look for a job because Selena can never watch the kids because Selena is never home because Selena has a job.

The Situation: Work has a negative impact on the relationship.

The Foxhole: George blames Selena for not being able to work out something with her boss. If Selena were home, even one afternoon a week, he'd be able to look for work. Selena blames George for being ungrateful. After all, who is working the 12 hour days ... who has the corns to prove it? Resentment builds on both parts as each feels frustrated, hurt, undervalued.

> It's your fault that you work this late. Why don't you talk to your boss? If you had guts, you'd talk to your boss.
> It's your fault that I have to work this late. If you had a job, I could come home earlier.
> It's your fault my dinner is cold. You have no appreciation for what I do for this family.

The Front Line: Selena and George would agree that they have a complicated problem, not easily solved. The complexity of their problem would be acknowledged. Rather than seeing this as a problem of Selena's fear to talk with her boss or George's frustration, they would see this as an awful situation they are both caught in which is putting additional pressure on both of them. This is such a difficult place for them to be.

And the question is: How can they help each other through it?

▶ Maybe we could afford a baby-sitter to watch the kids a couple of afternoons. Maybe a relative could do it. Whom can we ask to help us out here?

▶ If I have to talk to my boss, what do I say? We need to practise, because the very idea makes me nervous. What if my boss won't listen? What do we do if I talk to my boss and the worst happens?

▶ How can we make caring for the three kids easier for George? Where can he get a break?

▶ What can we do when we are together, given how exhausted we both are? How can we give each other a boost and be there for each other?

▶ How can we handle this frustration without taking it out on each other?

▶ How can we figure a way out of this mess?

George and Selena need to enlist each other to solve real problems. As long as they blame each other, however, real solutions cannot occur. When they are able to step to the front line, it means they have moved to a place where they can accept the differentness in how the problem is seen. They can approach the problem with a special regard for the 'we' that frames actions of the 'I'. They show an ongoing consideration of the quality of relating:

How you handle the problem is as important as the problem itself.

Perhaps Selena and George will go together to her dad, who is retired, and ask him to help out with the baby-sitting. Or, Selena and George will talk to a neighbour who is in the same boat, and George and the neighbour can help out each other. Or, George will coach Selena through a conversation with her boss until she feels more confident of her ability to speak up for herself. Or they will investigate using a childminder one day a week. George and Selena will find ways to care for the relationship without short-changing themselves.

More About the Front Line

Now that you have a picture of what the front line looks like, you need to know more about how to apply it to your relationship. Here are five tactics to get started:

Guerrilla Mating Tactic Number 1: Develop a couple's conscience

At around age nine or ten you knew without anyone telling you that it was wrong to punch Billy, steal sweets, cheat on a test. Sure, you still did those things from time to time anyway, just so as not to put the priests out of business, but you knew it was wrong to do them. The way you learned they were wrong was, you got in trouble when you did them. After you got in trouble enough times, you began to stop yourself from the behaviour. Do the same thing as an adult. Blaming gets you into trouble. Start to learn from your mistakes. A couple needs a conscience and you have to teach yourself, remind yourself, train yourself to grow one.

NINE-YEAR-OLD CONSCIENCE	ADULT CONSCIENCE
Punching won't make me popular.	Relationship problems belong to both of us and should be handled together.
Stealing is wrong.	I will study my individual impact on a problem.
Change dirty underwear.	Our problems aren't my fault or her fault, even if it seems to be so on the surface. There is a larger root system, like that of

a tree. I respect the complexity
of a problem. I can handle the
relationship with care as the
problem is explored.

You can see that the adult couple's conscience is more sophisticated than
the nine-year-old conscience. Meanwhile, if you can begin to integrate
these ideas, your point of view about the relationship will shift.

Guerrilla Mating Tactic Number 2: Understand process versus product

The path you walk, how you get there and the way you relate is as
important, if not more important, than the destination. How you travel
matters. How you travel is the idea of process, your destination is the idea
of product. Think of it as taking a holiday. It is not that you are going to
lie by the ocean in Lanzarote that matters most. It is how you choose
Lanzarote, how you pick the dates to go, how you compromise on what
hotel to stay in, how you decide to spend your days there, what you
decide to take, what you decide to leave, how you agree to get there. The
interaction between you, the process that got the two of you to Lanzarote
is as important as being there. In fact, you see the highest value in how
you relate to each other, *how you work at something together*.

When you take a look at what an awful time many couples have when
they do go on holiday, you can understand this more clearly. Maria and
Jack choose a destination, but never work together to plan the holiday,
how it will happen, who will do what to get ready, how they will relax,
what they will do if one of them gets ill while they're there. One of the
biggest problems couples have comes from planning destinations and
not holidays, *from desiring goals without thinking about how the goals
will be met*. It reminds me of a phrase I heard about a couple who got
divorced. The woman who told me the story said, 'They spent one year
planning the wedding and no time planning the marriage.'

Helen and Carl find family gatherings have always been a source of conflict. Now, after one such occasion, they both write down the five best things about it and the five worst things. They put their lists in a drawer. One month before the next gathering, they take the lists out, read them, go over them, plan to avoid the mistakes they made and appreciate the things that went right.

Guerrilla Mating Tactic Number 3: If necessary, take the first steps alone

For the relationship to work, it must be mutual. You both have to engage in the shift from the 'I' to the 'we'. But you can start things off and set an example. You can be aware of thinking in terms of 'we' before your partner starts to do it. Remember, as the one who bought the book, you are already first to take a step towards wanting to change things; you didn't buy the book so you could stew in your problems, you didn't buy the book so you could name your problems, you bought the book because you want things to be better. You may be more motivated than your partner at the moment. So you'll start things rolling, even if you've done a lot of that already. And you can start things off by starting to talk about problems using the voice of 'we' and encouraging your partner, by changes in you, to see the benefits of the front line without ever listing them – by showing him through your actions, rather than lecturing him with your words.

Note: Please do not start writing me letters suggesting that I am inviting co-dependence, my least favourite label in the world. The front line of love is not to be confused with co-dependence. In co-dependence your edges are blurred, muddled with the edges of your partner. You aren't sure where you end and your partner starts so you take responsibility for the other person's behaviour and blame yourself for it. You believe that if you can love enough you can solve the problem, and if she loves you enough she will solve the problem for you. The problems, the suffering, the blur are the interstitial tissue of the couple – connecting them like Siamese twins. You relieve your partner of responsibility and decision-making capacities by deciding that your partner's fate is out of her hands, it's in your hands. co-dependence is about one person's rescue effort. It is a stance of one individual rescuing the other individual. In co-dependence, the process of the couple is tied to the problem. On the front line, the process of the couple is the solution. The front line is the effort of the couple to join forces and find solutions. Co-dependent connections are based on the 'pain exchange'. In addition, I am not talking about confusion where you hold yourself responsible for her extramarital affair or his substance abuse. The front line is a willingness to look at your impact on the problem, not a willingness to merge with your partner and take over your partner's problems.

Guerrilla Mating Tactic Number 4: Get beyond blame

If you still think blame helps a relationship in any way, take this short quiz.

HAS BLAME HELPED SOLVE ANY OF OUR PROBLEMS?

Answer True or False:

T F   When I tell my partner that something is her fault, she is appreciative that I noticed.

T F   In our relationship, the one who is blamed takes immediate action on this information and fixes the problem. Things improve.

T F   My partner and I generally agree on who should take the blame.

T F   Knowing whom to blame has filled our relationship with funny stories to tell.

T F   The more we blame the closer we get. Our relationship has deepened with blame.

I've never seen anyone answer true to even one of these questions. It's easy to get caught in a contest of who failed whom because, if it's not your fault, you don't have to do anything. You can sit back, yell 'fix it, fix it' like a child, and wait for your partner to come through. You can stamp your feet and be righteously indignant if your partner doesn't accept the blame. You can blurt out the sorry situation to others and obtain great sympathy.

Blame, rather than a way of disengaging ourselves from the problem, is a way of saying: I'm a failure. I can't conceive of any contribution I could make to working this out. I'm not capable. I am incapable because of you.

Yes, nothing frustrates us more than someone who doesn't take responsibility for his or her behaviour, but blaming him won't get him to change that. **Rest assured! Blaming will not lead to his one day slapping his forehead with his hand, accepting your point of view and saying, 'What an idiot I've been. You're right. Of course, it's my fault.'**

When your partner acts like he has nothing to do with the problem, and you respond by trying harder to prove your point, you will only discover that there is no unpleasant destination that can't be intensified and escalated with blame. No matter what your partner has done, no matter how egregious his sin, no matter how justified you are: *When you resort to blame, you make your partner sound reasonable and you make yourself sound awful.*

For example, when Harry and Sally fight, Harry habitually resorts to blame: 'You did this, you did that, you said that...' Harry's blame-filled manner makes him sound whinging and out of control. The fact is that Harry often has good reasons to be angry with Sally, but you can't hear them because his blame-filled ways of relating injustice are such a turn off. Sally, who calmly defends herself, starts to look reasonable – even dignified – while Harry behaves like a loose cannon hurling assaults. By behaving this way, Harry inadvertently shifts the emphasis from what Sally did to his blaming behaviour. In other words, he takes his legitimate complaint and uses it to make himself look bad. Meanwhile, Sally gets away with murder.

Blame is a way of letting your partner off the hook.

MULTIPLE HONEYMOONS

Krista and Dennis have had 17 honeymoons – with each other. By calling their holidays 'honeymoons' they say they feel more romantic and sexual towards each other. Plus, when they make hotel and restaurant reservations stating that they are on their honeymoon, they often get a glass of wine, a single rose, a better room, or a choice from the pudding trolley – compliments of the house.

Guerrilla Mating Tactic Number 5: Work at it

Major changes in the evolution of human beings took thousands of years, and I know you don't want to wait that long. You need patience, but you also need actively to work at it. You will know you've joined forces on the front line when you can have a conversation about something you were previously unable to get anywhere with – when you can see multiple roots where you once saw blame. You will appreciate how the two of you work together to arrive at decisions, even if you aren't always happy with what those decisions are. It won't be this way all the time, but you will know what this feeling is and that it is what you are striving for.

As you learned in Chapter 2, when you invoke change in your relationship, your partner may not go along without a fight. She may still be captured by blame while you are ready, willing and able to move forward. In fact, a change in your style may initially feel threatening to her. She may feel that you are less engaged, less concerned, that you are pulling away instead of moving towards.

Instead of blaming her for blaming you, instead of blaming her for lagging behind, think about how you can help her to catch up. One way is by trying to be consistent in your stance, speaking in the 'we", instead of the 'you'. One way is to allow her to move more slowly, to let her lag behind without freaking out or becoming a self-righteous moralist ('I'm the better person'). The reality is that, as you move towards the front line you need to allow a minimum of three months for your partner to join you. Here's what she'll probably be saying to herself:

> Month One: What change? There's no change.
> Month Two: He doesn't love me. This is scary.
> Month Three: This is interesting. I'm curious about these new
> developments.

If you can operate from the front line and leave room for your partner to join you, you ought to begin to see change happening slowly, slowly. Yes, there will be times when your partner doesn't feel up to coming with you, when he moves more slowly or he can't let go of the old ways. There are even times when the changes in you may make him feel threatened and, thus, angrier. If, after a few months, you feel as if you are getting nowhere, you can still move towards joining forces by considering couples' counselling. Sometimes progress is best made with a little expert direction. And, if you keep at it, eventually one day in the middle of some disagreement when you are feeling quite unreasonable, you may notice that your partner is acting in an extremely empathic and reasonable fashion. He came around the curve and passed you – and you will be the one who has to catch him up.

On a personal note, there is no way I can convey to you what this was like the first time I recognized this happening to me. During a disagreement, my husband passed ahead of me on an inside curve as I stood there yelling. In that moment, I saw myself so clearly, I saw him, and what I felt more than anything else was – gratitude. As your relationship deepens on the front line of love, gratitude becomes a frequent, wonderful feeling that takes on new meaning when you see yourself as part of a team.

Late-Night Thoughts on Front Line

I remember an essay I read many years ago by the late Lewis Thomas – it has stuck with me. It was about the Hawaiian language, which Thomas explained was a language created by children who wanted to play with each other. Families from many countries who spoke many different languages moved to Hawaii, where they lived next to each other, working on the plantations. The children, playing in the yards, could not speak each other's language. So, they began to develop a new language, a language composed of pieces of many languages, and that language became what is now known as Hawaiian. The new language suited them all, and soon they were all speaking it, gay and playful. They took the best of what was there, they respected each other's differences, and they made up something brand new. Think about it. Aloha.

Epilogue

Interspersed throughout the book there are statements that I have emphasized which are important for every couple. Here, to send you on your way, I've collected many of them in one spot. I hope when you don't have time to flip through the book, but you need a little inspiration and soothing, you can turn here and get it.

The end of the honeymoon is not a wall, it's the next frontier of human experience, filled with great promise.

When you have the energy to want to throw each other out the window, you also have the energy to chart the next frontier of love.

The problem is where you start working, not the place you stop working.

The least you can do is to commit as much sweat to happiness as you've committed to keeping faltering relationships together.

A transition never feels like a transition; it feels like a crisis.

Frankly, it may be true that he started it, but even if it is, with all of the times he's started it, the question you ought to be asking yourself is: 'Have I become more competent at handling it?'

Women and men peak at different times sexually, so why be surprised that we peak at different times conversationally!

Never underestimate the power of saying you're sorry, even when you think you didn't do anything wrong.

Saying you're sorry is never a defeat. The courage to end an argument, to apologize first, to take the high road, is always a victory.

A worthy goal would be to actually learn to like the way you fight.

No matter what you thought when you fell for each other, two people can't join their lives, their lifestyles, their experiences, their realities on a daily basis without conflict.

Major breakthroughs between two people can take place after much conflict.

When you fight, the point is not to agree with each other, but to let each other feel heard.

Blame, rather than a way of disengaging ourselves from the problem, is a way of saying: I'm a failure. I can't conceive of any contribution I could make to working this out. I'm not capable. I am incapable because of you.

When you blame, you make your partner sound reasonable and you make yourself sound awful.

On the front line of love, you change your stance in the relationship from the 'I' to the 'we' – from the individual position to the couple's position, from 'his' problems to 'our' problems.

It's time to start talking about sex in the same way you talk about other relationship matters – through disclosure, negotiation, positive feedback, More of/Less of lists, seeking co-operation on a wish, increasing creative solutions to sexual problems, offering generosity, looking at the 'we' in sex, and most of all remembering that in sex as in every other part of the relationship, both partners will have times of feeling that they give more than they get (at least as you're working this stuff through).

When you convince your partner to take on something new, whether it be housework, doing the taxes or teaching your daughter to drive, you must then give up controlling the task yourself.

What would you be doing with your energy if it weren't all going to him?

When you think about fighting, think about fighting 'for' something, rather than just fighting. Keep your goal in mind. Keep at it. Things do get better.

It is impossible to enter the next frontier of love without making an incredible investment in yourself.

By the way, I think the most helpful thing I found out from couples about an enduring love is that you need a repertoire of solutions and creative ideas that is ever-expanding, because no matter what you find that works, it won't work for ever. Every good solution you discover for a problem runs its course and stops working after a while. You need to keep coming up with new solutions, using them, waiting, going back to the old solutions and trying them again after giving them a break – eventually, it all falls into place.

Multiple honeymoons, honeymoon moments – it's time to collect. Close the book. Go to your partner. Tell her or him that you want to take a journey, but you don't need a suitcase or hotel reservations or travellers' cheques – what you have in mind is the journey to the front line of love.

In Case of Emergency: When and Where to Seek Professional Help

I f you have read this book, worked at your relationship yet feel that the problems continue to be overwhelming, you may need to seek professional help as a couple or by yourself. You need to seek professional help when:

▶ Either partner adopts a pattern of becoming physically threatening in word, action, or deed
▶ You or your partner is having an affair (or seriously contemplating one)
▶ One or both of you is depressed or miserable
▶ You have ongoing distress that lasts for more than one month without any sign that things are improving even though you've tried the strategies in this book
▶ You feel that the love is dying and you can't stop it from happening
▶ Your children are acting up or acting out
▶ You are avoiding serious problems in the relationship which are only getting worse
▶ There is a relative or third person who is intrusive in your relationship
▶ You know things could be better but the two of you don't seem to be seeing much improvement on your own

Where to Get Good Help

The best way to find a good couples' therapist is to ask friends or family members for a referral. If they don't know of anyone, ask if they have friends who may have sought couples' therapy. When someone is helped through therapy they are often glad to tell you about it, hoping you will also be helped.

When you ask for a referral you don't have to disclose any details if you don't want to. You don't have to tell any more than you want to tell. Simply say that the two of you are looking for someone, and if pressed you can say that you'd prefer not to talk more about it.

When you get a name, ask the referrers why they liked the therapist and how long they went. When you call the therapist say:

> Lisa and Tom Jones gave me your name. My husband and I were interested in couples' therapy. May I ask a few questions?

Then:

1 Briefly (two minutes or less) describe your problem and ask if the therapist has experience in your problem.
2 Briefly ask the therapist's experience. Don't give the third degree – just find out if the therapist is licensed to practice and has training in working with couples.
3 Ask the fee (later, you can call your insurance company and find out if couples' family therapy cover is available).
4 If the fee is too high for you, ask if the therapist offers a sliding scale. If the therapist does not and you can't afford it, ask the therapist if she can offer a referral to someone who can accommodate your price range.
5 Ask how long treatment usually lasts.
6 Find out if the therapist has hours available at the time you and your partner can attend.

If you have received a high recommendation for a therapist whose fees are out of your budget range, you ought seriously to consider paying the higher fee – as with everything in life, you pretty much get what you pay for. With a good couples' therapist, many to most couples begin to see improvement within three to five sessions.

Note: Just because someone is a good therapist, it doesn't make them a good couples' therapist. Think of it like a medical doctor. You would not go to a nephrologist if you had a sore throat. Thus, it is important to find out if the therapist you see has training in couples' and/or family therapy. Couples' and family therapy is a different skill from individual therapy.

Call Training Institutes, Hospitals and Colleges

If you can't afford much, check out training institutes, hospitals (some have outpatient mental health clinics), and clinics in your area. Many GP practices have a counsellor on staff, who may be able either to help you directly or to recommend a qualified couples' counsellor. Some training institutes for psychotherapy offer advanced training for experienced psychotherapists and students. Many accept low-income couples at a reduced fee. To get this benefit you may have to be willing to be observed in sessions by students or to have your sessions videotaped for student training. If you don't mind this you can get good treatment at a low fee since all students have experienced supervisors who closely watch their work. One couple I know who are part of one of these programmes are currently being seen, as part of a pilot study, by two of the most revered couples' therapists in the world. The couple pay peanuts for their treatment. You can generally find institutes by looking in the Yellow Pages under 'psychotherapy' or 'mental health' or 'counselling'.

Other Referrals

The organization RELATE (Marriage Guidance) is the obvious place to find a well-trained couples' and/or family therapist. Check your Yellow Pages for the branch nearest you.

In the first session, try to get a sense of the following:

▶ The therapist's view on marriage. You want a therapist who has a bias towards helping couples to work their problems out. A good therapist won't have an investment in whether you work it out – that's up to you – but she or he will work with your hope of staying together.
▶ Whether the therapist will set goals with you and will stick with what you want to work on. If your therapist starts off by wanting to delve deep into your past to solve your present problems, expect to be in for long-term treatment. If that is not what you want, say so. You certainly may need to do some talking about your past, but you want a therapist who can stick with the problems at hand in the present.
▶ Does the therapist make both of you comfortable and not take sides? Both partners need to feel comfortable and to feel that the therapist can see and appreciate both points of view.

In addition to the above advice, I'd like to add this:

Avoid a therapist who wants to see you both individually as well as together on an ongoing basis. Couples' therapists are trained in many different ways, and it may be that your couples' therapist wants to see both of you alone a time or two. But beware a therapist who wants to do this on an ongoing basis and tries to get you into individual and couples' therapy simultaneously. This creates more problems than it solves because you'll both be wondering what's being said about you when you aren't there. My belief is that your couples' therapist can't be your or your partner's individual therapist, too. If either of you does need individual therapy, it should be with someone else.

Overcoming Objections to Therapy

People have many reasons for avoiding therapy, which include some of the following:

Objection Number 1: therapy is for sissies.
Therapy can be for anyone brave enough to sit down and take a look at what isn't working.

Objection Number 2: Therapy doesn't help.
It doesn't look like what you're doing is helping either. Could you entertain the idea that trying something new might help?

Objection Number 3: Every couple I know who went to therapy broke up.
That's probably a generalization, but even if it isn't, chances are good these couples, whether knowingly or unknowingly, went to couples' therapy in order to break up.

Objection Number 4: It's too expensive.
Have you heard what divorce costs these days?

Objection Number 5: If we can't solve the problem ourselves, we shouldn't be together.
Would you say that if you needed to have your gall bladder out?

Objection Number 6: I don't want to air my dirty linen.
When you don't air dirty linen, it starts to smell worse and worse.

Objection Number 7: I'm Jewish (Asian, Afro-American, gay, blah, blah, blah) and a therapist who is Catholic (Jewish, Asian, Afro-American, not-gay, blah, blah, blah) could never understand.

So tell your therapist that. Tell her what she needs to know to make this work for you. Tell her what you think it is that makes you different. Find out if she has experience working with your cultural or racial background. Don't make assumptions about her.

Objection Number 8: We tried therapy two years ago. If we have to go again, it means it didn't work for us.

If you had your tonsils out and then two years later you broke your foot, would you say the first doctor failed? Life is long and rigorous. New problems happen. Old conditions flare up.

If Your Partner Refuses to Go and You Know Your Problems Are Truly Serious

If you are in a relationship with serious problems and your partner won't go to therapy with you, you may need to go to therapy anyway to sort out the relationship. There will be signs that you need to do this in the way problems are handled in the relationship. Instead of discussing problems when you are certain your partner has lied to you or when he gets inappropriately pushy with you, you blow up or you have sex and forget about it. Or you send a love note, or you tell him how much you love him. Or you apologize and take the blame. Or you actually deny to yourself any threatening or conflicting information. If you are wondering if you are in trouble, here are 10 warning signals* that have been there all along if you'd only look at them:

1 You stop talking and/or socializing with friends.
   Variation: A variation on the theme of silence is when you talk about it constantly but you do nothing. Eventually people tune you out.
2 When your partner is impossible, you start focusing on the past, the man you first met.
3 You avoid family functions.
4 You focus on the hurt child beneath the adult.

* This list is partially compiled from the project on domestic violence at the Ackerman Institute for Family Therapy, a project led by Virginia Goldnor and Gillian Walker.

---

5 You start to do things you would never have done under normal circumstances.
6 You act as if he were not responsible for his actions, while you are responsible for everything in the relationship.
7 You put the relationship above protecting yourself.
8 You are captured by the power of the weak. In other words, when you do not assert your power for your safety and health, that does not mean you have no power. You always have the power to leave, but you don't leave. Your power becomes the power to humiliate your partner with what you allow him to do to you. You actually dominate him with weakness, with your inability to take a stand on his behaviour.
9 You rely on primitive defences to justify behaviour, insisting:
   He didn't hit me that hard
   I didn't see it coming
   Anyone would do what he did given the way I acted
   Being hit isn't the worst thing that's happened to me
10 You refuse to ask yourself the simple question, the question that would clarify everything you need to know. The question to ask, if any of this reminds you of yourself, is: *Do I feel scared?* If your answer is yes, then it signals that your relationship has serious problems – your relationship is hazardous to your health.

If you feel scared, then you need to tell someone what is going on; you need to seek help. Maybe therapy will save your relationship; maybe not. Even if you feel that this abuse is not the worst you've ever experienced, even if being lonely feels worse than the way your partner is currently treating you, you need to seek help from a counsellor who can work with you to make important decisions about how to handle a threatening situation. Please seek professional counsel immediately.

SELECTED BIBLIOGRAPHY

Brothers, Jo, *Attraction and Attachment* (New York: Haworth, 1993)

Buss, David, *The Evolution of Desire* (New York: Basic Books, 1994)

Dowrick, Stephanie, *Intimacy and Solitude* (New York: W.W. Norton, 1991)

Frankl, Viktor, *Man's Search for Meaning* (New York: simon and Schuster, 1959)

Gardner, Howard, *Creating Minds* (New York: Basic Books, 1993)

Gaylin, Willard, *On Being and Becoming Human* (New York: Viking Penguin, 1990)

Gilbert, Roberta, *Extraordinary Relationships* (Minnetonka, MN: Chronimed, 1992)

Gilligan, Carol, *In a Different Voice* (Cambridge, MA: Harvard University Press, 1982)

Goffman, Erving, *The Presentation of Self in Everyday Experience* (New York: Doubleday, 1959)

Goldberg, Carl, *Understanding Shame* (Northvale, NJ: Jason Aronson, 1991)

Goodman, Gerald, *The Talk Book* (New York: Ballantine, 1988)

Gottman, John, *Why Marriages Succeed or Fail* (New York: Simon and Schuster, 1994)

Gould, Roger, *Transformations* (New York: Simon and Schuster, 1978)

Grove, D. and Haley, J., *Conversations on Therapy* (New York: W.W. Norton, 1993)

Heitler, Susan, *From Conflict to Resolution* (New York: W.W. Norton, 1990)

Hochschild, Arlie, *The Second Shift* (New York: Viking Penguin, 1989)

Jordan, Kaplan, Miller, Stiver and Surrey, *Women's Growth in Connection* (New York: Guilford, 1991)

Lakoff, George and Johnson, Mark, *Metaphors We Live By* (Chicago: The University of Chicago Press, 1980)

Lifton, Robert Jay, *The Protean Self*, (New York: Basic Books, 1993)

Love, Patricia, *Hot Monogamy* (New York: Dutton, 1993)

MacArthur, Dorothea, *Birth of a Self in Adulthood* (Northvale, NJ: Jason Aronson, 1988)

Masterson, James, *The Search for the Real Self* (New York: Free Press, 1988)

Person, Ethel, *Dreams of Love and Fateful Encounters* (New York: Penguin, 1988)

Phillips, Adam, *On Flirtation* (Cambridge MA: Harvard University Press, 1994)

Schwartz, Pepper, *Peer Marriage* (New York: Free Press, 1994)

Shekerjian, Denise, *Uncommon Genius* (New York: Viking, 1990)

Tannen, Deborah, *You Just Don' t Understand* (New York: William Morrow, 1990)

Walters, Carter, Papp and Silverstein, *The Invisible Web* (New York: Guilford, 1988)

Watzlawick, Paul, Weakland, John and Fisch, Richard *Change: Principles of Problem Formation and Problem Resolution* (New York: W.W. Norton, 1974)

West, Malcolm and Sheldon-Keller, A., *Patterns of Relating* (New York: Guilford, 1994)

White, M. and Epston, D. *Narrative Means to Therapeutic Ends* (Adelaide: Dulwich Centre, 1990)

White, Michael, *ReAuthoring Lives* (Adelaide: Dulwich Centre, 1995)

Wiener, Daniel, *Rehearsals for Growth* (New York: W.W. Norton, 1994)

In addition to the above book references, I have attended or listened to the audiotapes of a number of lectures by renowned couples and family psychotherapists from across the country. For the knowledge and years of experience they shared, I am grateful to these lecturers: Paul Watzlawick, John Weakland, Insoo Kim Berg, Steve de Shaver, Michele Weiner-Davis, David Schnarch, William Pinsoff, Lois Braverman, Virginia Goldnor, Gillian Walker, Joel Bergman, Elie Wiesel, Betty Carter, Evan Imber-Black, Janet Surrey, Steven Bergman and, especially, Peggy Papp.

FOR MORE INFORMATION

Sharyn Wolf, CSW, maintains a private practice in New York City offering individual, couple and group psychotherapy. If this book helps you to feel more optimistic about your relationship, if you have a personal story you'd like to share, you can write to:

> Sharyn Wolf, C.S.W.
> 12 West 9th Street
> Room 1B
> New York, NY 10011
> (212) 674–6464

Sharyn's e-mail address is redwolf@datelynx.com. You can join in a weekly Internet chat session at www.datelynx.com.